Praise for
Cultural Christians in the Early Church

Once upon a time, early Christians were stereotyped as sturdy white-robed heroes, who seemed little less than angels walking the earth. In her very readable (and thoroughly researched) book, Nadya Williams performs the amazing feat of presenting those ancient believers as real human beings, with highly recognizable virtues and flaws, living in environments not that different from what we know today. Indeed, as she shows, those Christians often acted very much like their modern counterparts and faced many of the same dilemmas in their everyday lives. Her book is a major achievement of imaginative inquiry.

—PHILIP JENKINS, author of *A Storm of Images*, distinguished professor of history, Institute for Studies of Religion, Baylor University

Greed, lust, selfishness, prejudice, Christian nationalism—we wrestle with all these issues in the twenty-first-century church. But we moderns are not alone. In this poignant and perceptive work of historical and cultural analysis, Williams shows that such vices have plagued Christian communities from the beginning. She hopes that these ancients can put up a mirror for us to see our own blind spots and vices in their stories. But it's not all bad news. The early church had those few but powerful witnesses to the authentic, countercultural, and transformative way of Jesus. Williams creatively uses early Christian history to illuminate the narrow road of faithful discipleship.

—NIJAY K. GUPTA, professor of New Testament, Northern Seminary

Nadya Williams has written a fascinating account of how Christians have, since ancient times, faced the temptation to imitate resident cultures rather than adopt an authentic Christian life. Whether it is about food, sex, money, or politics, Christians have, from the Tiber to Tallahassee, faced the temptation to give themselves over to worldly vices rather than holy habits. An excellent example of how understanding the struggle of Christianity and culture in antiquity can help us to understand our own cultural struggles in the present. Thoroughly recommended!

—REV. DR. MICHAEL F. BIRD, academic dean, Ridley College, Melbourne, Australia

In this convincing and convicting book, Williams demonstrates that while Christianity ultimately transformed Roman society, early Christ followers struggled to resist the surrounding culture as much as believers do today. The author combines vivid stories of "cultural Christians" in the early church with expert analysis of the social, cultural, and historical context that shaped their worldview. The result is a nuanced account of the early church and the sinners who filled it. Williams calls on contemporary Christians to stop idealizing people in the past and challenges us to renew our efforts to resist sin in all its forms, from the familiar vice of avarice to the more insidious idolatry of Christian nationalism.

—MEGHAN DiLUZIO, associate professor of classics, Baylor University

In *Cultural Christians in the Early Church*, Dr. Nadya Williams turns to the first five centuries of Christianity to remind contemporary evangelical Christians that the well-known modern phenomenon of the "cultural Christian" has its roots in the very origins of Christianity. Though the most vivid stories about Christians of this period focus on persecution, martyrdom, and the radical rejection of the Roman secular world, our ancient texts provide abundant evidence that these "countercultural Christians" were not the norm. Indeed, as Williams demonstrates, there is another history of early Christianity to be told, one which highlights the extent to which most early Christians struggled to reject the values and social obligations of the secular Roman world. For Williams, it is in these struggles that modern readers can see the gap between Christian teaching and the everyday practices of many early Christians. Drawing on ancient evidence ranging from first to fifth centuries AD, and from Rome and North Africa to the Greek East, Williams makes a strong case for understanding that early Christians shared many of the same struggles that contemporary Christians face as they attempt to live in the secular world while holding fast to their faith.

Cultural Christians in the Early Church offers a gripping history of the early Christians who struggled to reconcile their faith with their communal responsibilities, career ambitions, and lifestyle preferences. By focusing on the messy lives of these "cultural Christians" rather than on the heroic martyrs who are most familiar to contemporary Christians, Williams encourages her fellow believers to consider the challenges that sin posed from the very origins of Christianity. Using a series of vivid case studies, she takes her reader on a whirlwind journey from the era of the New Testament to post-Constantinian Christianity and the rise of asceticism. Her heroes are not the famous martyrs but rather those Christians who struggled to live in the secular world, as members of communities, with family and civic responsibilities, in bodies prone to sin.

Williams is particularly interested in the ways these ancient stories allow the modern reader to recognize and reflect on their own failings as practicing Christians. Ultimately, *Cultural Christians in the Early Church* offers contemporary Christians a nuanced retelling of the complex early centuries of ancient Christianity, with particular attention to different types of behavior that modern evangelical Christians would consider sinful (e.g., ignoring the poor). Williams is a talented writer who tells a story that is engaging, witty, and instructive while also being accessible to nonspecialists with no previous knowledge of early Christian history. Ultimately, her goal is pedagogical: in explicating these stories of "cultural Christians," Williams aims to encourage her readers to reflect on their own lives, their own behaviors, and take steps to embrace a practice of "countercultural Christianity" that is grounded in serving one's community and fellow humans while declining to accommodate itself to the social norms of the secular world.

—DR. JENNIFER EBBELER, associate professor of classics at the
University of Texas at Austin, author of *Disciplining Christians*

Punchy and provocative, Williams's book offers an approachable, entertaining read on a serious theme. Her rich selection of historical examples and illuminating contextualization of early Christianity in its Greco-Roman context build to a point that could hardly be more timely, however much Christians then and now may disagree on what constitutes "cultural Christianity." Early Christianity was never an Eden, immune to the perennial problem of human sin. We should idealize neither the early church nor ourselves.

—HAN-LUEN KANTZER KOMLINE, professor of church history and theology at
Western Theological Seminary, Humboldt Fellow at University of Tübingen

Nadya Williams's thesis is unsettling and irrefutable. There was never an idyllic period in church history, when believers consistently shared goods, stayed true to the gospel, and joyfully gave their lives in martyrdom. Even the much romanticized "early church" (from AD 100 to 400) was sometimes tainted by compromise, apostasy, and mere going-through-the-motions. Nominal or cultural Christianity, in other words, is not just a problem in modern Sydney or Atlanta. It was present among the persecuted Christians of second-century Bithynia, the rapidly growing church of third-century Carthage, and even the famous desert fathers of fourth-century Egypt. *Cultural Christians in the Early Church* is not a work of "presentism," judging our ancestors by the values of today. In some ways, it is the reverse. By shining a gospel light on ancient Christians, Williams succeeds in providing a scorching critique of aspects of contemporary Christianity. This book is not for the fainthearted, but it is highly recommended.

—JOHN DICKSON, Jean Kvamme Distinguished Professor at Wheaton
College, host of *Undeceptions*, and author of *Bullies and Saints*

After reading this book I will be more careful when I invoke the so-called "countercultural" nature of the ancient church when criticizing the cultural captivity of American evangelicals. Nadya Williams is a model for how to think about the relationship between the past and the present.

—JOHN FEA, professor of American history, Messiah University

Cultural Christians in the Early Church offers the reader the chance to peer into ancient Christianity in a unique way. Reading this book, one has the sensation of peeking through the window of a church, while simultaneously seeing part of one's own reflection in the glass, as if partially mapped onto the people on the inside. Instead of offering a romanticized view of an ideal early church that only later fell into compromise, and instead of perpetuating a narrative about an emerging hierarchical church wedding itself to power and stamping out diversity, Nadya Williams introduces a series of captivating stories and vivid scenarios that help us see the past and the present in conversation. And it is a conversation important to any person of faith today, regardless of their prior knowledge of early Christian history.

—DAVID E. WILHITE, professor of theology, George W. Truett Theological Seminary of Baylor University

Cultural Christians IN THE Early Church

Cultural Christians IN THE Early Church

A Historical and Practical Introduction to Christians in

THE GRECO-ROMAN WORLD

Nadya Williams

ZONDERVAN ACADEMIC

ZONDERVAN ACADEMIC

Cultural Christians in the Early Church
Copyright © 2023 by Nadya Williams

Published in Grand Rapids, Michigan, by Zondervan. Zondervan is a registered trademark of HarperCollins Christian Publishing, Inc.

Requests for information should be addressed to customercare@harpercollins.com.

Zondervan titles may be purchased in bulk for educational, business, fundraising, or sales promotional use. For information, please email SpecialMarkets@Zondervan.com.

ISBN 978-0-310-14783-1 (audio)

Library of Congress Cataloging-in-Publication Data

Library of Congress Cataloging-in-Publication Data
Names: Williams, Nadya, author.
Title: Cultural Christians in the early church : a historical and practical introduction to Christians in the Greco-Roman world / Nadya Williams.
Description: Grand Rapids : Zondervan, 2023. | Includes index.
Identifiers: LCCN 2023016748 (print) | LCCN 2023016749 (ebook) | ISBN 9780310147817 (paperback) | ISBN 9780310147824 (ebook)
Subjects: LCSH: Christianity and culture—History—Early church, ca. 30-600. | Church history—Primitive and early church, ca. 30-600. | BISAC: RELIGION / Christian Church / History | RELIGION / Biblical Studies / History & Culture
Classification: LCC BR115.C8 W5449 2023 (print) | LCC BR115.C8 (ebook) | DDC 261—dc23/eng/20230629
LC record available at https://lccn.loc.gov/2023016748
LC ebook record available at https://lccn.loc.gov/2023016749

Cover design: Micah Kandros Design
Cover photo: © Ivan Soto Cobos; Mega Pixel / Shutterstock
Interior design: Sara Colley

Printed in the United States of America

23 24 25 26 27 28 29 30 /TRM/ 10 9 8 7 6 5 4 3 2 1

To Dan. I love you more than coffee.

Contents

The Roman Empire

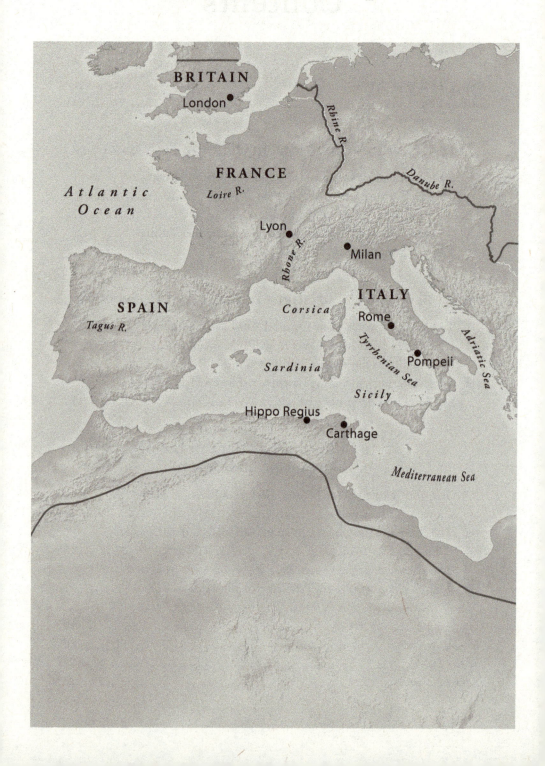

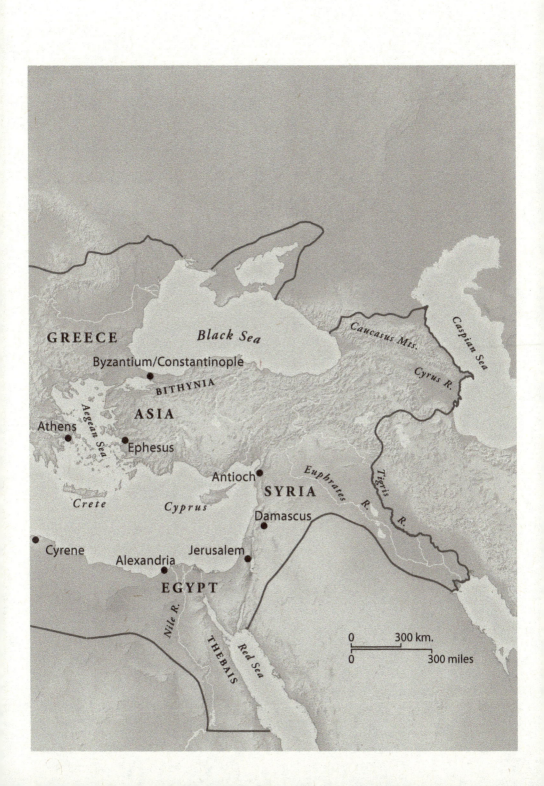

Introduction

Finding Cultural Christians
in Unexpected Places

In the middle of the third century CE, a North African bishop wrote a treatise for the women of his church, exhorting them to resist such culturally normalized yet immodest behaviors in their cosmopolitan Roman city as mixed public bathing in the nude and wearing excessive amounts of jewelry. The treatise appears even more striking once we realize that the scandalous individuals to whom it was addressed were single women who had dedicated their virginity to Christ. We are talking, in effect, about nuns, albeit before the concept fully existed.[1]

Almost a century and a half later, in 396 CE, an Italian bishop wrote a letter of rebuke to a nearby church that had split into bitter warring factions and could not agree on a new bishop to install after the death of the church's previous pastor. Leaderless for a season, the church was disintegrating into chaos and strife. Adding further insult to injury, members of the congregation were being influenced by the decidedly un-Christian scandalous teaching of two apostate monks. Apparently, living a more worldly life was the only thing on which the warring factions could actually agree. Ambrose, the outraged author of the letter, reminded the church members that while the Epicurean-style teachings on food and sexual pleasures that the two apostates presented to them were accepted in the pagan world around them, Christians from their earliest days have been called to resist such cultural views.[2]

---

1. The treatise in question is *On the Dress of Virgins* by Cyprian, bishop of Carthage in 248–58 CE.
2. Ambrose, Epistle LXIII, addressed to the church at Vercellae: https://www.newadvent.org/fathers/340963.htm.

These stories, and many others like them from the first five centuries of the church, challenge the general assumption of the public today that the earliest Christians were zealous converts who were much more counterculturally devoted to their faith than typical churchgoers today. Too often, Christians today think of cultural Christianity as a modern concept, one most likely to occur in areas where Christianity is the majority culture, such as the American Bible Belt. The story that this book presents, however, refutes both of these assumptions.

But first, who are these cultural Christians of whom I speak? This term refers to individuals who self-identify as Christians but whose outward behavior and, to the extent that we can tell, inward thoughts and motivations are largely influenced by the surrounding culture rather than by their Christian faith and the teachings of Jesus. In the Bible Belt, these are often the Christians who may faithfully attend church for an hour most Sundays, but who then compartmentalize their faith the rest of the week, adopting a variety of modern American culturally normalized behaviors that are antithetical to traditional Christian theological teachings and practices in key areas of life, including in attitudes toward dating and sexuality (e.g., cohabiting before marriage or accepting abortion), use of finances (e.g., gambling or a lack of tithing or compassion for others), politics (e.g., the rise of Christian nationalism), and even church attendance (e.g., those who believe that once they have been saved, church attendance is optional).

In a culture where church can sometimes seem to be as much a social club as a religious institution, and where to be a church member often means to gain rather than lose respectability particularly at the local level, cultural Christianity makes sense. But the shocking argument of this book is that cultural Christians could exist and even flourish in a world in which Christianity was a persecuted minority. Indeed, the first empire-wide persecution of Christians was taking place just as the beleaguered bishop of our first example, Cyprian, who was eventually martyred for his faith, was exhorting his flock, including the poorly behaved consecrated virgins, to resist their surrounding culture. Furthermore, cultural Christianity could exist also in a world in which Christianity had just recently become the legalized religion of the empire, as in the case of Ambrose. Instead of thinking of cultural Christianity as the exception, a phenomenon that could only flourish in very specific kinds of conditions, perhaps we should think of it as a default, a natural result of the fallen and sinful state of humanity.

And so, this book, which aims to be both historical and practical, argues that cultural Christians were the norm rather than the exception in the early church—from the first century CE to the fifth century CE. Using different categories of culturally inspired sins as its organizing principle, and focusing on a different sin in each chapter, the book considers the challenge of culture to the earliest converts to Christianity, as they struggled—and often failed—to live on mission in the Greco-Roman cultural milieu of the Roman Empire.

Why I Wrote This Book

I wrote this book for three related historical and theological reasons, and these three reasons are also the reasons why you should read it. First, as a professor of ancient history who has been teaching for over a dozen years now at a state university in a predominantly evangelical region of the American South, I have heard too many of my students and fellow churchgoers over the years make comments about the superiority of early Christians to us. This book is an attempt to explain both why this view is wrong and why holding this belief can end up misleading us in the present. Second and related, both the American public at large and American Christians in particular have a very limited understanding of ancient history and the world of the early church. Particularly lacking is an accurate understanding of Greco-Roman culture and its responsibility for shaping people's worldview, which means also shaping the sins to which they were particularly prone. And third, if we understand the presence and impact of cultural Christianity in the early church and understand that so many of our own sins are cultural sins, this will have an impact on everything, including our views on finances, marriage and sexuality, and politics, to name just a few examples. Because if so many of us too are cultural Christians, then trying to fix the world through politics or just through particular policies on marriage, for instance, will never work. Rather, we need to pursue genuine conversion and sanctification.

In defining cultural Christianity, I noted that it is the faith of those who are confessing Jesus with their words while living by the standards of the surrounding culture. Those culturally normalized behaviors of cultural Christians become, in turn, what I refer to as *cultural sins*. Put simply, cultural Christians commit cultural sins whenever they bypass God's standards to engage in certain culturally conditioned and approved behaviors. These might be so common that the surrounding culture considers them utterly normal, perhaps not even deserving commentary—like the mixed-gender nude public bathing of the sacred virgins to which Cyprian objected or the modern American attitude toward cohabiting before marriage. And yet the New Testament presents a countercultural view of such everyday subjects and many others.

In the dissonance of the gospel teachings with those of the surrounding culture, we find culturally inspired sins. Focusing on these culturally inspired sins, in turn, allows us to consider which aspects of the surrounding Greco-Roman culture were particularly challenging for early Christians to overcome. We will meet, for instance, men and women who relied entirely on Greek and Roman ideals of patronage in thinking about how to use their money. We will also meet men who eagerly embraced Christianity but continued to frequent prostitutes in their cosmopolitan city—a practice that was socially and culturally normalized. And we will also meet men and women who were eager for martyrdom at a time of persecution but categorically refused to serve the sick and the dying in their community. Finally, while many of the individuals whose stories we will consider were part of the nameless multitudes in the early churches, we will also hear from some more familiar voices, such as Augustine, whose views on Christian nationalism we will consider in chapter 8.

While this is, first and foremost, a historical narrative, the stories of these believers, men and women from all walks of life and all parts of the Roman Empire from the first five centuries of the church, provide a fresh perspective for considering the difficult and timeless questions that stubbornly persist in our own world and churches. How do we resist the views of property, food, gender and sexuality, and self-care that are dominant in the surrounding culture? Why is Christian nationalism a problem and a cultural sin? And why is running away from the church a solution for cultural Christians? Ultimately, recognizing that cultural sins were always a part of the story of the church and its people is a reminder that we should never idealize the people of the past. Furthermore, for Christian readers in particular, seeing the early church wrestle with the same challenges of cultural Christianity should be both a source of comfort and a call to action in pursuit of sanctification in the present.

I contend that looking at the stories of these far-away and far-removed people, the cultural Christians from the ancient world, as strange as they may appear at first glance, is a fruitful way to gain a better understanding of our own struggles as Christians today. This understanding is ultimately what I would like you to get from reading this book, beyond the sheer entertainment value of studying the Greco-Roman world, which will also be apparent, I hope.

But understanding the stories of these earliest cultural Christians requires first understanding something about the world in which they lived. The Roman world was no stranger to the phenomenon of cultural religion. But for the Romans, unlike the Christians, the idea of cultural religion had no negative connotations. Some of our best witnesses for this, as it happens, are not human, but poultry.

Fowl Business: Cultural Religion
in the Roman World

The chickens were hungry. Marcus Furius Camillus, recently appointed dictator for the purpose of leading the Roman army in its prolonged war with Veii, stood nearby and watched them with rising confidence. The chickens never lied, in his experience. He knew that this omen could only mean one thing: the pagan gods were about to grant the Romans one of their most important victories yet. Camillus's family, one could say, was particularly close to the gods—a relative of his, Quintus Furius Paculus, possibly an uncle or distant cousin, even served as Pontifex Maximus, head of a powerful priestly college.[3] But more than anything, Rome's cultural religion was part of Camillus's worldview, just as it was for all residents of the Roman Republic. But what exactly does this idea of cultural religion mean, and what did it mean to the Romans? Camillus's experience offers a glimpse.

Sometime around 396 BCE, the Romans, then still largely restricted to a little-known and malaria-ridden village on the Tiber, undertook the siege of Veii. A major Etruscan stronghold located less than ten miles from Rome, Veii posed a significant threat to Rome's safety and growth. As a result, the Senate appointed a dictator—a military office reserved for extreme emergencies and only for six months at a time. That dictator was Camillus, whose extraordinarily successful previous military record spoke for itself.

During the siege, the Romans prayed to the gods for help, as was their custom. Indeed, Roman generals were subject to a vast array of essential rituals, the violation of which, the Romans believed, jeopardized the success of the entire campaign. To give just one particularly well-known example, mentioned above, generals had to consult the sacred chickens prior to battle. If the chickens ate the proffered grain, the omens from the gods promised victory. If the chickens refused to peck at their food, however, a defeat was sure, so the battle had to be postponed for another day.

We hear of generals trying to rig the system a bit: sacred chickens were

---

3. As Christians, we may feel uncomfortable talking about pagan religion, with its many deities. I am using the term *gods* here because that is the language that these pagan believers used. And so, even this very terminology reminds us of the very different worldview in which the earliest Christ-followers lived, as well as the challenges of language that they surely faced as well, as they tried to share the gospel with those around them. For an overview of the differing views of faith in the Roman versus early Christian worldview, see Teresa Morgan, *Roman Faith and Christian Faith: Pistis and Fides in the Early Empire and Early Churches* (Oxford: Oxford University Press, 2015).

known to be starved on occasion, so they would eat grain, when finally offered, particularly eagerly, providing the desired good omen. But as anyone who has had experience minding chickens knows, they are not the smartest nor the most predictable creatures. Later on, during the First Punic War, one Roman general, understandably annoyed with the diva fowls disrupting his well-laid battle plans, exclaimed, "If they won't eat, let them drink!" and threw the chickens in the sea. The chickens promptly drowned, but their prediction proved true. The Romans lost the battle spectacularly, losing ninety-three of their one hundred and twenty-three ships.[4]

At the siege of Veii, under the leadership of Marcus Furius Camillus, the protocols were followed precisely. In addition to the usual religious rituals, such as the consultation of the chickens, the Romans also performed an *evocatio*—the ceremonial "calling out" of a god or goddess of another city or state to come join the Roman side. Specifically, the Romans called out Juno, the patron goddess of Veii, to join their side, promising her a swanky new temple in Rome in return for her aid. The bargain worked. Veii fell to the Romans, and (as the Roman historian Livy tells us) a particularly cheeky Roman soldier, who was helping package the cult statue of Juno for transport to her new digs in Rome, asked the statue if she wanted to come to Rome. Juno, to the utter amazement of all bystanders, nodded her head in assent.[5]

This story reveals several key aspects of traditional Roman religion. First, Roman religion was, from its earliest days, as expansionist and colonizing as Rome itself. As Rome conquered territories increasingly farther removed from the village on the Tiber, it brought in new gods, or new manifestations of known gods, into the state pantheon. But they usually had to be Romanized at least a little bit so they would fit in. Juno was, most likely, part of Roman religion from its earliest days, but the Veiian Juno was still welcomed in as a new entity, in need of her own temple.

Second, Roman religion was paradoxically both rigid and flexible, and

---

4. Publius Claudius Pulcher had a distinguished political and military career prior to this incident, but his loss at the Battle of Drepana in 249 BCE ended his career. He was recalled to Rome and put on trial, narrowly escaping capital punishment on a technicality. The story about his disregard of the omen of defeat appears to have been well-known in antiquity. Cicero tells it in *On the Nature of the Gods* 2.7, Suetonius includes it in *Life of Claudius* 2, and Valerius Maximus thought of it as striking enough to include it in his collection of *Memorable Deeds and Sayings*.

5. These stories survive in book 5, chapters 21–22, of Livy's *Ab Urbe Condita*, a history of Rome from its foundation to Livy's own age (the Augustan period). While the purpose of these stories here is merely to provide context for how Roman religion functioned in its cultural milieu, I direct anyone interested in Juno between Veii and Rome to Lisa Mignone's book, *Rome's Juno: Religious Imperialism and Self-Preservation* (Ann Arbor: University of Michigan Press, forthcoming).

ultimately rooted in bargaining. Certain rituals had to be followed, and the *pax deorum* (peace with the gods) had to be upheld by correct ceremonies. Sure, most residents of the Roman state had significant flexibility in their personal religious practice. But in times of crisis, everyone was expected to join in the sacrifices. And on a regular basis, for priests, weighty responsibilities were attached to the job. The most bizarre of ceremonies to please particular gods were relegated to the very few members of priestly colleges, who were subject to a variety of fairly outrageous archaic rules, purported to date back to the days of King Numa, the legendary second king of Rome who first formulated the concept of *pax deorum*. More specifically, a woodland nymph, Egeria, told him all about it. True story, or so such Roman historians as Livy tell us, although it is unclear just how many Romans fully bought into it.[6] At any rate, these few priests had to display a high level of commitment.

The *Flamen Dialis*, high priest of Jupiter, was subject to particularly restrictive regulations on all aspects of his life, including special attire with a bizarre-looking conical hat (without which he could never go out in public) and a ban on being away from Rome for longer than a single night. His hair and nail clippings had to be preserved and ceremonially buried under a specially designated sacred tree. And these are just the tip of the iceberg when it comes to the many regulations he had to follow for the sake of securing Jupiter's favor for the city of Rome. But the well-being of Rome was presumably worth it for him, although, alas, no *Flamen Dialis* has left us a detailed journal of just how he really felt about his job. At any rate, the complex Roman rituals and the extreme requirements for priests and priesthoods remind us that, in the Roman worldview, all transactions with the gods were essentially *quid pro quo* bargains.[7] It is only in the world of such bargains that the story of Veiian Juno makes perfect sense. And this brings us to the third aspect.

Like other ancient polytheistic religions, Roman religion was a quintessentially cultural religion. While today, we may think of religion as just one particular aspect of life in our society that can be sequestered from others—think,

---

6. Livy, *Ab Urbe Condita* 1.21.

7. The bibliography on Roman religion is immense. Particularly accessible yet comprehensible is the monumental two-volume collection by Mary Beard, John North, and Simon Price, *Religions of Rome* (Cambridge: Cambridge University Press, 1998). Volume 1 provides a sweeping thousand-year history of Roman religions from the early Republic to the Christianization of the Empire, whereas volume 2 is an accompanying collection of primary sources. Also readable is John North's introductory text, *Roman Religion* (Oxford: Oxford University Press, 2000). Wonderfully comprehensive, including ancient Mediterranean religions beyond Rome, but more academic in tone is Sarah Iles Johnston's edited volume, *Religions of the Ancient World: A Guide* (Cambridge, MA: Belknap, 2004).

for instance, of the American concept of separation of church and state (leaving aside the debate over whether that is exactly what the Establishment Clause of the Constitution means)—this was not the case with other religions in the pre-modern world.[8] Roman religion, in particular, was very practical and embedded into every aspect of daily life from birth to death, governing in the process what it meant to be a Roman. The worship of the Roman gods was an integral part of being a Roman citizen or resident. Rather than being predicated on a system of theological beliefs or any creed, this polytheistic worship was based around cultural values, of which the chief was the acceptance of the paramount impor-tance of the city of Rome and, over time, what Rome stood for. Individuals who rejected these basic values, as the early Christians did, directly positioned them-selves as enemies of Roman society at its core, which is why the Romans saw them as such a threat to the entire social edifice.[9] But Veiian Juno was willing to play by the Roman rules, at least.

Juno's acceptance of the bargain in Veii meant that she was ready to agree to this rule, and she became Romanized. Given the significance of the city of Rome to Roman cultural religion, it is no coincidence that Constantine, the emperor who moved the capital of the empire from Rome to his own new city, Constantinople, was also the first Christian emperor. Adding insult to injury, he did not even bother asking the sacred chickens' permission. After a thousand years of blessing or threatening Roman generals' battle plans, the chickens were now out of a job.

Cultural Religion: New and Old

At first glance, the idea of cultural religion—where someone may identify with a particular religious tradition culturally but not follow most of its theological tenets or even see the relevance of theology beyond cultural identification—may seem very thoroughly modern, perhaps because we are so used to seeing it. After all, more American Catholics and Protestants could be classified as cultural Christians than not, and the same applies to a significant percentage of American Muslims and Jews. As one Pew Center study noted, more American Jews think

---

8. See Brent Nongbri, *Before Religion: A History of a Modern Concept* (New Haven, CT: Yale University Press, 2015).

9. See Larry Hurtado, *Destroyer of the Gods: Early Christian Distinctiveness in the Roman World* (Waco, TX: Baylor University Press, 2016). For primary sources documenting the concerns of Romans with Christians' un-Roman beliefs and practices, see Robert Wilken, *The Christians as the Romans Saw Them* (New Haven, CT: Yale University Press, 2003).

that remembering the Holocaust is more essential to their Jewish identity than believing in God.[10] I can certainly attest to this from my own experience as well, which offers one concrete example of what cultural religion today can look like.

I grew up in a secular Jewish home in Russia and Israel and came to Christ as an adult. While Jewish heritage clearly meant enough to my parents to move to Israel, my family never belonged to a synagogue and did not observe Jewish holidays—or, rather, did not observe them in the originally intended way. I have fond memories of joining neighborhood friends and classmates on Yom Kippur to roller-skate through our neighborhood, followed by a late-night impromptu supper of cheese sandwiches. This was the one day each year when there were no cars on the street, guaranteed. So when the sun went down and the Day of Atonement—the holiest day in the Jewish religious calendar and, from antiquity, a day of strict fasting from all food and drink—began, all of the kids from families that were not observant Jews would pour out onto the streets on skates and bikes. There is something incredibly freeing in skating full speed down a hilly street and knowing that, unlike any other day of the year, no car would appear in the way. Still, I have a knee scar to prove that no cars are necessary to wipe out spectacularly on the pavement.

Yes, in the process of such fun activities, one could say that kids like me inadvertently built new rituals together to mark an important date in the Jewish calendar. But our cultural ritual had nothing to do with God, like all the other similar rituals from various holidays that I got to mark with family and friends. For instance, gathering wood and anything that could be burned for Lag BaOmer, a minor holiday marked with late-night bonfires, began months in advance. I did not even know for sure what the holiday was meant to celebrate until I was an adult. To be fair, its origins are murky. The celebration postdates antiquity, although it possibly involves, among other causes, the commemoration of the Bar Kokhba revolt against the Romans. The revolt failed, but a memory of the Jewish spirit of resistance and persistence against oppression survives.

---

10. According to one study, 45 percent of Americans have a connection to Catholicism, but only 20 percent of Americans consider themselves to be currently Catholics: Michael Lipka, "45% of Americans Have a Connection to Catholicism," *Pew Research Center*, September 5, 2015, https://www.pewresearch.org/fact-tank/2015/09/02/45-of-americans-have-a-strong-connection-to-catholicism/. Another Pew study highlights the diversity of levels of belief among American Muslims: "Muslims in America: Immigrants and Those Born in U.S. See Life Differently in Many Ways," *Pew Research Center*, April 14, 2018, https://www.pewforum.org/essay/muslims-in-america-immigrants-and-those-born-in-u-s-see-life-differently-in-many-ways/. American Jews' emphasis on the importance of remembering the Holocaust over holding any religious belief is documented in this study: "A Portrait of Jewish Americans," *Pew Research Center*, October 1, 2013, https://www.pewforum.org/2013/10/01/jewish-american-beliefs-attitudes-culture-survey/.

A similar desire to commemorate perseverance against tragedy and oppression also defines the secular Jewish commitment to remembering the Holocaust,
as the Pew poll noted. In this as well, my family fits the trends. While my parents
did not talk about God, my mother has sent my children more books about the
Holocaust than any other topic. One of them is a poignant collection of black-
and-white photographs of Jewish children in Eastern Europe.[11] In the early parts
of the book, the children play in the streets, perform chores, and walk with their
parents. On the last pages, the same streets are shown as empty. The children and
the world that they inhabited are gone. The tragedy of the story shown is clear.
But without a discussion of God, the Jewish identity that these books aim to
commemorate becomes merely ethnic and cultural. The persecution has always
existed and still exists in this narrative. But it is not about religion.

While cultural religion did not look the same in the ancient world as today,
it ultimately functioned in similar ways. Cultural religion created identity
without demanding excessive personal commitment. The Roman world, with
its polytheism and a religion built around the divine protection of the capital
of the empire, was a natural environment for cultural religion. So how did the
early Christians fit into this picture? Some scholars, such as Éric Rebillard, have
argued that the early Christians, just as the Jews and even pagans around them,
were not quite so clearly defined as we might think. The categories of religious
belief were, instead, overlapping and sometimes fluid.[12] The evidence that such
previous studies have examined convincingly shows that fluidity of religious
practices and identities in practice—yes, some Christians did not behave as we
might expect Christians to behave on many occasions!—but it does not provide
an adequate explanation for why this was the case.

A question remains unanswered: Why did some people who converted to
Christianity still keep up with pagan practices, whether knowingly or unintentionally? The premise of this book is that we will understand God's people
in the early church better if, instead of looking at such stories as those at the
very beginning of this chapter as examples of the fluidity of ancient religious
identities, we look at them as examples of cultural Christianity. This is an
important difference, and one that stems from my own clear theological beliefs
and assumptions, which govern this study no less than my academic training.
I am a Reformed Christian, and unlike Rebillard's argument, which tries to
normalize the combination of pagan and Christian practices by some early

---

11. Chana Byers Abells, *The Children We Remember* (New York: Greenwillow, 1986).
12. Éric Rebillard, *Christians and Their Many Identities in Late Antiquity, North Africa, 200–450 CE* (Ithaca, NY: Cornell University Press, 2012).

Christians as simply the objective reality of their lives, I see such behaviors as obviously sinful.

The key, therefore, for answering the question of how the early Christians fit into this world of cultural religion is to study the particular sins that resulted from cultural, rather than deeply countercultural, belief. Because the earliest Christians lived in the Roman Empire, whether they were Romans, Greeks, Jews, or members of the dozens of other groups, the Roman cultural milieu matters a great deal for understanding the particular sins to which they were prone, precisely as a result of their cultural background.

In other words, with each major category of sin that we consider in the church from the first to the fifth century CE, we can identify Greco-Roman cultural attitudes that made the sin possible in the form we see it take. And what may be one of the most shocking revelations of all is that cultural Christians were present in the church both before and after legalization of Christianity. Adoption of Christianity as the official state religion did not make a difference in the existence of cultural Christians. It only adjusted the form that their cultural sins might take.

Cultural belief in Roman religion and an accompanying belief in the greatness of Rome came somewhat easily to various polytheists who were absorbed into the Roman Empire over time.[13] Indeed, many of them had a much greater problem with being conquered and ruled by the Romans than with the idea of having to add Roman gods to their own.[14] But part of what set Christianity apart from all other religions of the day was the movement's opposition to the idea of a casual commitment to the faith—a common feature of cultural belief.

As the New Testament repeatedly reiterates, one either was a Christian or not. Why? Part of the answer certainly has to do with the nature of Christianity as a monotheistic religion. Cultural belief, by contrast, would have allowed the combination of belief in Jesus plus something, effectively amounting to idolatry. Yet that is the trap into which so many early Christians fell, precisely because living counterculturally has always been much harder than following the culture. Their story is the story that this book aims to tell.

---

13. Recent studies that consider the complexities of the place of the individual in Roman religion and culture include Craige Champion, *The Peace of the Gods: Elite Religious Practices in the Middle Roman Republic* (Princeton: Princeton University Press, 2017); Jörg Rüpke, *Pantheon: A New History of Roman Religion* (Princeton: Princeton University Press, 2018); and Jacob Mackey, *Belief and Cult: Rethinking Roman Religion* (Princeton: Princeton University Press, 2022).

14. One tantalizing study of how the Romans gradually Romanized the Gauls in the late first century BCE and first century CE documents the resistance of the conquered to such Roman institutions as schools and the imposition of the Latin language: Gregg Woolf, *Becoming Roman: The Origins of Provincial Civilization in Gaul* (Cambridge: Cambridge University Press, 1998).

In (Historical) Pursuit of
Cultural Christians: From the New
Testament Era to the Fifth Century CE

Proceeding in chronological order, this book tells the story of cultural Christians in the early church from the first to the fifth centuries CE. Using sins as the chief organizing principle for the overall narrative, each chapter focuses on a particular type of sin stemming from cultural belief. We will try to understand the average people in the early churches, to the extent that anyone can ever be deemed truly average.

Part 1 focuses on cultural Christians in the New Testament era and considers sins resulting from Christians' culturally inspired treatment of property, food and drink, and sexuality. In particular, chapter 1 uses the episode of Ananias and Sapphira in Acts 6 as a starting point for considering how the earliest cultural Christians absorbed the teachings of the world around them, sometimes without even intending to do so, through the examination of their culturally imbued views of property and giving.

Chapter 2 turns to difficult questions stemming from the Christian view of food and drink, including the Lord's Supper and provenance of meat. Ultimately, we see that for converts both from Judaism and from traditional Greco-Roman backgrounds, cultural views of food were a stumbling block that was difficult to overcome.

Concluding this section, chapter 3 turns to the thorny question of sexual mores in the early church and the challenges that cultural expectations brought to it. While the Romans, in particular, heavily regulated the sexuality of respectable women, men were largely exempt from those expectations. Slaves' bodies, furthermore, were considered to be the property of their masters, with all attendant implications. By holding all believers to the same standard of personal holiness, the church presented a countercultural expectation that proved challenging to many believers.

Part 2 moves past the New Testament period and considers apostasy, the gendered nature of sin, and the sin of self-care among cultural Christians in the second and third centuries CE. Specifically, chapter 4 examines apostasy as a cultural sin in early churches, using as its case study a church that is known both from the writings of non-Christians and the New Testament: the Bithynian church, which was documented in the famous letter exchange of Pliny and Trajan ca. 111 CE, and also was one of the churches in the audience of 1 Peter. The case study of the Bithynian church shows that erstwhile Christians who renounced the faith in times of persecution did not necessarily do so mainly because of the threat of punishment; indeed, some of the causes of apostasy may have occurred decades before the governor's actions. And this has convicting results for Christians today.

Next, chapter 5 analyzes the ways in which women in the early church challenged cultural expectations of what it meant to be a devout believer in both the pagan and Christian world. The central case study for this chapter is the Passion narrative of Perpetua, a young mother who was martyred in Carthage in the early third century. Perpetua's story highlights the dilemmas that female converts faced because of the Roman legal requirement that women had to be under guardianship of a male relative. Her story shows, as a result, the gendered nature of culturally inspired expectations. Ultimately, for the church to accept that women could have new roles, including a life of singleness, required a radical rejection of Roman cultural views of gender expectations.

Finally, chapter 6 asks the challenging question: When is self-care a cultural sin? The ugly side of self-care, we will see, is the sin of callousness and selfish individualism in the Christian community—ignoring the suffering of others, while focusing wholly on one's own suffering or well-being. We investigate this cultural sin through the pastoral ministry of Cyprian, bishop of Carthage during the worst decade of the Third Century Crisis. Because Cyprian was writing during a pandemic in the Roman Empire, his insights about Christian community are particularly apt, as we emerge from a pandemic that killed, in the most conservative estimate, over one million people in the US and well over six million globally.[15]

Then part 3 looks at the shifts that occurred after Constantine's conversion, when Christianity went from being a persecuted minority to a privileged minority, and eventually, a privileged majority religion in the empire. How did the conversion of Constantine change the story of cultural Christianity in the church? The answer, we will see, is the rise of new forms of cultural Christianity, which were not possible when the Christians were a persecuted minority.

So chapter 7 considers one of the most uncomfortable challenges in the Late Antique church: sectarian strife and violence over doctrine. Using the Donatist controversy as the main case example allows to ask difficult timeless questions, such as: Can Christians ever simply agree to disagree on some doctrinal issues?

---

15. The numbers I note are official counts. Examinations of excess deaths reveal an even more grim estimate of the global death toll: https://www.economist.com/graphic-detail/coronavirus-excess-deaths-estimates.

I argue that the violent response to the Donatists reflected both traditional Roman comfort with violence and the regional pre-Roman traditions that normalized violence as part of regular life. In other words, the collision of multiple pre-Christian traditions that accepted extreme violence as a regular part of civic life amplified the high level of violence that came to define the Donatist controversy.

Chapter 8 turns to the cultural sin of Christian nationalism (that is, equating God's kingdom and the Christian faith with a particular earthly kingdom or nation), as it looks at Augustine's desire to educate Christians and eradicate this sin not only from the local church but from the body of Christ across the Empire following the fall of Rome in 410 CE—an event that (as Augustine's writings show) challenged Christians and pagans alike in their assumptions and premises. The existence of the Roman Empire and its success had been an integral part of the theology of pagans and Christians alike. The fall of Rome to the Goths in 410 was seen rightly as a harbinger of the fall of the Empire in the West and inspired a number of evaluative responses, of which the most monumental was Augustine's *City of God*.

Finally, the concluding chapter examines an alternative to the stories considered throughout this book—the "what if" scenario that existed already in antiquity. If churches were filled with people who longed for holiness but were too prone to sin, what if the most dedicated faithful were to separate themselves wholly from the world and, therefore, all forms of temptation from sin and culture? Would living apart from the culture not be the key to living a holy life in this world? A small number of desert saints, both male and female, elected to live such holy lives in the fourth and fifth centuries CE, and their stories enticed the imagination of believers from that time on. These stories allow us to confront the essential conundrum that we face in our churches today: people are sinful, and whenever sinners gather together, there will be debates over sin. At the same time, however, a Christian cannot live alone without the church. The stories of the desert saints provide us with a poignant response to the growing number of individuals today who claim to be Christians yet reject the church. As some of the desert saints themselves acknowledged, it is just as easy to be a cultural Christian in the church as outside of it.

At this stage, it seems fitting to say a few words about what this book is not. There is no shortage of books that criticize Christianity and Christians, ancient and modern. These books often bring forth legitimate and deeply rooted sins of individual Christians or entire groups that cry out for attention. Evangelical Christians in the twentieth and twenty-first centuries, in particular, have been subject to significant criticism, rooted in exemplary research. To mention just a few examples, the recent books of Kristin Kobes du Mez and Beth Allison Barr have brought attention to the culture of toxic masculinity and the resulting mistreatment and disrespect toward women in some evangelical church circles.[16] Meanwhile, John Wigger's investigation of the scandalous unraveling of two prominent televangelists, Jim and Tammy Faye Bakker, and Matthew Avery Sutton's work on the likewise scandal-ridden ministry of the Pentecostal megachurch pastor Aimee Semple McPherson are just two examples of books on specific sinners and their place in the culture that made them into stars.[17] Last but not least, Jemar Tisby and Esau McCaulley have brought much needed attention to the historical and still present sin of systemic racism in the church.[18] The stories of sin that all of these writers expose are gut-wrenching, because they are true.

At first glance, a book about cultural Christians might seem to be in the same vein as these books about the more recent history of specific types of culturally inspired sins in the church, and maybe in certain ways it is. One distinction here is that in this particular study of sinners, I am including all of us in the discussion. This book is, put simply, about the average church-goers not only in antiquity, but also today.

Talking about sin and sinners is not cheerful. But in engaging in this kind of conversation, the aim of this book is not to leave the reader in utter despair about the state of the church and its people. Furthermore, my goal most certainly is not to motivate anyone to give up and just walk away from Christianity rather than continue fellowshipping with all these hypocrites, of whom I am admittedly one. I found my own faith strengthened by the process of writing this book, and I hope that this will be the case for its readers.

So why write a book about cultural Christians in the early church with the express aim of bringing attention to the prominence of these same sins of cultural Christianity in the church today? Can we observe and criticize believers in the past in a way that does not merely amount to an exercise in historical gossip and, at its worst, voyeurism, as we look in on examples of painful culturally

---

16. Kristin Kobes du Mez, *Jesus and John Wayne: How White Evangelicals Corrupted a Faith and Fractured a Nation* (New York: Liveright, 2020); Beth Allison Barr, *The Making of Biblical Womanhood: How the Subjugation of Women Became Gospel Truth* (Grand Rapids: Brazos, 2021).

17. John Wigger, *PTL: The Rise and Fall of Jim and Tammy Faye Bakker's Evangelical Empire* (Oxford: Oxford University Press, 2017); Matthew Sutton, *Aimee Semple McPherson and the Resurrection of Christian America* (Cambridge, MA: Harvard University Press, 2009).

18. Jemar Tisby, *The Color of Compromise: The Truth in the American Church's Complicity in Racism* (Grand Rapids: Zondervan, 2018); Esau McCaulley, *Reading While Black: African-American Biblical Interpretation as an Exercise in Hope* (Downers Grove, IL: IVP Academic, 2020).

inspired sins and the ways they show the sinful heart of God's people? I write with the confidence that the answer to this question is yes. Through these many and varied stories that span the first half-millennium of the church, we will see that many early believers were just as eager as Christians today to claim belief in Jesus while continuing to make idols out of their wealth, food, appearance, sexual relationships, and patriotism. Their stories allow us to get to know real people who lived and tried to follow Jesus, however imperfectly.

Ultimately, their stories and cultural sins are also deeply relatable in ways that are productively uncomfortable. While we may think that we are removed from the world of the early church, the nature of human sinfulness has not changed. The stories of these early Christians, therefore, are surprisingly familiar and convicting, if only we look closely. While it is at times jarring to admit, their stories are our stories too.

PART 1

Cultural Christians in the New Testament Era

1

More for Me, Less for Thee

The Curious Case of Sharing without Caring in the Early Church

NESTLED IN THE SANDS OF EGYPT ARE THE REMAINS OF AN ancient civilization that long predated the Greeks and Romans, even as it came to be ruled by them. Some of these remains are still visible today, looking incongruously embedded in the landscape of modern cities, like Cairo. Other remains from this civilization look less glorious to the naked eye. Of course, appearances are not everything.

From the days of the Pharaohs, ancient Egyptians generated amounts of records that would have made a Byzantine bureaucrat weep with joy in solidarity. Written painstakingly by trained scribes on papyrus scrolls, these documents had to be disposed of once they had outlived their usefulness. So they were eventually thrown out into local rubbish heaps or recycled to be used as wrappings for sacred animal mummies. Layered in strips, recycled papyri were used to create a sort of ancient papier-mâché encasing for the mummies. In particular, sacred crocodiles, living personifications of the crocodile god Sobek, were lovingly cared for in life and mummified in death. The crocodile cemetery in the ancient city of Tebtunis alone contains thousands of such crocodile mummies. Thankfully, the dry sands of Egypt provided the perfect environment for preserving the mummies and the documents buried with them.

Ancient papyri do not look terribly impressive at first glance. Their state often reflects their thousands of years spent marinating in a garbage dump. Of course, the papyri recycled into mummy casings look even worse—ripped, shredded, stained, and crumpled. But the contents of the documents preserved in them merit our attention.[1]

The documents preserved in papyri from the period when the Greeks and then the Romans ruled Egypt tell fascinating stories of property concerns, many of which would likely be echoed in other parts of the Mediterranean had such records survived. "On such and such a day and month, someone broke into my yard at night and stole my cow," indignantly complains one village police report. A list of the cow's identifying markers follows. One cannot help but hope the poor fellow got his cow back. The frequency of similar reports, however, suggests that such occurrences were commonplace. Both Hammurabi's law code and the Mosaic laws have much to say about theft and disregard for the property of others. The toddler code of "I see it and like it, so it is mine" came much too naturally to many in ancient societies.

Other documents deal with tax collection. Egypt's complicated system of calculating tax obligations for its residents each year makes the IRS look like boy scouts. Since taxes were collected in grain—Egypt was dubbed the breadbasket of the Roman Empire for good reason—a system existed for tracking the annual flooding of the Nile. Through complex formulas, state officials were able to predict the harvest amount for that year based on the flood level. Tax obligations were calculated accordingly, much to the chagrin of farmers, who were always eager to dispute the excessive demands. All societies in world history, it appears, have shared this lack of enthusiasm about taxation.

But most intriguing for our purposes are Egyptian prenuptial agreements. It should not surprise us, perhaps, that such documents were reasonably common. These documents confirm that brother-sister marriages from the Hellenistic period on were not just for the Pharaohs. Egypt was known throughout antiquity for this odd quirk, which others considered bizarre (although, of course,

---

1. The best single-volume introduction to the discipline of Greek papyrology remains P. W. *Pestman's New Papyrological Primer* (Leiden: Brill, 1994). For readable histories of the social world the papyri reveal, see Naphthali Lewis, *Greeks in Ptolemaic Egypt* (New York: American Society of Papyrologists, 2001); and *Life in Egypt Under Roman Rule* (New York: American Society of Papyrologists, 1999).

Abraham married his half-sister Sarah). More surprising, however, are Egyptian divorce agreements.

While no one has done a statistical analysis in correlating Egyptian prenups and divorce documents, it does appear that marriages between brothers and sisters were just as likely as any other marriages to result in divorce.[2] The quarrels over property, in these cases, were no less acrimonious. Sharing, it appears, has never been an ingrained human impulse, not even sharing with one's own relatives, whether those related by blood or marriage or both. One of the countercultural desires of the early Christians had to do with challenging these ideas of sharing. But they learned very early on that resisting the culture is always harder than going along with it.

In this chapter, we will see how ever-present culturally reinforced personal desires—for money, for respect, and for glory—impacted early believers' attitudes toward sharing property and financial resources. While early Christians agreed on the importance of giving and had a distinct view of sharing property with each other, we will also see questions arise in the earliest days of the church about the precise degree of sharing of personal wealth that was expected.[3] Just how much do we need to give to be seen as generous and kind to others? Wouldn't just tithing be enough? The answer to these complicated questions is inextricably connected to the early church's views on sin, sanctification, and the tangled relationship of Christianity and culture.

A Cultural Jew Converts: The Story of One Levite

Early Christians were residents (and sometimes citizens) of the Roman Empire, which had its particular cultural expectations vis-à-vis religious practices, disposal of property, dietary customs, and sexual mores. Many of the earliest Christians, furthermore, were Jews who converted to Christianity. They brought with them their own cultural expectations regarding these same concepts. Jews

---

2. For an analysis of marriage and divorce in the Greco-Roman world, including in the world of Egyptian papyri, see Claude-Emmanuelle Centlivres Challet, *Married Life in Greco-Roman Antiquity* (London: Routledge, 2021).

3. New Testament examples of these discussions include Acts 2:45 and 4:32–35, as well as the story of the rich young ruler (Mark 10:17–27; Matt. 19: 16–22; Luke 18:18–30); Eph. 4:28; 1 John 3:17; and 1 Tim. 6:17–19. Also see Hannah Switchinbank and Steve Walton eds., *Poverty in the Early Church and Today: A Conversation* (London: Bloomsbury, 2018).

of Paul's time were not like the Jews of today, who value Holocaust remembrance over religious belief and practice.[4] And yet they too sometimes treated Judaism as a cultural religion, seeing it as something inherited and mandated—a duty and a source of cultural identity rather than as their sole source of security and joy. As residents of the Roman Empire, Jews were mostly exempt from Roman religious obligations that violated their conscience, but they were clearly affected by the attitudes of those around them regarding their own religious practices.[5] The attitudes toward property, which form the focus of this chapter, exemplify this push-and-pull impulse.

The book of Acts begins with exciting momentum, narrating a series of events showing that Jesus's death and resurrection were only the beginning of something historically and theologically astounding. Following Jesus's resurrection and ascension, the long-awaited gift of the Holy Spirit is poured out on the believers in Jerusalem at Pentecost, and the story of the church begins in earnest.[6] A key component of this early community of Jewish Christians in Jerusalem is the remarkable unity of the people, and an integral part of that unity is their view on property and money:

> All the believers were one in heart and mind. No one claimed that any of their possessions was their own, but they shared everything they had. With great power the apostles continued to testify to the resurrection of the Lord Jesus. And God's grace was so powerfully at work in them all that there were no needy persons among them. For from time to time those who owned land or houses sold them, brought the money from the sales and put it at the apostles' feet, and it was distributed to anyone who had need. (Acts 4:32–35)

The narrative of Acts 4 is full of hope and enthusiasm, as it notes that the believers took care of each other. Those who had more possessions sold off some

---

4. For a study that documents these priorities, see "A Portrait of Jewish Americans," *Pew Research Center*, October 1, 2013, https://www.pewforum.org/2013/10/01/jewish-american-beliefs-attitudes -culture-survey/.

5. For a perspective of a Jewish historian from the first century CE who wrote a history of his people up until that period, see Josephus, *Antiquities of the Jews*. Also see Lester Grabbe, *An Introduction to Second Temple Judaism: History and Religion of the Jews in the Time of Nehemiah, the Maccabees, Hillel, and Jesus* (London: Bloomsbury Academic, 2010).

6. There are a number of excellent commentaries on Acts. One that pays particular attention to the social and historical context is Ben Witherington III, *The Acts of the Apostles: A Socio-Rhetorical Commentary* (Grand Rapids: Eerdmans, 1997). See also Craig Keener, *Acts: An Exegetical Commentary: Volume II* (Grand Rapids: Baker Academic, 2013); and Steve Walton, *Reading Acts Theologically* (London: Bloomsbury, 2022).

property to take care of their needier brothers and sisters. Even more extreme, "No one claimed that any of their possessions was their own." The chapter ends with an exemplary story of how this worked in practice. Joseph, also named Barnabas, a convert (and a Levite, no less!), sold a field and donated the money into the common pot (Acts 4:36–37). This story presents a hopeful glimpse of the transformation that a genuine conversion could bring to this man, who, as we will see shortly, appears to have previously been a cultural Jew.[7] In particular, did you catch the contradiction in the idea of a Levite with property?

The tribe of Levi originally received no inheritance and thus had to depend upon the largesse of the other tribes in exchange for their work as teachers of the law and leaders of worship in the temple. A true Levite should have owned no property, so this anecdote shows just how far the Jewish community had drifted at this point from its roots. Of course, by now many Jews had long lived in exile, as we are reminded of by the comment that this Barnabas was a native of Cyprus. Should not he, as a Levite, have considered himself a native of Israel?

We do not get much information beyond this intriguing comment about Barnabas's place of origin. Maybe he had never even been to Cyprus, and his family simply had ancestral estates there, as some aristocrats were wont to do. But that is not the most likely explanation. The identification of Paul of Tarsus gives us a parallel and a more plausible scenario. Paul was born into a family of Pharisees based in Tarsus in modern Turkey, and his father was the first in the family to receive Roman citizenship. Eager for his son to receive the best possible theological education, his father sent him to study in Jerusalem, where the family also still had relatives. Though Paul never lived in Tarsus again, he continued to refer to himself by this place of origin.[8] Barnabas's story may have been similar, down to the reason for his initial move to Jerusalem from Cyprus.

In any case, the description of Barnabas's place of origin, along with his display of wealth, is most likely a clear mark of his (and, presumably, his family's) generations-long departure from their tribe's original purpose to serve God with their entire time and energy. Indeed, we know from the Jewish historian Josephus that there was a vibrant Jewish community on Cyprus at this time.[9] Away from

---

7. This hopeful passage illustrates the transformation in all the converts that only the Holy Spirit can produce—see John Stott, *The Message of Acts: The Spirit, the Church, and the World* (Downers Grove, IL: Intervarsity Press, 1990), 106–8.

8. For an in-depth reconstruction of Paul's biography and frame of thought and orientation, see Ben Witherington III, *The Paul Quest: The Renewed Search for the Jew of Tarsus* (Downers Grove, IL: Intervarsity Press, 2001), especially pp. 21–35 on Paul's views of his identity and place of origin, and 69–73 on his Roman citizenship.

9. Josephus, *Antiquities of the Jews*, 13.285–288.

Jerusalem for so long as to have forgotten his God-ordained purpose from the Old Testament, this Levite is the quintessential cultural Jew. Like other Levites of this time period, he remembers his tribal identity but has not lived it out so far. As New Testament scholar I. Howard Marshall notes in his commentary on Acts, "The ancient law forbidding Levites to own land (Nu. 18:20; Dt. 10:9) seems to have been a dead letter (Je. 32:7ff.)."[10] This story in Acts demonstrates how the Levite's conversion to Christianity redeemed his wealth and ironically remade him into what he was originally ordained by God to be. By selling this field and donating the proceeds to his new brothers and sisters in Christ, this Levite had come full circle, as he dedicated himself to serving God fully.

This is an encouraging story, and presumably the original audiences found it to be such—after all, we hear that it was the apostles who had given Joseph his new name of Barnabas, "son of encouragement" (Acts 4:36). Barnabas's behavior shows the transforming power of the gospel and the work of the Holy Spirit in the lives of the earliest converts. Their oneness in "heart and mind" is reminiscent of the way the New Testament elsewhere describes the bond of marriage and the bond of Christ with the church. The believers were, without a doubt, bound together into a new kind of family. But lest we be deceived to think that perfection is possible this side of eternity, this story is followed immediately in Acts 5 by a rather different episode, one showing us that sin was never far from even this seemingly perfect new community.[11]

Meet the First Cultural Christians: Ananias and Sapphira

A husband and wife, Ananias and Sapphira, sold off some property. Although they claimed publicly to donate the entirety of the proceeds, they only donated a part. This distinction will turn out to be very important, and the consequences of the deception for them will turn out to be dire. A close reading of the episode suggests that for Ananias and Sapphira, their greed and their cultural views of

---

10. I. Howard Marshall, *The Book of Acts: An Introduction and Commentary* (Grand Rapids: Eerdmans, 1980), 110. Luke Timothy Johnson makes the same point: holding property, by this point, has long been seen as normal for Levites. See Luke Timothy Johnson, *The Acts of the Apostles* (Collegeville, MN: Liturgical, 1992), 87.

11. Stott sees the contrast between Barnabas and then Ananias and Sapphira as a very deliberate effort on Luke's part to show the best and the worst of attitudes, one divinely inspired, the other demonically. See Stott, *The Message of Acts*, 105, 109–12.

property—namely, its usefulness for winning community acclaim—were their chief motivators rather than genuine love for the community.

Peter confronts the couple separately, first questioning the husband. Ananias lies to Peter in response to his questions. Peter rebukes him harshly. At this point, things go from curious to downright surprising. Ananias drops dead—struck down by God. When his wife arrives shortly thereafter, without any knowledge of what has transpired, the earlier scenario is repeated with the same results. Peter questions her as well, and Sapphira expressly insists that the amount of money she and Ananias donated was exactly the amount they had received from the sale. Following the lie, she as well dies on the spot. The story closes with the following comment: "Great fear seized the whole church and all who heard about these events" (Acts 5:11).

What is the point of this story in the general context of Acts? Why tell about this disaster in the midst of what was a rather encouraging narrative so far? Furthermore, what is the problem with Ananias and Sapphira's actions? It seems clear that God is passing judgment on them for a sin, but what is the precise sin being punished, and why is it a sin? To all of us who have at any point not given our all to God, whether in terms of money or time or energy or attention, this is a worrisome question. The punishment of death certainly seems a bit harsh for this transgression, as presumably the believers who saw these events unfold thought—thence the profound fear that they experienced as a result.

The end of Acts 4, with the story of Barnabas, and the first part of Acts 5, with the story of Ananias and Sapphira, deliberately take us into the hearts of real sinners in the church. After seeing the transformation of a cultural Jew into a devout Christian, we now get a glimpse into the deeply sinful nature of some of the earliest Christians. While we have yet to explain exactly why Ananias and Sapphira are sinners deserving of death, Acts gives us no choice but to see that in God's eyes, they must be.

This sequence of events, featuring a new and exciting beginning followed immediately by a tale of sin, has multiple parallels in the Old Testament. To give a couple of particularly famous examples, in Genesis 9, immediately after the flood that God had sent to wipe out sin-filled humanity with the exception of Noah and his family, we get a description of God's covenant with Noah, commemorated with a rainbow.

Most children's Bibles stop there, on that hopeful note. But stopping with the covenant overlooks the ending of the story, which is no less significant. The very next episode in the same chapter is the story of Noah planting a vineyard and getting drunk on its product. His drunkenness is described in a way that shows its undeniable sinfulness. Furthermore, his drunkenness led at least one of his sons into another kind of sin, as he made fun of his father, violating the fifth commandment. Sin did not stay away long even from the one man whom God had judged righteous enough to save from the flood. Next, we get a glimpse of unity among all people.

After the description of the different nations descended from Noah's sons, Genesis 11 proceeds to tell the story of outright sin and rebellion against God after the flood—the building of the Tower of Babel. And that story opens with the statement "Now the whole world had one language and a common speech" (Gen. 11:1). Unity among people is not always unity in pursuit of holiness, a theme that is likewise picked up in Acts. Overall, the juxtaposition of the stories of Barnabas and Ananias and Sapphira plays a key role in showing that while conversion achieves genuine transformation in some, sin has not been absolutely put to death.

But this still leaves unanswered the other question at hand: What is the problem with the actions of Ananias and Sapphira? The Bible does not contain many stories in which someone is struck down directly by God for their transgression, so it is a legitimate question to raise: Why did God judge their actions, including the lie, to be severe enough to deserve death? And why did Ananias and Sapphira consider their own actions acceptable? Answering these questions requires us to consider the cultural expectations about property in both the Jewish community of the day and the Roman world at large, as Ananias and Sapphira, along with the rest of the Christian community in Jerusalem, were navigating these worlds and their expectations.

Property and Cultural Expectations

The story of Barnabas from Cyprus has already reminded us that the Old Testament customs of property ownership did not continue in the Jewish community of the early Roman Empire. Instead, the evidence of the New Testament shows Jewish ideas about property to be remarkably self-serving. Let us consider just two examples of financial transactions that the Jews of the first century CE considered acceptable and that Jesus expressly condemned as perversions of Old Testament teaching. In both cases, we can see cultural religion at work, corrupting the original teaching.

In Matthew 15:4–6, Jesus rebukes the Pharisees for perverting the Old Testament teaching about honoring one's parents. Instead of supporting their parents in old age, the Pharisees claimed that their financial obligation to their parents could be fulfilled by giving money to God—effectively, tithing. There are several important takeaways from this practice. First, Jesus issues it as a general statement, which suggests that this was a widespread practice rather than an isolated occurrence. The implications are jaw-dropping for a society in which the only support and care for the elderly was that provided by their families. By not taking care of their parents financially, the Pharisees are abrogating one of their most important filial obligations for the sake of personal financial gain.

Obviously, whether to support the temple or to support one's parents is not meant to be a choice. Both are essential. The Pharisees, however, had created a system that allowed them to enrich themselves while pretending to serve God. Jesus is not fooled. He poignantly notes, "Thus you nullify the word of God for the sake of your tradition" (Matt. 15:6). The reference to tradition that the Pharisees claim to serve is an indicator of cultural belief that we see here. The Pharisees were citing God's word about honoring their parents, yet they were claiming to fulfill it while actively voiding it, all for the sake of their greed.

Greed and cultural Judaism go hand in hand in another famous episode in Jesus's ministry, one significant enough to be told in all four Gospels—when he threw the money changers and traders out of the temple, rebuking the Pharisees for making God's house into a place of trade—or, to use Jesus's more forceful language, "a den of robbers" (Mark 11:15–19; Matt. 21:12–17; Luke 19:45–47). Strikingly, the idea of financial transactions at the temple clearly seemed appropriate to the Jewish leaders of Jesus's day. Instead of being upset by the market at the temple, they are upset with Jesus's actions of healing and teaching (Matt. 21:15).

The disordered priorities that the Pharisees have about activities that are or are not suitable for the temple shows yet again their greed and their unscrupulous bending of cultural norms for its sake. The money changers and sellers of small sacrificial animals (such as doves) were all at the temple with an eye toward profit, and this means that they provided their services for an outrageous price, knowing that those who traveled from far away had no choice but to pay these fees in order to be able to offer the required sacrifices. The Pharisees' siding with the sellers rather than Jesus is, yet again, an example of their preference for profit, but in a way that still looked outwardly godly.

In both cases, we see a common activity that the Jews of Jesus's day considered culturally acceptable but that violated Old Testament principles and, as Jesus shows, was ultimately an act of greed. Cultural Judaism was filled with such hypocrisies, allowing one to claim to give much to God, while keeping one's fortune. Other examples from Jesus's teaching readily come to mind in addition to these two: the story of the poor widow's offering, for instance, shows the faithfulness of some Jews, while again highlighting the cultural faith of a wealthy giver who gives publicly just to be seen doing so (Mark 12:41–44; Luke 21:1–4).[12] We can assume with a reasonable certainty that these cultural expectations and behaviors greatly influenced the actions of some Jews who converted, including Ananias and Sapphira. Furthermore, though, their rather loose views of financial obligations to others and to God were affected by Roman cultural ideas about property and appropriate ways to get rich.

Whatever we may think of the Jewish views of disposal of property that Jesus criticized, Roman ideas of property were significantly more cutthroat: using wealth to acquire power and using power to acquire more wealth. Traditionally, Romans looked down at wealth acquired through trade and idealized wealth brought in through activities rooted in working the land. To qualify for membership in the Roman Senate, candidates had to own landed property of at least one million sesterces in value—somewhere in the vicinity of eleven million dollars in today's currency.[13] In addition, senators were not supposed to be engaged in trade, but this could be (and was) easily circumvented by relegating business ventures to the care of relatives of equestrian census rank or even trusted freedmen. Gift exchange for political favors also regularly played a part in this calculus.[14]

Roman politicians also used their power to acquire further wealth, which was often essential to continue supporting one's career. Especially notorious were provincial governor appointments, which senators used as an opportunity to get rich, actively encouraging or extorting bribes in exchange for favors. While such practices were technically considered unethical, everyone did it. Only the most outrageous case of a governor's plundering of his province, Verres's governorship of Sicily, made a splash in Rome in 70 BCE. The prosecutor was none other than the great orator Cicero, who thoroughly documented Verres's stripping of the

---

12. Half a millennium after Jesus, Rabbinic Judaism will attempt to create a new and more community-oriented system of care for others, challenging the practices we see here. See Gregg Gardner, *The Origins of Organized Charity in Rabbinic Judaism* (New York: Cambridge University Press, 2015).

13. There are different ways to calculate equivalencies between ancient and modern currencies, and a complicating factor is the current inflation rate, that renders number calculations from as recently as 2015 less accurate at the time of writing. Still, this online ancient currency conversion calculator is a useful tool and estimates that one million sesterces would have been $10,875,000: https://testamentpress.com/ancient-money-calculator.html. For a more detailed explanation of how scholars achieve such calculations, see https://www.the-colosseum.net/history/monete_en.htm.

14. Neil Coffee, *Gift and Gain: How Money Transformed Ancient Rome* (New York: Oxford University Press, 2017).

province of its works of fine art while practicing a series of complex embezzlement schemes and accepting bribes. Ultimately, the only thing exceptional and objectionable about Verres was the scale to which he abused his power. Using the post of power to extort just a little bit less, in other words, would have been perfectly normal and would not have necessitated discussion.[15]

Lest we think that it was only the few at the top of the Roman power pyramid who were employing such dubiously ethical practices in their treatment of wealth, an example from much lower on the totem pole is that of tax collectors. Few professions in the Roman Empire were hated so fiercely. Anything tax collectors extorted above the contracted amount was their take-home pay. The references to tax collectors throughout the New Testament show that these ubiquitous representatives of the empire in the provinces were unscrupulous in their treatment of others. While Ananias and Sapphira were not provincial governors or tax collectors, both Jewish and Roman cultural practices regarding wealth were a part of their world.

We need to keep one final cultural concept in mind when considering Ananias and Sapphira's likely thought process in disposing of their property. Euergetism, the use of one's wealth for the public benefit of one's city or community, was an important feature of Hellenistic city-states and continued into the Roman period. After all, the idea of using taxes for public works did not exist in the Greco-Roman Mediterranean. Many public works, instead, had to be sponsored by wealthy citizens, who used these golden stars on their public service resumé to maximum effect when running in elections for subsequent political office. Also, some citizens had to perform public works as part of official elected positions and unofficial community leadership capacities, as we will see below.

Euergetism involved more than just using one's wealth philanthropically because the ultimate goal was not merely to benefit one's community. Rather, it involved a highly public display of wealth for the purpose of bringing glory and gratitude to the giver, who became widely known and publicly recognized as a patron and benefactor of his city or community. Statues and dedicatory inscriptions celebrating such givers exist and emphasize just how significant this

---

15. For a history of Roman attitudes toward money, see Neil Coffee, *Gift and Gain*. For a more detailed analysis of the different aspects of Cicero's case against Verres, see J. R. W. Prag's edited collection of essays, *Sicilia Nutrix Plebis Romanae: Rhetoric, Law, and Taxation in Cicero's Verrines. Bulletin of the Institute of Classical Studies. Supplement 97* (London: Institute of Classical Studies, University of London, 2007). The Verres case particularly inspired a number of conversations, ancient and modern, about the appropriation of art and cultural resources, beyond mere money and financial extortion. See, for example, Margaret Melanie Miles, *Art as Plunder: The Ancient Origins of Debate about Cultural Property* (Cambridge: Cambridge University Press, 2008).

concept was for political and social advancement of individuals and families. Two examples from Pompeii from the mid-first century CE show this model of euergetism at work.[16]

In 62 CE, the temple of the goddess Isis in Pompeii was destroyed by an earthquake. The event likely presaged the great eruption of 79 CE, which would eventually bury the entire city, but no one seemed to realize that in the 60s. Instead, Numerius Popidius Celsinus rebuilt the temple at his own expense. The inscription on the building commemorates his generosity and thoughtfulness and notes that because of it, the city council enrolled him in its number, despite his being just six years old. Needless to say, it was most assuredly Numerius's papa who provided the financing, but the glory gave the erstwhile moppet a good start on his political career.[17]

Another major public project in Pompeii from earlier in the first century is the Building of Eumachia, so named by archaeologists after the name of its benefactress. Eumachia was a patroness of the local fullers' guild—the Latin term *fullones*, translated as "fullers," is a fancy word for laundry workers, an important profession in a world where no one was equipped to do laundry at home, just as most people could not take a bath at home and went to public baths. At any rate, in their gratitude, the fullers set up in public a lovely statue of Eumachia. While women in the Roman world were precluded from political office, this example shows the ability of women to wield political power within their community through their financial patronage. It seems likely that Sapphira, who is treated as an equal in the crime and in its punishment in Acts 5, was well aware of this custom and harbored similar aspirations of public recognition for her generosity.

To summarize, we see that cultural expectations about property were ingrained into the early Christian communities, for Jewish and gentile converts alike. Ananias and Sapphira were not the exception but rather the rule in this regard. In this context, the actions of Barnabas, who joyfully gave the entire proceeds from a property sale to the Christian community at the end of Acts 4, should strike us as deeply countercultural to both Jewish and Roman views of

---

16. For a history of euergetism in the Hellenistic Greek world, see Marc Domingo Gygax, *Benefaction and Rewards in the Ancient Greek City: The Origins of Euergetism* (Cambridge: Cambridge University Press, 2016). On the Roman side, a great resource is Kathryn Lomas and Tim Cornell, *Bread and Circuses: Euergetism and Municipal Patronage in Roman Italy* (London: Routledge, 2003).

17. For an overview of Pompeii and the stories it reveals about life and property in the Roman world, hands-down the most readable modern book is Mary Beard, *The Fires of Vesuvius: Pompeii Lost and Found* (Cambridge, MA: Belknap, 2010). For a more academic history of the city through its buildings and material remains, see Paul Zanker, *Pompeii: Public and Private Life* (Cambridge, MA: Harvard University Press, 1999).

property. Barnabas's actions were countercultural not just because he donated the entirety of his profits from the sale but also because of his motivations. He is described as feeling profound joy at his own actions, suggesting that he truly and genuinely wanted to serve his community. Nothing in the text suggests any desire on his part to be recognized and awarded special power in the church in exchange for his generosity.[18] The countercultural way in which he displays generosity highlights further the transformation that conversion wrought in him. Ananias and Sapphira, by contrast, behave in ways that exemplify Roman cultural expectations.

While attributing motives to individuals whose own voice we never hear is always tricky, what follows is an explanation that considers likely motives stemming from their cultural milieu. It seems likely that they wished to set themselves up as benefactors of their community, in the model of Greco-Roman euergetism. As theologian John Stott put it, "They wanted the credit and the prestige for sacrificial generosity, without the inconvenience of it. So, in order to gain a reputation to which they had no right, they told a brazen lie. Their motive in giving was not to relieve the poor, but to fatten their own ego."[19] Indeed, the thought of giving anything to support the work of the church does not seem to have occurred to them until they saw Barnabas give an immense sum. Seeing someone else appear to be a benefactor of the community in such a public way presumably gave them the idea of winning gratitude and glory from the same community through a similar financial gift. Also, Sapphira's acting together with her husband shows her desire to seek recognition as a benefactress of the community, in the model of such Roman women as Eumachia at Pompeii.

There is nothing surprising about the way Ananias and Sapphira acted given their cultural context. While they certainly knew at some level that they should not have kept some of the money—after all, that is why they lied about it—they likely expected to be celebrated and publicly thanked for their gift and hoped to use it to leverage a greater level of public respect and standing in the Christian community. But as we now have had a chance to unpack their motives within their cultural context, the question remains: If they merely followed the cultural values and precedents on how to treat one's wealth, why did God judge their actions so severely? Our greatest clue in answering this question lies in Peter's response to their action.

Peter's response to Ananias, as he confronts him about the deception,

---

18. Commentaries emphasize the trustworthiness of Barnabas for the future that this episode already establishes. See Stott, *The Message of Acts*, 108; Johnson, *The Acts of the Apostles*, 91.

19. Stott, *The Message of Acts*, 109–10.

emphasizes the significance of lying to the Holy Spirit, but property is at the center of the story as well: "Ananias, how is it that Satan has so filled your heart that you have lied to the Holy Spirit and have kept for yourself some of the money you received for the land? Didn't it belong to you before it was sold? And after it was sold, wasn't the money at your disposal? What made you think of doing such a thing? You have not lied just to human beings but to God" (Acts 5:3–4).[20]

Peter's rebuke situates the deception of Ananias and Sapphira within the language of spiritual warfare: the deception is motivated by Satan, and the lie is a lie directed not against the church but against the Holy Spirit. Peter notes that at each stage Ananias and Sapphira could have made a different decision with regard to this property. He emphasizes that the property was theirs before the sale and that the proceeds belonged entirely to them after the sale. Any of the three possible courses of action would have been acceptable: they could have kept all of the profits for themselves, they could have given away some of them, or they could have given away all. The problem emerged from secretly dividing the proceeds into two portions, one for themselves and the other for God, while presenting themselves as sacrificial givers à la Barnabas, all with the goal of gaining applause for themselves rather than serving the church.

In the traditionally practiced model, Greco-Roman euergetism amounted to creating an idol of money and honor, all with the goal of elevating oneself and one's family above others. While the use of finances to win prestige was culturally acceptable among Jews and Romans of the day, Christians were meant to be countercultural. Regarding possessions in particular, this meant a rejection of the Greco-Roman model of euergetism, along with a recognition that all believers and their property are set apart for God. Just as Barnabas of Cyprus reverted to his Levite roots by using his property to benefit the church, Ananias and Sapphira were meant to follow traditional Jewish law in fulfilling the vow that they appear to have made. Our strongest clue that this is the issue at hand lies in the particular word choice.

Commentators note parallels between this episode and the story of Achan in Joshua 7.[21] In that story, the Israelites had conquered and destroyed the city of Jericho, and all of the property in the city was dedicated to God for destruction. But one man, Achan, secretly stole some of the property, inciting God's anger against the entire community and leading to the Israelites' crushing defeat at Ai.

---

20. John Stott considers the Satanic attack on the early Christian community to be the defining theme of this passage. See Stott, *The Message of Acts*, 105.

21. Johnson, *The Acts of the Apostles*, 91–92.

The episode ends with the revelation of Achan's secret crime, and the stoning of Achan and his family by the rest of the Israelites.

The connection between Ananias and Sapphira and Achan is more than merely hypothetical. As it happens, the precise verb used to describe the actions of both parties is the same. As John Stott explains:

> Luke, in declaring that Ananias kept back part of the money for himself, chooses the verb *nosphizomai*, which means to "misappropriate." The same word was used in LXX of Achan's theft, and in its only other New Testament occurrence it means to steal. We have to assume, therefore, that before the sale Ananias and Sapphira had entered into some kind of contract to give the church the total amount raised. Because of this, when they brought only some instead of all, they were guilty of embezzlement.[22]

The lie of Ananias and Sapphira was, in other words, worse than we might think. It was a reneging on a promise or vow previously made. Peter's speech is quoted in such detail because it is meant to be a warning against the self-glorifying mentality exemplified by Ananias and Sapphira's actions. God demands everything, including correct motivations for outwardly good actions and including the fulfillment of financial promises. This episode ultimately serves to remind all audiences, ancient and modern, that the truths stated in the first commandment still stand. God is a jealous God and will tolerate no other gods. Cultural religion is idolatry and a direct violation of this commandment because it involves worshiping something (in this case, public honor and prestige, along with personal wealth) as being on par with God by withholding from God something that already belongs to him. According to the Old Testament, the penalty for idolatry was death, and that is the penalty that Ananias and Sapphira received.

Conclusion

The continued allure of culture and the desire to live lives as cultural Christians rather than countercultural ones is a timeless trouble that continues to rock our own world and churches. The question of how best to use our money, in particular, has been coming up in the context of such discussions since the earliest days of Christianity. Peter Brown's masterful book *Through the Eye of the*

---

22. Stott, *The Message of Acts*, 109.

Needle: Wealth, the Fall of Rome, and the Making of Christianity in the West, 350–550 AD considers the complex feelings of discomfort about wealth in the Late Antique Christian community.[23]

Brown's study focuses on the extremes—the Bill Gates figures of antiquity, such as Paulinus of Nola or the two Melanias—and shows that these individuals sought ways to make their wealth respectable through the construction of holy sites and other ways of benefiting the Christian community. While the Roman world saw nothing wrong with the ostentatious accumulation and display of wealth, and actually encouraged it, the Christian community struggled to square extravagant wealth with Jesus's teachings.

Of course, it is easy to feel discomfort over excessive wealth. But the contrast between Barnabas and Ananias and Sapphira reminds us that the issue at hand is not merely wealth per se but rather internal motivation for how we use it. And this should be convicting for the average American churchgoer of the twenty-first century.

As we consider Ananias and Sapphira's culturally motivated rather than God-centered views of property, it becomes clear that what should be most shocking to us about this situation is not that God punished Ananias and Sapphira but rather that he spared others who have been guilty of that same violation. If we are honest with ourselves, we should readily think of moments when we have acted similarly. But as God had said on other occasions, "I will have mercy on whom I will have mercy" (Exod. 33:19; quoted in Rom. 9:15). The original onlookers of Ananias and Sapphira's deaths understood the implications, and that is why the episode concludes with the observation that all who saw or heard of this incident were greatly afraid. They were not surprised or puzzled first and foremost—although perhaps they felt these emotions as well—but afraid.

Fear has been the appropriate reaction since the garden of Eden, for moments when people are particularly struck by their own deep sinfulness in contrast with God's holiness. Understanding that cultural religion is *de facto* idolatry is key for understanding the concerns that we see about it in the early church and why we should be more concerned with it in our own lives today. While the implications extend far beyond our treatment of property, it certainly is a good starting point.

The story of Ananias and Sapphira should make us uncomfortable. And it should make us uncomfortable for the right reasons. It is easy to blame God for injustice if we think that the punishment does not fit the crime. It is striking that

---

23. Peter Brown, *Through the Eye of the Needle: Wealth, the Fall of Rome, and the Making of Christianity in the West, 350–550 AD* (Princeton: Princeton University Press, 2012).

the early Christians did not think so, however. Rather, they wanted to think of themselves as saints, holy people set apart, but were repeatedly convicted of their individual and collective sinfulness through such events as this. If we entertain this thought, that the punishment was unjust, it is merely an example of our own cultural "baggage" distorting our theological understanding. This story challenges us to ask: Are we like Ananias and Sapphira? Are we focused on gaining honor and public recognition for our benevolent acts rather than genuinely desiring to serve those who need our generosity and compassion? At least sometimes, if we are honest, the answer is likely yes.

Ultimately, generosity and giving do not come any easier to us than they did to most ancient Jews, early Christians, or pagan Romans. The story of Verres, the scandalous politician accused of extortion during his time as provincial governor, would feel at home in the modern news. But there are also glimpses of hope. Recent studies have consistently shown the correlation between religious belief and philanthropic giving. Church-attending Christians give more than secular individuals. Furthermore, their giving is not limited solely to supporting the local church. These same individuals are also more likely to give to various organizations.[24] Clearly, believers today are eager to share some of their wealth to support others. But the story of Ananias and Sapphira forces us to be less satisfied with sharing just bits and pieces and asks us to consider motivations: Are we sharing out of love, or are we too seeking honor and recognition? Could we ever share all joyfully, the way Barnabas did? What might that look like? There are many possible applications, but I will limit myself to just three.

One ministry that exemplifies the giving of all is adoption. Parenting always requires sacrifices, but much more than parenting biological children, adoption often requires the sacrifice of finances and personal time and health. The sacrifices may be staggering. One couple in my church made the decision to cash out their retirement savings to adopt—a decision that may seem foolish in the eyes of the world but is an example of a remarkable sacrifice for the cause of Christ. Another couple chose to adopt two girls with special needs from China after their three biological children were grown. Instead of living a more restful life in their middle age and retirement, they embraced the sacrifice of their time, energy, and finances for this ministry.[25]

---

24. For some useful statistics summarizing this phenomenon, see Karl Zinsmeister, "Less God, Less Giving?" *Philanthropy Magazine*, Winter 2019, https://www.philanthropyroundtable.org/philanthropy -magazine/less-god-less-giving.

25. For more inspiring stories of Christians who gave much to live out the calling to adopt, see Katie Davis Majors, *Kisses from Katie: A Story of Relentless Love and Redemption* (Brentwood, TN: Howard, 2012). As an eighteen-year-old, Katie gave up on the regular "American Dream" of college

Another application might be to embrace a different view of taxation, in light of the different purposes of taxes in the modern world. The resentment toward taxation in the ancient world involved the aspects of it that were decidedly corrupt—after all, tax officials effectively raised their own salary as part of what they collected. By contrast, taxation in modern America takes on, on a large scale, much of what the church attempts to do at the local level, such as the work of caring for orphans, widows, and the destitute, providing them with food, healthcare, and better access to education. Whenever tax cuts are passed, however, these works of mercy most often suffer in the name of balancing a state budget. Instead of complaining about all taxes as a senseless burden, might we embrace them as an additional opportunity to care for the less fortunate both within and outside the church? We should see these works not as trying to replace the church but as types of parachurch ministries. And this could be especially true if more Christians go into social work career fields—a vocation that, given its low pay, also involves sacrificing financial security.

Finally, as we rethink what it means to share some or all with other Christians, this should impact our attitudes toward immigration and foreign aid. Sacrificial giving and sacrificial sharing require recognizing the suffering and needs of others. If we refuse to consider the needs of people who are willing to risk their lives just to get into this country, we resemble the pagan Romans, who had no qualms saying that some people (i.e., noble Roman citizens) were better than others and therefore more worthy of assistance or, even, a chance for survival. Today, as in antiquity, the sharing of property and resources with those less fortunate has the potential to improve or even save lives, quite literally. Ultimately, the theological truth that we so often forget, as we are blinded by our own materialistic culture, is that nothing that we own is truly ours anyway.

Of course, cultural religion involves much more than our views of property and sharing resources. So in the next chapter we consider how the adoption of cultural standards over God's standards could corrupt our treatment of one of the most basic of human needs: food.

---

and gradual transition to adulting. Instead, she moved to Uganda and ended up adopting a village (just about literally!) of orphans. Russell Moore, who with his wife has also adopted internationally, has written a powerful call for Christians to pursue adoption as a ministry: *Adopted for Life: The Priority of Adoption for Christian Families and Churches* (Wheaton, IL: Crossway, 2015).

2

BBQ and Wine

When Food Leads to Sin

ACCORDING TO EARLY GREEK MYTH, THE FIRST EVER MEAT sacrifice that humans offered to the gods involved a trick.[1] Prometheus, an older-generation god who had repeatedly sided with the humans against the younger Olympians, offered the gods a choice of two piles of meat. In one of the piles, he disguised the better parts of the sacrificial animal, making them look quite unpleasant. In the second pile, he cleverly draped what was largely just bones with some fat. Zeus and the other gods were fooled into selecting the second pile as theirs, leaving the rest for the humans. This, believed the Greeks, was how the Greek custom of sacrifice for the gods as a barbecue feast for humans was born. The precedent of the sacrifice procedure, once acknowledged by the gods, had to be followed in the same way forever. After all, accepting the sacrifice was a contractual act.

This etiological myth explains certain cultural values that were shared among those who lived in the Greco-Roman world and worshiped its traditional gods. Central among these cultural values was the association of the consumption of meat with religious rituals. Since any typical sacrificial animal would have been much too large for one individual or family to eat alone, these rituals generally were celebrated with communal meals that included many people,

---

1. Hesiod, *Theogony*, vv. 509–72; and *Works and Days*, vv. 58–76.

often of different social ranks. As a result, these occasions of feasting also created and perpetuated specific social customs that dictated socially motivated seating arrangements at the banquet and a likewise strategic distribution of the best and worst parts of the animal at the meal.[2]

The cultural idea of sacrifices to the gods as major communal feasting occasions continued throughout antiquity. Just like their polytheistic neighbors, the Jews had their own tradition of animal sacrifice and communal feasts, after giving God a portion of the meat. And some, albeit more informal, ranking of individuals by quality of meat given to them was a feature of Jewish gatherings as well. We encounter one such example in 1 Samuel 1:5, where we learn that the future prophet Samuel's father expressed his affection for Hannah, the favorite of his two wives, by giving her the best portion of the meat at sacrifices. Yes, this went over as well in his household as it would in yours, should you decide to try it out.

The Jewish religious custom of animal sacrifices ended forever with the destruction of the Second Temple by the Romans in 70 CE. But even before this, early Christianity challenged the dietary customs of both cultural Romans and cultural Jews. Through the dismantling of previously expected dietary traditions and restrictions, early Christian teaching on dietary customs showed the importance of being countercultural in a world that valued conformity with existing culture. Cultural views on food, much like cultural views on property, were problematic, because they could lead down the slippery slope to idolatry. A related issue had to do with the concept of personal holiness. "You are what you eat" was a very literal concept for Jews who followed the Mosaic dietary laws, and in its redefined form, it became an integral part of teachings on personal holiness for the early Christians.

This chapter considers some of the earliest debates in Christian communities about the role of food in fueling the sin of cultural religion. Ultimately, we will see, the conviction that the consumption of certain items could lead to sin stemmed not from any particular food or drink itself, but from the ways the cultural baggage associated with these foods and beverages could distort the relationships of people with each other and with God. Christianity encouraged countercultural relationships, bringing together believers who had nothing in common except their faith. Food, especially the celebration of the Lord's Supper

---

2. I direct anyone interested in reading more on Greek religious views on sacrifice to Marcel Detienne and Jean-Pierre Vernant, *The Cuisine of Sacrifice Among the Greeks* (Chicago: University of Chicago Press, 1998); and Fred Naiden, *Smoke Signals for the Gods: Ancient Greek Sacrifice from the Archaic through Roman Periods* (Oxford: Oxford University Press, 2015).

as part of worship, was integral for the building of this new and deliberately countercultural community of saints.

In Praise of Vegetables

Sometime around 160 BCE, Cato the Elder, a staunch Roman conservative politician, perhaps best remembered for nagging the Roman Senate into destroying Carthage (he kept ending every speech with an addendum "and I think Carthage must be destroyed!" for about a year, until no one could take it anymore), wrote a treatise *On Agriculture*. Cato's praise of agriculture is part of his carefully staged public persona as an authentic Roman conservative and advocate of Roman traditionalism. Agriculture was a noble Roman occupation, and land ownership was required for senators. Still, in his manual, Cato shows off his knowledge of much more than merely the everyday running of the estate.

The crowning jewel of the document is the discourse on the various uses of cabbage. A vegetable that "surpasses all other vegetables," the cabbage is not only versatile—it can be eaten either raw or cooked—but has incredible medicinal value, explains Cato. Headache? Eat some cabbage. Can't sleep? Eat some cabbage. Digestive ailments? Eat some cabbage or drink special cabbage broth, for which Cato helpfully provides a recipe. It is also useful when applied topically on wounds, ulcers, and even cancers. Finally, a fan of "waste not" policies, Cato provides some medicinal uses for the urine of habitual cabbage eaters. Bathing weakly babies in such urine will apparently ensure health. Gently warmed and applied topically, cabbage urine is guaranteed to assist with eye ailments and headaches.

Cato lived to the ripe old age of eighty-five, so perhaps the cures worked for him. At the very least, presumably his robust natural disposition was able to ward off any potential dangers of, say, regularly washing out his eyes with cabbage urine. But his praise of vegetables, including the humble miracle that is the cabbage, was not entirely original. It stems from an ancient philosophical school, the Pythagoreans, who advocated a wholly vegetarian diet and the complete avoidance of meat. The reason? Souls, they believed, migrated from one living being to another after death. So there was always the danger, when eating the meat of an animal, that one might inadvertently eat a loved one.[3] While the Pythagoreans'

---

3. Colin Spencer, *The Heretic's Feast: A History of Vegetarianism* (Lebanon, NH: University Press of New England, 1996), 50. For additional explanation of the Pythagoreans' approach to vegetarianism, see Michael Beer, *Taste or Taboo: Dietary Choices in Antiquity* (Totnes, UK: Prospect, 2009), chapter 2.

reasoning for abstaining from meat was unique to them in the ancient world, the ancient Jews at times maintained a similar vegetable-heavy diet for reasons of their own.

The dietary laws that God first revealed to the Jews through Moses in Leviticus 11 set the stage for arguably the most restrictive diet in the history of the ancient world. To qualify as kosher (fit for eating) the animal had to chew cud and have split hooves. Some common land and sea animals were deemed unclean under this system and thus were not to be eaten or even touched. This included, most notably, the pig, that quintessential cheap source of meat for civilizations ancient and modern. The laws also specified a specific way of slaughtering and cooking animals. In particular, blood could not be consumed. The purpose of this system was to keep God's people holy and set apart. But just how demanding did the Jews find these rules to be? In a nutshell, very. When the prophet Daniel, enslaved in Babylon, determined to adhere to God's dietary laws, the only solution he could find was to go on a vegan diet of vegetables and water.[4]

Daniel's choice reminds us that the Mosaic dietary laws did more than allow God's people to maintain personal holiness. A related purpose of these laws was to set God's people apart from everyone else around them in the ancient world. Although this setting apart was meant to be a virtue, an idolization of it could swiftly turn into sin. We see this arise in the Pharisees' reactions to Jesus's association with people considered disreputable, such as Zacchaeus the tax collector. Pharisees were particularly scandalized that Jesus ate meals with such questionable characters. This was a controversial act because of a fear that devout Jews had of the less devout in their midst. After all, such people may not be keeping the dietary laws perfectly and thus were likely to pollute those who eat with them.

The concern of the Pharisees over Jesus's actions and his seeming disregard for the traditional dietary laws show their culturally rooted idolization of their own separate status. Their strict adherence to dietary laws, after all, led them to reject the Son of God, literally judging full obedience to the dietary laws to be

---

4. For a historical overview of ancient Jewish dietary laws and customs surrounding them, see Jordan D. Rosenblum, *The Jewish Dietary Laws in the Ancient World* (Cambridge: Cambridge University Press, 2017). For books that take the story of Jewish eating customs and laws from antiquity to the present, showing ways in which the rules have been reinterpreted and adapted since antiquity, see John Cooper, *Eat and Be Satisfied: A Social History of Jewish Food* (New York: Aronson, 1993); David C. Kraemer's *Jewish Eating and Identity through the Ages* (London: Routledge, 2007); and most recently, Aaron Gross, Jody Myers, and Jordan D. Rosenblum eds., *Feasting and Fasting: The History and Ethics of Jewish Food* (New York: NYU Press, 2020). Finally, for an intriguing modern approach to food inspired by Daniel's diet, see Rick Warren's coauthored book, with Daniel Amen and Mark Hyman, *The Daniel Plan: 40 Days to a Healthier Life* (Grand Rapids: Zondervan, 2013).

more important than God himself. The absurdity of the Pharisees' choice is clear. Further highlighting the absurdity of privileging the dietary laws over God's commands, Acts 10 tells us of the miraculous vision given to Peter. The vision abolished the old laws but created new ones regulating the consumption of meat in the early church. As we will see, both measures served to bring the gentiles into the church, while acknowledging the difference between their cultural baggage vis-à-vis food and that of the Jews. Again at the center of the battleground was meat.

Meat Consumption and the Early Church

In the first century CE, during the time of the emperor Tiberius (and thus during Jesus's lifetime), a Roman culinary expert Apicius published a cookbook of popular contemporary recipes. We do not know much about Apicius, and many of the recipes preserved in his *On Cooking* are later additions. The oeuvre, nevertheless, gives us a fascinating insight into Roman dietary practices. Especially illuminating is the section on meats.[5]

Apicius devoted book 8 specifically to quadrupeds, and his recipes are conveniently grouped by animal, much like in some modern cookbooks. The similarities, however, end with the arrangement. The animals included are mostly unfamiliar to our Western tastes: wild boar, venison, gazelle, wild sheep (note that they are separated here from domesticated sheep, suggesting that this was a different animal), beef and veal, kid and lamb, pig and suckling pig, hare, and finally—for those with cheaper tastes—the dormouse (a closer relative of the modern squirrel or rat than a mouse).

The dormouse apparently came into culinary vogue in the Roman Empire, giving rise to the *glirarium*—a commercial farm where the *glis*, the dormouse, was raised for meat. Roman gourmets noted that dormice raised in a *glirarium* were much fatter than those in the wild and thus more desirable for eating. In addition, little clay jars with grooves inside have been found in cities, such as Pompeii, which were specifically designed for storing and fattening an individual

---

5. For a translation of Apicius with helpful contextual notes, part of public domain, see Apicius, *De Re Coquinaria*, trans. Joseph Dommers Vehling, https://penelope.uchicago.edu/Thayer/E/Roman/Texts/Apicius/home.html. Please note that Apicius, just like many premodern cooking guides, does not provide detailed measurements or precise instructions for his recipes. An intrigued chef intent on recreating a Roman meal at home may be best served by consulting Christopher Behr and Annie Schlechter, *Carne: Meat Recipes from the Kitchen of the American Academy in Rome* (Rome: Little Bookroom, 2016).

dormouse for dinner. The grooves allowed the trapped rodent to get some exercise while awaiting its inevitable fate.

Spices can go a long way in making sketchy meats palatable. Years ago, a student in my introductory Roman history class re-created Apicius's stuffed dormouse recipe. He substituted chicken for the original meat to great acclaim by classmates, turning on its head the joke about all unfamiliar meats tasting like chicken.

At the same time, the sophisticated spices, herbs, and sauces used in Apicius's recipes remind us that they were largely designed for the upper-crust gourmands of Roman society. Some recipes are even named after particular individuals whose chefs (usually enslaved) presumably had served them to great success. A recipe for smoked rabbit is named after one Passenius. A rather simple recipe for a suckling pig with leeks and dill is named after Fronto, who was *praetor urbanus* (a senator in charge of judging civil cases) during the brief rule of the emperor Vitellius in 69 CE. Another recipe, also for a suckling pig, is named after Vitellius himself, an emperor who was as famous for his lavish appetites as for his administrative incompetence.

Not all animals mentioned receive the same level of attention in the cookbook. Apparently, there are not a lot of ways to prepare a dormouse, for instance. But the section of recipes for cooking a pig or suckling pig is especially lengthy, reflecting the wide availability of the animal, and the versatility of this particular meat. Still the range of the meats included is remarkable compared to our tastes today. It reminds us just how adventurous ancient eaters were. But it is also a reminder of a world with which many of us are not personally familiar—a world that was no stranger to food insecurity and thus had learned to be resourceful. Not only are a lot of different animals consumed, but there are also recipes for using every part of the animal, such as the two different recipes for hare's liver and other entrails. Blood, furthermore, makes an appearance in sauces, including the recipe for hare's liver and entrails cooked in blood.

For Jews living in the Roman Empire and seeing what their non-Jewish neighbors ate, the dietary differences revolving around meat were a constant reminder of their own uniqueness. Not only could they not eat any of the conveniently prepared meals, such as meat pies, sold on city streets as Roman "fast food," but they could not eat any of the meats sold in Roman markets. After all, at least half of the meats that the Romans ate did not fit the qualifications in the Mosaic laws. While the hare, for instance, chews its cud, it does not have split hooves and thus is out. An additional barrier had to do with the ways animals were slaughtered. Because the Mosaic code required a specific way of slaughtering the animal to drain away blood, to this day Jews who keep kosher will only buy meat from kosher butchers. Jews living in the Roman Empire did likewise, and there may have been kosher butchers in some major cities, such as Rome and Alexandria. But for those Jews who were the earliest converts to Christianity, their conversion was soon accompanied by a surprising new mandate regarding meat. And this new rule, ultimately, was key for the spread of the gospel to the gentiles.

The cultural value of Jewish uniqueness enforced by the Mosaic dietary laws was challenged early in the history of the church by the cancelation of the old dietary mandate, and the accompanying mandate to take the gospel to all peoples. The story illustrating this connection most overtly is found in Acts 10, where the apostle Peter experienced an unusual vision while awaiting a meal:

> He saw heaven opened and something like a large sheet being let down to earth by its four corners. It contained all kinds of four-footed animals, as well as reptiles and birds. Then a voice told him, "Get up, Peter. Kill and eat."
>
> "Surely not, Lord!" Peter replied. "I have never eaten anything impure or unclean."
>
> The voice spoke to him a second time, "Do not call anything impure that God has made clean." (Acts 10:11–15)

Peter's objections to God during the vision, refusing three times to eat foods that were not lawful to consume under the Mosaic laws, suggest both a strong cultural adherence to these laws, to which he had been subject his entire life, and also perhaps a fear that God was testing him. But finally, Peter is convinced that the mandate is no test of his faithfulness and is meant in earnest.

While understandably shocked by this vision, Peter correctly interprets it to be about more than just food. When a Roman centurion, Cornelius, summons Peter immediately afterward to come to his home and tell him about the gospel, Peter tells the vision to Cornelius, by way of introduction: "He said to them: 'You are well aware that it is against our law for a Jew to associate with or visit a Gentile. But God has shown me that I should not call anyone impure or unclean. So when I was sent for, I came without raising any objection. May I ask why you sent for me?'" (Acts 10:28–29). Peter proceeds to tell Cornelius and his household about Jesus, and the chapter concludes with the first occurrence of the outpouring of the Holy Spirit on gentile converts and a group baptism of the members of Cornelius's household.

Peter's initial statement to Cornelius suggests that there was a strong possibility that Peter would have refused to come to Cornelius's home had he not received the earlier vision. That would have been a lost opportunity to share the gospel. This episode shows that the cultural Jewish dietary customs could be a hindrance to the spread of the gospel because of the attitude that people, rather than just foods, were unclean. Besides, we have to keep in mind that hospitality in the ancient world required the sharing of foods. If visiting with someone for hours to discuss a complex topic, as was the case for Peter's visit with Cornelius, the sharing of food together at some point in the visit was expected. Offering a guest some cold cuts or sausage with bread, cheese, and olives would have been customary but, of course, a violation of multiple Jewish dietary rules. Yet for Peter to reject Cornelius's hospitality would have been more than simply rude—it would have been an insult from a social inferior to his superior.

In reading this episode, we need to remember that Cornelius himself had cultural prejudices to overcome when calling Peter into his home. After all, as a distinguished centurion and a Roman citizen, he was, from a Roman cultural standpoint, far above Peter in social rank. Yet we hear of no hesitation on his part about associating with Peter. It may have been easier for this Roman God-fearer to reject the Roman cultural expectations about food and people than it was for a formerly devout Jew to reject the Jewish cultural expectations about these concepts. Ultimately, we see a redefinition of sin stemming from a redefinition of what foods, especially meats, are acceptable to consume. The precise command whose violation used to be sin under the Mosaic code is now a sin if followed precisely, because it is a barrier to bringing people to God.

Peter's experience shows the challenges that even some of the leaders in the early Christian community faced in resisting previous Jewish cultural expectations about meat. But what about the pagan converts? We might imagine that the Romans who converted to Christianity did not have to face sins related to food. After all, if God himself declared all animals to be clean, should this not be a sign that one could be an Apicius-style gourmet and a Christian as well? Suckled pig boiled in milk can be back on the dinner table now, right?

Alas, this is not quite that simple. Paul's first letter to the Corinthian church provides us with insights on the challenges that converts from the traditional Greco-Roman religion faced. When it comes to dietary practices, the cultural baggage of the pagan world had its own significant potential to lead people into sin, precisely because in the pagan world certain dietary practices were inseparable from idolatry in a literal sense. But both concerns about personal holiness and the potential to create barriers to the faith of others were a part of the puzzle as well.

In 1 Corinthians 8, Paul brings up the question of whether Christians should eat meat from pagan sacrifices. The fact that he brought up this issue clearly indicates that at least some in the Corinthian church engaged in this practice, but there were also perhaps questions about whether this was acceptable. For Jews, the issue would not have even come up: since pagan ways of slaughtering meat did not meet God's standards, that alone was already a good reason to not partake. We can recall yet again the example of Daniel and his refusal to eat meat from the king's table in Babylon. It appears that the Corinthian Christians were gentile converts, for whom such previous prohibitions did not apply. Instead, they were used to cultural celebrations revolving around the consumption of meat that had been offered to the pagan gods.

Eating food offered to idols did not mean merely eating meat that came from animals sacrificed to pagan gods. Rather, it meant participating in the full array of activities that accompanied such occasions of consumption inside pagan temples, no less. And that, rather than the mere act of eating, could be a stumbling block whether to those choosing to eat meat from sacrifices or for their weaker fellow-converts, who see them eating. As Paul warns:

> But not everyone possesses this knowledge. Some people are still so accustomed to idols that when they eat sacrificial food they think of it as having been sacrificed to a god, and since their conscience is weak, it is defiled. But food does not bring us near to God; we are no worse if we do not eat, and no better if we do.
>
> Be careful, however, that the exercise of your rights does not become a stumbling block to the weak. For if someone with a weak conscience sees you, with all your knowledge, eating in an idol's temple, won't that person be emboldened to eat what is sacrificed to idols? So this weak brother or sister, for whom Christ died, is destroyed by your knowledge. When you sin against them in this way and wound their weak conscience, you sin against Christ. Therefore, if what I eat causes my brother or sister to fall into sin, I will never eat meat again, so that I will not cause them to fall. (1 Cor 8:7–13)

In theory, Paul notes, food is food. In reality, however, it has too many cultural associations that are likely to lead the eaters and others around them into sin.

What would have been the cost of foregoing meat from sacrifices? Why is this such a significant issue to discuss in detail? We have to remember that if city dwellers in the Roman Empire were not going to partake of the meat offered to idols, they would likely have had to forego eating some kinds of meat entirely—with the exception, of course, of those ever-present and decidedly sketchy street-sold mystery meat pies. But even the meat pies were no guarantee, as a number of emperors throughout the first century CE tried to ban or restrict the sale of hot foods at *popinae*, the ubiquitous street establishments that sold drinks and snacks.

One theory to explain the restrictions is practical: the *popinae* may have been a fire hazard in the crowded ancient cities, like Rome, which had one million residents by the first century CE. Another theory, however, is political: if people gathered to eat hot food, they would have spent longer at the shop, and there was potential for plotting against the emperor. After all, what else would someone do when going out for a hot lunch? Whatever the reason, it made the religious sacrifices and the opportunity to eat meat that they provided all the more special.

While the wealthy could purchase an entire animal for cooking or (more likely) had a ready supply of animals raised on their own country estates, this was not an option for most ancient city dwellers. We must keep this urban setting in mind to understand what Paul says about his own dietary decision at the end of 1 Corinthians 8—if eating food might make another believer stumble, he would rather skip it. Paul is assuming that any meat purchased in the city could have come from a sacrifice and, therefore, subject to this concern of idolatry. Lest we think that this is a problem specific to the Corinthian church, which admittedly seemed to have a fair share of challenges, Paul brings up the same concern in his letter to the Romans, a church that appears to have been exemplary for its faith-fulness: "Accept the one whose faith is weak, without quarreling over disputable matters. One person's faith allows them to eat anything, but another, whose faith is weak, eats only vegetables. The one who eats everything must not treat with contempt the one who does not, and the one who does not eat everything must not judge the one who does, for God has accepted them" (Rom 14:1–3).[6]

Paul's remarks to the Romans make it clear that eating a particular food or diet does not a saint or sinner make. However, dietary choices are important and are a personal choice. Most significant, Paul notes that each person should make the decision using his or her own faith as the chief criterion. The others should respect that decision to build up a brother or sister rather than tear down their faith. Dietary decisions yet again cannot be separated from faith. A dietary choice only becomes sinful if it leads the eater or those around him into sin.

As someone who has admitted to trying to become all things to all people in the name of Christ, Paul has noted in 1 Corinthians 8 that he chooses to err on the side of caution. That meant paying close attention to those with whom he was dining and cutting meat out entirely when necessary. This effective shift yet

---

6. The issue at hand in Romans could involve two possibilities that are not mutually exclusive: Paul could be concerned about Christians eating meat sacrificed to idols, or he could be concerned about Jewish Christians eating meat that they were not supposed to eat per Levitical laws.

again to the "Daniel diet" for Paul, and any other early Christians who made the same decision, would have had both dietary and social costs. The dietary costs, of course, meant simply cutting meat out of one's diet. But fish was abundant in Corinth, a city located right on the Isthmus, and widely available in Rome as well. Besides, chickpeas, lentils, and other legumes were a regular part of the ancient Mediterranean diet. Meeting one's protein needs would not have been a challenge.

But the social costs of Paul's decision to forego meat were more serious. Missing occasions at which sacrificed meat was consumed meant missing the opportunity to connect with other community leaders and be recognized for one's social status in their midst. Paul's dietary choices, therefore, meant embracing a humble status willingly in a world that judged everyone by their status. As we see from his discussion of the Corinthian Christians, such a choice was not easy, as cultural practices seeped into the early churches. It appears, in particular, that the Corinthian Christians transferred the cultural expectations that applied during the pagan banquets to their celebration of the Lord's Supper in a way that was decidedly sinful.

From the Pagan Banquets to the Lord's Supper

In 1 Corinthians 11, Paul accuses the Corinthians of perverting the Lord's Supper by celebrating it in a highly individualistic way. His description of the proceedings is forceful: "So then, when you come together, it is not the Lord's Supper you eat, for when you are eating, some of you go ahead with your own private suppers. As a result, one person remains hungry and another gets drunk. Don't you have homes to eat and drink in? Or do you despise the church of God by humiliating those who have nothing? What shall I say to you? Shall I praise you? Certainly not in this matter!" (1 Cor 11:20–22). As Paul proceeds to explain, this is a distortion of Jesus's original celebration of the Lord's Supper with his disciples, which emphasized both the equality of the disciples and the symbolic significance of the meal. The Corinthians have forgotten Jesus's command to "do this in remembrance of me" (1 Cor 11:24). Instead, they have been going through the motions, distracted by the cultural baggage of Greek and Roman feasting practices.

The Corinthians lived in a world marked by the intersection of Greek and

Roman culture. Corinth was a prominent port city in the Greek world from the Archaic period on, but by the time of Paul, it was also a center of Roman presence in the province of Achaea. As we think of cultural practices revolving around feasts, the Corinthians' world included knowledge and practice of values of both the Greek symposium and the Roman convivium. These two types of communal celebrations had certain differences, which are relevant to outline here.

The Greek symposium, an aristocratic drinking party (the term literally means "drinking together"), was an integral part of respectable men's social activities in the Greek city-states. Plato's famous dialogue, *Symposium*, outlines a semifictional account of just such an occasion, on which a number of leading Athenian aristocrats and thinkers, including Socrates himself, gathered together for a night of casual drinking and conversation. After an agreement in the group that they have all had too much to drink on the previous night, the company decides instead to pass the evening by presenting refined extemporaneous speeches on the topic of love. The orderly activities are eventually derailed, when Alcibiades, the *enfant terrible* of late fifth-century Greece, drops in uninvited. The symposium concludes with everyone but Socrates drunk to oblivion. So much for a night of civilized conversation.[7]

Although Plato's work was not meant to describe precisely how symposia proceeded in real life, the dialogue emphasizes the equality of all participants who were worthy to be included in this gathering. Even the uninvited guest, Alcibiades, is a social equal and thus could have been invited. He is not entirely breaking conventions, therefore, by showing up. Only men were allowed to be present for a symposium (although disreputable women could be present for entertainment, some of it of highly disreputable nature), but those allowed were treated as equals. This means that all seating locations were more or less equally honorable, and all guests received the same quality of wine and food. In fact, they received their wine from a communal mixing bowl. Since the Greeks usually mixed their wine with some water, this ensured also that the strength of the wine was equal for all. The symposium, in other words, while a feature of aristocratic

---

7. The definitive academic study on the subject remains Pauline Schmitt-Pantel, *La cité au banquet: histoire des répas publiques dans les cités grecques* (Paris: Sorbonne, 1992). See also the essays in Oswyn Murray ed., *Sympotica: A Symposium on the Symposion* (Oxford: Oxford University Press, 1990); and William J. Slater ed., *Dining in a Classical Context* (Ann Arbor: University of Michigan Press, 1991). A less academic history of feasting, focusing in particularly on history of beverages, is Tom Standage, *A History of the World in Six Glasses* (New York: Walker, 2006). Finally, for a history of feasts, pagan and Christian, into Late Antiquity, see Jason König's intriguing study, *Saints and Symposiasts: The Literature of Food and the Symposium in Greco-Roman and Early Christian Culture* (Cambridge: Cambridge University Press, 2012).

life, was nevertheless a highly democratic institution in practice, as long as one met the high bar required to be included.

This democratic aspect of the Classical Greek symposium continued to fascinate people across the Mediterranean long after the Roman conquest. In the early third century CE, Athenaeus of Naucratis wrote a massive fifteen-volume work, *The Learned Banqueters.* A fictional story of a series of exceedingly long dinner parties set in imperial Rome, the book is a dialogue about everything related to the Greek symposium. While the democratic aspect of the symposium comes through—all guests are equally prominent in society—another aspect of the symposium that this work highlights is its potential to incite "consuming passions."[8] The symposium was a place where regular societal limitations on moderating the pleasures of the flesh were suspended. So immoderate eating, drinking, and misbehaving with the flute girls (who did more than just play the flute) was an accepted part of the festivities.

To be clear, this is not a new element of the symposium that Athenaeus invented. Scenes of the symposium abound in Classical Athenian vase paintings, fittingly on pottery that would have been used at these parties. The decorations portray the extremes of the consuming passions that were an integral part of the symposium in very graphic action. One popular theme in the vase paintings is a party game known as the *kottabos.* While we are not entirely sure how the game was played, it apparently involved throwing the dregs at the bottom of one's cup at a target. The dilemma for the players was, of course, that to get another pass at the game, one needed to drain another cup down to the dregs. But consuming too much was bound, eventually, to affect one's aim. A surviving floor mosaic from a house near the Athenian agora reminds, incidentally, of the mess that the excesses of eating and drinking at the symposium created: the mosaic, exquisitely executed, shows a debris of fish heads and bones, oyster shells, and various other food fragments. We might as well imagine some spots of wine dregs in the mix as well. For those used to the symposium, these excesses were a reflection of a life well lived and a social structure where those enjoying the party were not the ones cleaning up after it.

The Roman banquet, *convivium* (a term that literally means "living it up together" in Latin), represented a different set of cultural values that were intrinsically less chaotic and messy at first glance. While seemingly more inclusive than the Greek symposium—women and people of different economic classes could

---

8. See James Davidson, *Courtesans and Fishcakes: The Consuming Passions of Classical Athens* (Chicago: University of Chicago Press, 2011).

be invited together—the Roman convivium firmly reinforced the hierarchical social standing of all guests through both seating arrangements and quality of wine and food served to them. In other words, where you sat at a Roman banquet and what you were served were dictated solely by your socioeconomic standing. In the Roman convivium, just as in Roman society proper, status was visible. The purpose of the dinner, furthermore, was ultimately to allow the host to show off, thus maintaining or even enhancing his status in the community.

A Roman literary text from this period that shows the extremes of the Roman convivium is the "Dinner at Trimalchio's," an episode from Petronius' novel *The Satyricon*. Trimalchio, a freedman with the ultimate rags-to-riches life story, uses his wealth to show off his superiority to others by serving the most outlandish dinner imaginable—in fact, some of the dishes and their presentation deliberately defy imagination. One of the courses is a tray with the twelve signs of the zodiac, with representative foods set on each sign. Another course features a whole roasted wild boar, with baskets of fancy dates hanging off his tusks and pastries shaped as piglets surrounding it on the appropriately massive serving tray. As cheesy commercials would say, "But wait, there's more!" When the boar is cut open, a flock of thrushes fly out dramatically. Overall, Trimalchio's display of wealth and status is undoubtedly over the top and vulgar. Yet toned-down displays of the same nature were perfectly acceptable and expected, as Apicius's recipes demonstrate.

The Corinthian Christians' behavior at their celebrations of the Lord's Supper as described by Paul combined the worst features of both the Greek symposium and the Roman convivium. Some of the believers borrowed from the Greek symposium the acceptability of communal drunkenness. At the same time, the distribution of food at these occasions—where some ate plenty, while others went hungry—replicated the Roman convivium, serving food of the quality (and, actually, quantity) commensurate with each guest's status.[9] Paul notes that this approach served to humiliate the poorer members of the congregation. While this would have been acceptable in a Roman convivium, where the humiliation of some would have merely served to further highlight the wealth of others, it was not acceptable in Christian worship.

The Corinthians seemed to forget that the Lord's Supper was a feast hosted by God rather than mere people. While meals hosted by the gods were a feature of certain festivals in both Greek and Roman religion, those meals were still subject

---

9. Hunger was a very common reality of life for many in the Roman world. See Peter Garnsey, *Famine and Food Supply in the Greco-Roman World: Responses to Risk and Crisis* (Cambridge: Cambridge University Press, 1989).

to typical Roman banqueting customs. In their embracing of the cultural practices of Greek and Roman feasting, the Corinthians rejected the value of equality of believers and the requirement to care for each other that Jesus established. At the same time, they also showed a lack of respect for what the food at the Last Supper was meant to represent—the body and blood of Christ, shed in common for all believers.

How the culture treated food was integrally connected to its view of people—an idea that is true today as well. We see this come through in Paul's discussion of the Lord's Supper. Peter's statement to Cornelius that God didn't make anyone or anything "common" comes to mind in this context as well. In the Roman world, where the convivium simply replicated the socially accepted belief that some (very few) people were more valuable than others, the idea of all believers being precious in God's eyes was utterly countercultural and difficult to comprehend. We have to remember, after all, that slavery was an integral part of Roman society, and enslaved people were a part of urban churches throughout the empire. Any member of an urban church in the Roman Empire, therefore, had to be prepared to break bread in worship with individuals from higher social classes and lower ones. No other situation in Roman culture would have involved such a radical mixing of social groups. Resisting cultural sins when food was consumed communally in the church required countercultural views of both food and people in Christ's vision for the church and the world.

Conclusion

Christians today often have an instinctive view of the importance of food in caring for others. It is not coincidental that churches and parachurch ministries that feed the hungry continue to proliferate. This desire to feed the hungry harkens back to Jesus's mandate to feed his sheep.[10] It is also a subtle reminder of the ways gospel priorities have infiltrated our culture. After all, this mindset, so instinctive to our culture today, did not exist in the Roman world. Many a Roman aristocrat would have considered it normal that others around him were starving. Both the quality and quantity of food available were meant simply to reinforce social order. But even as we indignantly reject this view, are we doing enough? Too

---

10. John 21:15–17. In addition, feeding the hungry is the subject of the only miracle present in all four Gospels: Jesus feeding the five thousand (Matt. 14:13–21, Mark 6:30–44, Luke 9:12–17, and John 6:1–14).

often, we are content to feed bodies without feeding spirits and minds. In the cultural Christianity of today, the emphasis on feeding bodies alone has become our cultural sin, even as we try to fulfill Jesus's command.

A decade ago, I attended a conference on the book of Romans at Princeton Theological Seminary. One of the speakers, in a pensive moment, wondered how one might tell apart a church-run soup kitchen or a similar food ministry from one that is run by a secular group. The question was telling and ought to be a challenge to churches who run such ministries. While serving others should never be contingent on their faith, the opportunity to help with providing the most basic of needs, such as food, should not be divorced from providing other resources, including spiritual ones. As Christians, in fact, we should see spiritual food as a basic need, right alongside the physical food.

Christians today are also too quick to dismiss the idea of food or drink leading a brother or sister into sin in their embracing of cultural ideals of food. Being a "foodie" has become trendy, and a marker of the professional class. This interest in refined and exotic foods and beverages has even led some urban churches to create café churches or even bar churches. The argument for this trend rests in its potential as a welcome gesture to those who might otherwise be turned off from the formality of church. This welcoming potential is important, and I admit that I was one of those who cheered the loudest when my church brought back the coffee station in the lobby after it had been shut down for over a year because of the COVID-19 pandemic. And yes, all foods (and drinks) are allowed through God's grace. But we cannot forget to ask the essential question that Paul articulated: Can the foods we consume make someone else stumble? Let us consider three examples that show this question under consideration in Christian circles today: the consumption of alcohol, meat, and gluten.

In 2003, Wheaton College, one of the leading evangelical institutions of higher learning, made headlines over the changes to its long-standing conservative policy on a trifecta of controversial activities: drinking, dancing, and smoking.[11] The ban on dancing was repealed altogether. The ban on drinking and smoking was repealed for non-undergraduate students, allowing graduate students and faculty to drink in private, something that they were previously not allowed to do, per institution's regulations. Wheaton's decision prompted response from other evangelical colleges and universities, some of whom, at the time, reiterated their

---

11. Ted Olsen, "Wheaton College Allows Dancing for All, Drinking and Tobacco for Non-Undergraduates," *Christianity Today*, February 1, 2003, https://www.christianitytoday.com/ct/2003/februaryweb-only/2-17-32.0.html.

commitment to prohibition of alcohol.[12] But as public opinion surveys since then have shown, Wheaton's decision reflects trends in churches.

Over the past twenty years, evangelicals have become much more tolerant and even supportive of alcohol consumption. A 2019 Pew Research survey found a clear connection between religious belief and the belief that consumption of alcohol is morally wrong: less than 1 percent of atheists believed that drinking is morally wrong, whereas 16 percent of all Protestants, 23 percent of white evangelical Protestants, and 13 percent of Black Protestants believed that it was morally wrong.[13] A sizeable minority of evangelical Christians remain wary of alcohol, but their number has been declining for a while.

Social occasions among Christians are now more likely than ever to include wine or beer. Those who embrace this trend claim that this is a rebellion against the legalism of evangelical churches in the not-so-distant past. Drinking, therefore, is often presented as a casting off of the Pharisee's mask and an embracing of God's grace, which has offered all foods and drinks to us. One seminary student at my current church holds the belief, in fact, that not consuming alcohol is morally wrong. The pendulum has swung indeed!

Alcoholism and irresponsible drinking still exist, nevertheless, among churchgoers just as in the rest of the population. The social drinking that may not be a challenge to some could lead others into sin and destroy lives in the process, as even Wheaton's original document that eased the ban on alcohol noted. The document reaffirmed the institution's denunciation of drunkenness, while encouraging responsible enjoyment of God's creation, a theme that has also been central to the work of theologian Gisela Kreglinger.[14] Another recent study suggests that those who attend church regularly are less likely to engage in binge drinking or even binge eating.[15] That is an encouraging trend that raises additional questions about ways being a part of the body of Christ builds up the individuals who are part of that body.

A different kind of debate surrounds the consumption of meat today. The

12. See, for example, Michael Foust, "Wheaton Changes Alcohol Policy; Others Not Ready to Follow Its Lead," *Baptist Press*, March 3, 2003, https://www.baptistpress.com/resource-library/news/wheaton-changes-alcohol-policy-others-not-ready-to-follow-its-lead/.

13. Philip Schwadel, "Americans' Drinking Habits Vary by Faith," *Pew Research Center*, 03/06/2019, https://www.pewresearch.org/fact-tank/2019/03/06/americans-drinking-habits-vary-by-faith/.

14. Gisela Kreglinger, *The Spirituality of Wine* (Grand Rapids: Eerdmans, 2016); and *The Soul of Wine: Savoring the Goodness of God* (Downers Grove, IL: InterVarsity Press, 2019).

15. Alexa Lardieri, "Religious People Drink Less than Those with No Religious Affiliation," *US News*, March 6, 2019, https://www.usnews.com/news/national-news/articles/2019-03-06/study-actively-religious-people-drink-less-than-those-with-no-religious-affiliation.

Catholic theologian Charles Camosy has argued that as part of embracing radical creation care and stewardship, all Christians should be vegetarian or vegan. Camosy has overtly connected his argument for veganism with his pro-life stance. Refusing to take any life, he argues, should include sparing the lives of animals that God created.[16] The argument has not been popular in evangelical circles, even as the number of ethical vegetarians—those who believe that eating meat or animal products is morally wrong—has been growing for decades in the general population. To be fair, ethical vegans were few in both Daniel's and Paul's days as well, so the few believers who adhere to such diets today are in good historical company.

On the other side of the meat issue, few brands have been as emphatic about their Christian identity as Chick-fil-A. Memes and jokes about Chick-fil-A as "God's chicken" proliferate. One meme shows a Renaissance image of God, pensively stating "I'm going to put two chickens in the ark, so I can bless the world in 2,000 years with Chick-fil-A." The caption at the bottom notes, in case anyone missed the joke, "He really had a plan for us to be filled with love and chicken tenders." Another meme, marveling at the mouthwash dispenser that has become standard issue in Chick-fil-A bathrooms, states that the mouthwash dispenser is there, "so you can wash your filthy heathen mouth before eating God's chicken." And then, in deference to American society's struggles with weight, are the memes noting that "Chick-fil-A doesn't affect my diet, because those are the Lord's calories."

Some Christians insist that it is morally wrong to drink, while others insist that it is morally wrong not to drink. Some Christians believe that it is morally wrong to eat animal products, whereas others see meat as a blessing God gave for our enjoyment. Who is right? And, more precisely, considering that moral arguments are passing judgment statements, who is sinning? Since people with any of these positions can remain in communion with each other and attend the same churches, this is a reminder that not every challenge that some Christians consider to be important is as important to all others. But there is always the threat of idolatry. If obsessed with a particular stance on one of these challenges, one could end up falling into sin by breaking fellowship with others over an issue that is theologically less central to orthodoxy.

Ironically, perhaps the food-related challenge that is most likely to be fellowship breaking is one over which people have the least control. I am speaking here

---

16. Charles Camosy, *For Love of Animals: Christian Ethics, Consistent Action* (Cincinnati: Franciscan, 2013).

of food allergies, especially those that preclude someone from taking communion. The debate persists: Is it the genetically modified wheat that has caused the spike in gluten intolerance and Celiac disease over the past couple of decades? Or have these allergies always existed, but we are just better equipped to diagnose them? Regardless of the answer, the simple medical truth is that those with certain allergies cannot take communion in its traditional wheat-based form. Surprisingly, division in the body has occurred over this. In particular, for Catholics, gluten free communion is not an option, per repeated rulings from the Vatican.[17] For evangelical churches, this has not been divisive, as many commercial communion-makers offer premade gluten free options. Who is right?

Difficult questions remain for churches to answer when it comes to issues of food and sin. Just as in the earliest Christian communities, Christians today are finding ways to be countercultural in their use of food to minister to others and build relationships both within the church and outside of it. Rosaria Butterfield's recent book on hospitality passionately argues for extending the table into the community in a way that is distinctly countercultural and gospel centered. In a world where hospitality is becoming suspect, the Christian community can continue its early mission of welcoming the stranger, remembering the connection God revealed to Peter between seeing the value of all foods and the preciousness of all people in God's sight. Sharing a meal for Peter was a conscious act of acknowledging the worthiness of gentiles to be grafted into the church. It can still be this meaningful and impactful in our cultural context, as Butterfield's own powerful conversion story reminds us.[18]

Roland Barthes, a distinguished twentieth-century French literary critic and philosopher, wrote an essay "Steak and Fries" as part of his *Mythologies*, a collection of essays on new mythologies and symbolism created in the everyday.[19] His over-the-top praise of the simple pairing of steak (the more raw and bloody it is, the better) and the humble fry is a reminder of the power of food as a symbol. But a symbol of what? The answer is culturally determined. Food is never just food, and the church perhaps is more aware of this than any other entity.

---

17. Kevin Lui, "The Vatican Says Gluten-Free Wafers Can't Be Used for Communion," *Time*, July 10, 2017, https://time.com/4850893/vatican-gluten-free-eucharist-communion-wafers/.

18. See Rosaria Butterfield, *The Gospel Comes with a House Key: Practicing Radically Ordinary Hospitality in Our Post-Christian World* (Wheaton, IL: Crossway, 2018). Also see Butterfield's powerful conversion story, which began with hospitality that others showed her: *The Secret Thoughts of an Unlikely Convert: An English Professor's Journey into Christian Faith* (Pittsburgh: Crown and Covenant, 2012).

19. For a recent translation of Barthes' *Mythologies*, see Richard Howard and Annette Lavers, *Mythologies: The Complete Edition in a New Translation* (New York: Hill and Wang, 2013).

3

(Un)Holy Bodies, (Un)Holy Minds

Resisting the Cultural Views of Sexuality

IN 2 CE, ONE OF ROME'S MOST FASHIONABLE POETS OF THE age, Ovid, published the concluding scroll to what turned out to be his most controversial work. A manual to dating, presented as an elegiac poem in three books, the *Art of Love* dedicated its first book to advice for men on how to find a girlfriend. Pick-up lines abound, as does a list of suitable locations for finding eligible and not exactly eligible women for dating—Ovid has no qualms providing tips on picking up married women.

The second book provides advice on how to keep a girlfriend, while the third is directed at women and offers advice on keeping a man interested. Crude throughout, and not shy about advising lies and any kind of trickery to men in order to seduce women, the manual became an instant bestseller in Ancient Rome. So successful was this book that Ovid, like many bestselling authors today, wrote a sequel: *The Cure for Love*, a how-to manual on how to abandon a relationship or fall out of love well. He also spun off his franchise to write poems on such topics as *On Cosmetics*, an epic poem for women on . . . well, makeup. As a connoisseur of women's beauty, Ovid was obviously the man for the job. Only a hundred lines of this work survive, but they are sufficient to make it clear that modern-day total makeovers are nothing compared to the Roman version.

Ovid's advice in all of these works, especially in *Art of Love*, reads like something out of a risqué modern magazine and is also highly misogynistic at its core. A man on the prowl (both hunting metaphors and those of military service abound) has his work cut out for him. Thankfully, Rome's many locations for popular entertainment, from theaters to the race track, dinner parties, and even the popular beach at Baiae, provided many places for men and women to go and be seen. Ovid notes that the theaters in particular were "fatal to chaste modesty." In fact, one of his recommended pick-up strategies for use at theaters and circus races is to sit so closely to a woman as to end up touching her seemingly by accident. The excuse is that seating was too crowded at such events. And if a woman resists one's charms, one can always find another, more willing. Although, he notes also, a man never has to take no for an answer. If we take Ovid's word for it, Rome's hook-up and date-rape culture was more scandalous than anything we might imagine today.

The picture of the dating scene in Rome that Ovid paints was perhaps satirical in part, but jokes have to be sufficiently close to reality to be funny. As it happens, Ovid's jokes, although they made his books bestsellers, turned out to have hit a little too close to home. The Emperor Augustus, who had passed comprehensive moral legislations in order to encourage more fruitful and faithful marriages among the higher social classes, exiled Ovid from Rome in 8 CE. The reason for the exile appears to have been the immoral nature of the *Art of Love*. Clearly Augustus did not take the poem in jest and considered Ovid a bad influence on Roman society. But then he also had to exile his own daughter, Julia, from Rome because of her serial adulteries. Several Roman aristocrats received their own small island as a place of exile in the first decade of the new millennium for the same reason.[1]

At first glance, Ovid's description of Roman attitudes toward sexuality seems surprisingly modern. But archaeology confirms Ovid's picture of the normalization of Roman public displays of sexuality in striking ways. Tourists walking down the streets of Pompeii today can still see the phallus etchings on cobblestones and on external walls of buildings. While some scholars have theorized

---

1. For a study of this complicated push and pull of state and private mores in the Augustan period, see Kristina Milnor, *Gender, Domesticity, and the Age of Augustus: Inventing Private Life* (Oxford: Oxford University Press, 2005). For a broader overview of Augustan culture, see Karl Galinsky, *Augustan Culture* (Princeton: Princeton University Press, 1998).

that the phallic symbols on the streets were meant to be directions to the nearest brothel, a theory that has more recently taken hold is that these were simply meant for good luck. This theory fits well with the ubiquitous displays of sex in the city's decor. Yes, Pompeii had a fair share of brothels, attesting to the popularity of this trade in the famous resort town. Clearly, what happened in Pompeii was meant to stay in Pompeii. But one building that decidedly was not a brothel has an over-sized phallus-shaped doorbell. And graphically explicit scenes of various sexual acts abound on frescoes inside the many wealthy private villas of the city and are especially popular inside formal dining rooms.[2] Apparently, in first-century CE Pompeii, at least, it was fashionable to commission an erotic scene for one's formal dining room wall. Of course, these were also Ovid's readers.

Any attempts to explain such choices of decor have to consider the same Roman cultural attitudes that we examined in the discussion of the Roman *convivium* in the previous chapter. The Roman Empire was a highly stratified society in which every person knew (or should have known) his or her place and every social interaction, public or private, reflected the power dynamic. The erotic scenes in Roman art reflect this same idea: the individuals in these scenes are never equals, and many of these scenes portray mythological stories of rape, such as Zeus (or Jupiter) visiting Leda disguised as a swan. Sexual acts, just as hosting elaborate dinners, were yet another way for some Romans to display their superiority over others. In the same way, for the men to whom Ovid gives advice, the women to seduce were merely objects of conquest. Once a victory is achieved, it is time to set one's sights on the next one, Ovid said.

Instead of seeing the Romans as sexually liberated, we need to remember the horrific use and abuse of bodies that the Roman Empire perpetuated. Ovid's poems describe freeborn women as mere objects of lust to be used and discarded. While it may have been written tongue-in-cheek, if we read Ovid's *Art of Love* closely, we realize that it is essentially a how-to rape manual, in which all women, including those who are married, are portrayed as prey to be hunted and overpowered by any means necessary. Their fate, though, was not the worst. Most prostitutes, in particular, were enslaved and thus literally did not own their own bodies in the eyes of the law. The use of enslaved men and women for sex by their masters was so commonplace as not to merit commentary. For example, Petronius's novel *Satyricon* features Encolpius as its protagonist. Encolpius is a

---

2. Perhaps the most readable overview of Pompeii is Mary Beard, *The Fires of Vesuvius: Pompeii Lost and Found* (Cambridge, MA: Belknap, 2008). More academic but exquisite is Andrew Wallace-Hadrill, *Houses and Society in Pompeii and Herculaneum* (Princeton: Princeton University Press, 1994).

Roman man who is engaged in a sexual relationship with his enslaved teen boy Giton. Giton's opinions on the matter, of course, do not matter.

Ovid's writings bring to the fore a fundamental reality about the Roman world: lust was the quintessential Roman cultural sin, and it was rooted in the displays of power that enforced the social structure in ways similar to those we saw at work in the Roman *convivium*. Stories of rape and sexual exploitation, in fact, formed part of the basic lore of Greco-Roman pagan religion. That is why they were ubiquitous in Greek and Roman literature and art. Ovid himself served to further popularize such tales in his mythological epic *Metamorphoses*.[3] Stories of transformations—metamorphoses—of victimized individuals into animals or various objects include such tales as the god Apollo's attempted rape of the nymph Daphne. After a harrowing chase through the woods, Daphne was only able to escape Apollo's unwanted attentions by praying to be transformed into a tree. Luckily, her prayer was answered. But not even her metamorphosis into a laurel tree accorded her complete escape, as Apollo adopted her as his sacred tree, claiming her branches for his crown, thus literally cutting off parts of her, albeit in tree form, to keep as souvenirs.

Other stories are even more harrowing. In another myth Ovid includes in this epic, the Thracian king Tereus raped his wife's sister, Philomela. When Philomela threatened to tell of his crime to the world, Tereus cut out her tongue and imprisoned her. Deprived of speech, Philomela wove her sad tale into a tapestry and sent it to her sister, Procne. Understanding the message, Procne cooked their son Itys and served him to Tereus for dinner. Only when Tereus found out the truth of this final horrific act did the gods intervene and transform all three into birds. Philomela became a sorrowful nightingale, Procne is transformed into a swallow, and Tereus a hoopoe. In hearing tales like these for entertainment, seeing them in art all around, and reflecting on some of them in religious contexts, the Romans were perhaps desensitized to such abuses. But whatever degree of horror and sorrow they felt over them, these stories were undoubtedly an ingrained part of their worldview.

Christianity challenged this use and abuse of human bodies as displays of personal power by requiring all believers to have holy bodies and holy minds. This meant, in particular, erasing the double standard that the Roman world had toward men's and women's sexuality. And so, after a consideration of Paul's teaching on this subject for the Corinthian church as a representative example of

---

3. For a readable translation of the epic into modern English poetry, see Stephanie McCarter, *Metamorphoses by Ovid* (New York: Penguin Random House, 2022).

the countercultural views of sexuality reflected throughout the New Testament, we turn to an anonymous text from the mid-second century CE, *The Shepherd of Hermas*. This allegorical document, read widely enough by the early church to have been considered part of the canon by some early church fathers, reflects the concerns of the early Christian community beyond the New Testament era about the sins inherent in the cultural views of sexuality and the impact of these sins on the church as a whole. At the same time, we will see in both Paul's writings and in *The Shepherd of Hermas* the encouraging message of gradual sanctification as a challenge to cultural Christianity. Sinners who truly believed could in time become saints, transforming the church into the glorious bride that she was meant to be.

The Challenge of Cultural Views on Sexuality in the Early Church

While Ovid's *Art of Love* may have been the most famous and most controversial popular text on illicit seduction and adultery in the early first century CE, it was certainly not the only one. The entire genre of Latin elegiac poetry was built on train-wreck-worthy dysfunctional romances in which the poets who composed these works were ostensibly engaged themselves. An earlier Augustan era poet, Propertius, devoted most of his elegies to describing his tumultuous affair with a woman to whom he refers by the pseudonym Cynthia and who may have been a high-profile courtesan. So messy was his relationship with Cynthia that he fantasizes about her coming back to haunt him after her death. Another first-century BCE poet, Catullus, wrote a significant portion of his poetry about his stormy relationship with Lesbia, a pseudonym he used to disguise his lover's identity.

Modern scholars believe that the mysterious Lesbia was none other than Clodia, daughter of the Roman aristocrat Appius Claudius Pulcher and sister of a notorious plebeian tribune Clodius, who went on to get killed in an ancient Roman gangster street fight. She was also the wife of Quintus Caecilius Metellus Celer.[4] Clodia's blood was bluer than blue, and her multiple extramarital affairs

---

4. For an analysis of lust and power in Roman love poetry of this period, see Ellen Greene, *The Erotics of Domination: Male Desire and the Mistress in Latin Love Poetry* (Baltimore: Johns Hopkins University Press, 1998). For a biography of Catullus's paramour, see Marilyn Skinner's masterful attempt to re-create the story of her life from limited sources, none of them written by the woman herself, *Clodia Metelli: The Tribune's Sister* (Oxford: Oxford University Press, 2011).

were a matter of no small scandal. If reality television existed in first century BCE Rome, this family would have dominated it. In fact, they managed to fascinate the public just fine without social media. When in 56 BCE Clodia accused a former lover, Marcus Caelius Rufus, of attempted poisoning, the orator defending Caelius, the great Cicero himself, made sure to drag Clodia's dirty laundry out for all of Rome to see. He seemed to relish in the task a bit too much, but it got the job done—he won his case.

In considering the popularity of Roman love poetry and the social scandals of the day, it is important to note not only what is there—descriptions and even glorification of dysfunctional relationships abounding with emotional and possibly physical abuse—but also what is not there. Strikingly absent is any mention of marriage or, at least, any mention of marriage between the lovers. Yet we know that Lesbia, at least, was a married woman, so whenever marriage is mentioned in these poems, it is mentioned only as a barrier to romance.

The message of this popular poetry was clear: love and marriage do not go together, but marriage is no reason to let go of the pursuit of pleasure, especially for men. Furthermore, the language of homosexual rape seems to have been a common tactic for threatening or humiliating opponents. In one particularly obscene poem, Catullus threatens to inflict all kinds of demeaning sexual violence on two male opponents who apparently criticized his poetry. One of the individuals he threatens by name was a prominent politician who served as a consul. Clearly, the negative publicity did not hurt.

For anyone who may not have been as interested in reading or listening to poetry, the same messages about use and abuse of sexuality, whether for personal pleasure or to threaten and humiliate opponents, were readily available through such popular entertainment as comedies and farce routines, performed at no cost for the public at certain religious festivals throughout the year. In the midst of such cultural values, with which they were bombarded in everyday life, art, and literature, it is not surprising to see that the early Christians struggled to resist Roman cultural views of sexuality and were apt, instead, to continue to hold these views after conversion.

Paul comments on the commonplace nature of such behaviors in his letter to the Romans, specifically connecting sexual immorality and idolatry. Those people who, despite their knowledge of God, refused to honor and serve him, faced the following consequences:

> Because of this, God gave them over to shameful lusts. Even their women exchanged natural sexual relations for unnatural ones. In the same way the

men also abandoned natural relations with women and were inflamed with
lust for one another. Men committed shameful acts with other men, and
received in themselves the due penalty for their error.

Furthermore, just as they did not think it worthwhile to retain the knowledge of God, so God gave them over to a depraved mind, so that they do what
ought not to be done. (Rom 1:26–28)

Paul's general comments here are not meant specifically to note that the church at
Rome is guilty of such behavior. His comment is more general and describes the
sociocultural environment that normalized and popularized the values glorified
in the poetry of Catullus, Propertius, Ovid, and many others. This description
makes it clear that Christians who were not secure in their faith could easily fall
back into the disordered sexuality that was the norm in the Roman world.

For Paul, idolatry and cultural views of sexuality go hand in hand, just as we
saw with the cultural views of property and food. Embracing these cultural mores
meant, as we see in the poetry of the Augustan age, doing what one wanted to do
and abiding by no other standard of conduct. Sure, Ovid seems to have crossed
a line, and was exiled for it, but the penalty that he and several other aristocrats
received for adultery was relatively uncommon. More than anything, Ovid's case
proves that a Roman aristocratic male had to surpass a high bar of prodigiously
immoral behavior to get in trouble for it.

This cultural baggage is directly pertinent to our understanding of the issues
in the Corinthian church. Paul provides specific examples of the range of sinful
behaviors that emerge from the cultural views of sexuality in his first letter to the
Corinthian church, which he opened by addressing the Corinthian Christians
as "saints." First, he notes that one of the men in the church is having a sexual
relationship with his father's wife—a transgression that Paul notes is "of a kind
that even pagans do not tolerate" (1 Cor. 5:1). Next, Paul rebukes members of the
church for frequenting prostitutes, thus defiling the entire body of Christ (1 Cor.
6:15–20). He concludes this section of the letter with a discussion of marriage.
While he suggests singleness as the ideal, he recommends marriage over temptation: "Now to the unmarried and the widows I say: It is good for them to stay
unmarried, as I do. But if they cannot control themselves, they should marry, for
it is better to marry than to burn with passion" (1 Cor. 7:8–9).

The three specific issues that Paul identifies all have to do with fighting
the Greco-Roman cultural ideal of placing one's own desires first and leaving
God out of the decision-making process. The first example, a son who is sleeping
with his father's wife, is a good example of the disordered views of sexuality that

Paul identifies in Romans 1. It would have reminded Paul's original audiences of several Greek myths, including the one popularized in Euripides's tragedy *Hippolytus*. In that tragedy, Phaedra fell in love with her stepson, Hippolytus. When he rejected her, she orchestrated his death by falsely claiming rape, leading her husband, the hero Theseus, to call the gods' vengeance on Hippolytus. Phaedra ultimately committed suicide, consumed with passion and regret. But Paul's Corinthian Hippolytus and Phaedra, who are engaged in a consensual sexual relationship, have re-created a worse tragedy—one that Paul notes even the pagans would have found horrifying, even if the father is presumably deceased.

The consensual union of a stepson and stepmother would have recalled to Greek audiences the most horrific marriage in all of Greek mythology: that of Oedipus and his mother, Jocasta. But that marriage, also following the death of the father (accidental murder by the son, no less!), occurred without the awareness of the two parties that they were mother and son. That the situation Paul described would have been considered incest in the pagan world is undeniable, and the awareness of the stepmother and son of their connection simply made it all the worse. It is striking, therefore, that despite these negative associations, no one in the Corinthian church intervened until Paul spoke against this particular sin. We see here another Roman cultural value at work—that of leaving others to their sins.

While the first example of disordered sexual behavior that Paul describes in the Corinthian church is admittedly exceptional, the next example he brings up is one that was common in Roman society: frequenting prostitutes.[5] The price of hiring a cheap prostitute in the Roman Empire was about equal to the price of lunch, making this particular type of sexual sin readily accessible to all, including the poorest men in Roman society. Again, of course, much of the sex trade relied on enslaved women. A trope in Roman comedy, exemplified in the modern musical and film *A Funny Thing Happened on the Way to the Forum*, was the kidnapping of honorable free girls by robbers or pirates and their sale into slavery for work in brothels. In comedies, such as Plautus's *Braggart Soldier*, the identity of the girl as free and honorable would ultimately be uncovered, resulting in her

---

5. The work of Thomas McGinn on Roman prostitution is authoritative and relies extensively on the evidence of Pompeii: Thomas McGinn, *The Economy of Prostitution in the Roman World: A Study of Social History and the Brothel* (Ann Arbor: University of Michigan Press, 2004); and *Prostitution, Sexuality, and the Law in Ancient Rome* (Oxford: Oxford University Press, 1998). More recently, Anise Strong has challenged the traditionally accepted binary between respectable matrons and definitely not respectable prostitutes in the Roman world, *Prostitutes and Matrons in the Roman World* (Cambridge: Cambridge University Press, 2016).

freedom and marriage. In real life, however, the enslaved women in brothels were rarely rescued and simply lived miserable and short lives.

While it is not clear just how common this sin of frequenting prostitutes was in the Corinthian church, Paul's phrasing suggests that it was habitual enough in the community to address in general terms rather than describing it as an exceptional behavior specific to just one or two people. Paul tends to note whenever sinful behaviors are specific to a few people, as we saw already in the discussion of the stepmother-stepson relationship. It appears, in fact, that Paul had previously spoken with some of the Corinthian Christians, whether individually or in groups, as he quotes their actual justifications in addressing particular assumptions underlying this sinful behavior: "'I have the right to do anything,' you say—but not everything is beneficial. 'I have the right to do anything'—but I will not be mastered by anything. You say, 'Food for the stomach and the stomach for food and God will destroy them both.' The body, however, is not meant for sexual immorality, but for the Lord, and the Lord for the body" (1 Cor 6:12–13).

We see a connection here in the Christians' attitudes toward food and toward the body and sexuality. If all food is lawful to consume for believers, and no food may pollute them, then why should anything else that they do to their bodies pollute them? This attitude will continue to grow in fringe Christian movements in the second century CE, as some Gnostic groups will embrace the idea of separating the body and the spirit in their theology, reaching the conclusion that it does not matter what one does to one's body because only the spirit matters. But this idea is also rooted in Roman cultural views, where the concept of religious pollution existed but was very rarely attributed to such activities as eating or sex, and even then, not for most people. Only for a few members of particular priesthoods could such activities result in ritual impurity for a brief period of time.

A countercultural view of one's body, as Paul notes in 1 Corinthians 6, is one that sees one's body as part of the church as a whole. The idea of the church as the Bride of Christ is central to understanding the importance of the holiness of individual bodies for the holiness of the whole. Each individual is part of the Bride of Christ, and sex, the act that unites two into one flesh, has been established as a covenantal activity since the original union of Adam and Eve in Genesis 2:24. A union of a Christian with a prostitute is a ludicrous offense against the entire body of Christ, for it mocks the covenantal union of the Bride of Christ with Christ himself. This understanding of the covenantal significance of sex specifically in a Christian community has obvious bearing on the appropriate views of singleness and marriage for Christians, as Paul notes in the third and final issue that he addresses on this topic.

Resisting the Culture in
Singleness and Marriage

One of the most famous legends in early Roman history has to do with the first marriages that took place in the brand-new city. When Romulus, following a bout of fratricide, founded Rome with his band of warriors, the city had no women. The men came up with an ingenious solution: after inviting the neighboring Sabines for a festival, they kidnapped all the young women, thereby getting wives. The Sabines were not exactly thrilled, but as the Roman historian Livy explains it, once the new wives had gotten used to their Roman husbands, they mediated in the brewing war between the Romans and their families of origin, effectively ending the conflict.

This episode in early Roman history became known as the Rape of the Sabine Women. While likely a later legend, it reflects the general attitudes toward marriage in the Roman world. First, marriage was seen as a practical transaction and civic duty, especially for aristocratic families, about whose propagation and survival rulers were most concerned. Second, as in the rest of the ancient world, women did not have a voice in the selection of a husband. Once married, however, they could facilitate diplomatic relations between their new family and their family of origin. With few exceptions, such as surviving papyri consisting mostly of legal contracts about dowries and divorce, we must work hard to get the wives' side of the story from the surviving evidence, although Emily Hemelrijk recently did just this in publishing an impressive collection of primary source inscriptions concerning women's experiences in various areas of life in the Roman west.[6] Still, as even Hemelrijk's collection shows, the vast majority of documents like Roman epitaphs for women are set up by male relatives and are remarkably one-dimensional. "She loved her husband." "She worked in wool." "A dutiful wife and mother."

In his discussion of marriage and well-ordered sexuality in 1 Corinthians 7, Paul provides advice for both the single and the married in the Christian community. It is important to note in this context that the vast majority of people living in the ancient world would have been married at some point in their lives. Depending on the location and social status, women were married as early as puberty, while men were typically a bit older. Roman society had no place for single men and women, and such social expectations had further backing after

---

6. Emily Hemelrijk, *Women and Society in the Roman World: A Sourcebook of Inscriptions from the Roman West* (New York: Cambridge University Press, 2020).

Augustus's extensive marriage legislation came into place in 18 BCE—the same legislation that Augustus believed Ovid's poetry had threatened. From that point on, career advancement in the imperial bureaucracy, as well as in politics, highly incentivized not only being married but also producing three children. Rampant disease and, in the case of women, death in childbirth, resulted in many becoming widowed early on, and Augustus's laws encouraged swift remarriage, at least for aristocrats.[7]

The arranged nature of many marriages, however, meant that love was not part of the equation, and divorce was reasonably common in some circles. Also common was the double standard of sexuality. Many married Roman men frequented prostitutes, while women were expected to remain faithful. This was common in the ancient Mediterranean world. To give a non-Roman example that shows just how deeply ingrained such values were, the Athenian law on adultery, promulgated sometime in the sixth century BCE and still in effect throughout the Classical period (480–323 BCE), allowed a husband to kill on the spot any man whom he caught with his wife in his own home. This was a rare case of justified homicide in the Athenian law code, which otherwise discouraged murder as an obvious source of blood pollution on the entire city.[8] Blood pollution, otherwise, was bad news. In the case of an unavenged killing, as the plot of Sophocles's tragedy *Oedipus the King* reminds us, the gods' wrath would fall on the entire city—in that case, in the form of a deadly plague that kept killing citizens until the murderer was found. But nowhere in the Athenian laws is there any concern about respectably married men sleeping with prostitutes. The only case in which prostitution is mentioned as a concern has to do with a disreputable woman who had previously worked as a high-class courtesan passing herself and her daughter off as reputable.[9]

This cultural view of marriage, just as of sexuality more generally, was long ingrained for the Corinthians, located a day and a half of travel from Athens. While Paul does not mention this issue in his rebuke to Christians who

---

7. For an overview of ancient sexuality, see Marilyn Skinner, *Sexuality in Greek and Roman Culture* (Oxford: Blackwell, 2005). An excellent study on the history of Roman marriage, grounded in studies of Roman legislations on the topic, remains Susan Treggiari, *Roman Marriage: Iusti Coniuges from the Time of Cicero to the Time of Ulpian* (Oxford: Clarendon, 1991). For a study specifically of Constantine's marriage reforms, see Judith Evans-Grubbs, *Law and Family in Late Antiquity: The Emperor Constantine's Marriage Legislation* (Oxford: Oxford University Press, 2000). Finally, Kyle Harper provides an insightful story of the transformation of values from the Roman standards to those of Christianity in *From Sin to Shame: The Christian Transformation of Sexual Morality in Late Antiquity* (Cambridge, MA: Harvard University Press, 2013).

8. The authoritative study on pollution in Greek religion remains Robert Parker, *Miasma: Pollution and Purification in Early Greek Religion* (Oxford: Clarendon, 1996).

9. Demosthenes 59 ("Against Neaira"). Also see Debra Hamel, *Trying Neaira: The True Story of a Courtesan's Scandalous Life in Ancient Greece* (New Haven, CT: Yale University Press, 2003).

frequented prostitutes, it is reasonable to assume that at least some, if not all, of the Corinthian Christians who engaged in this behavior were married. In addition to disregarding the holiness of their own bodies as part of the Bride of Christ, these men were also betraying their own marriage vows, disrespecting the covenant of marriage by treating it in the same way as the culture around them.

While Paul's inclusion of advice on marriage is to be expected, especially in the context of presenting principles for gospel-centered views of sexuality, his mention of singleness as an option would have been wholly countercultural for residents of the ancient world: "I say this as a concession, not as a command. I wish that all of you were as I am. But each of you has your own gift from God; one has this gift, another has that. Now to the unmarried and the widows I say: It is good for them to stay unmarried, as I do. But if they cannot control themselves, they should marry, for it is better to marry than to burn with passion" (1 Cor. 7:6–9).

Paul's advice would have had significant repercussions for the place of individuals in Greco-Roman society, akin in some ways to the repercussions we considered in connection with the decision to give up eating the meat of sacrificed animals. First, any unmarried man would not have qualified for a significant number of jobs in the imperial bureaucracy or for any political position in the local government and would have been viewed with suspicion in the local community. So singleness would have carried significant social cost. Besides, for anyone who had property, the cultural expectation would have been to marry and have children who may inherit said property. The eradication of a family name is repeatedly described in Greek and Roman literature as a curse.[10] Yet the values of Christianity presented this curse as a new kind of blessing.

As countercultural as singleness would have been for men, it would have been even more so for women, in a society where there was no place for single women at any stage of life. Remaining single or not remarrying after losing a husband would have carried significant financial concerns in a world where most women did not support themselves or their families. This precarious financial status of widows comes up repeatedly in the New Testament.[11] This concern was shared by many bishops of early churches, and Ambrose of Milan even wrote a

---

10. This is usually the final stage of the series of curses that follow unfortunate families in Greek tragedy, such as the royal house of Thebes, to which Oedipus belonged. His children end up being the last of the royal line, and it dies with them. This curse, the end of a family line, is also at the center of the myth of Niobe, told in at least two different Greek tragedies, but only surviving in Ovid's *Metamorphoses* 6.146–312. Niobe refused to worship Leto, the mother of the twin gods Apollo and Artemis, boasting instead in her fertility as the mother of seven sons and seven daughters. In revenge, Apollo and Artemis shot all of her children, and she, in her sorrow, turned into a statue.

11. Examples include Luke 7:12–14; Acts 6:1; 1 Tim. 5:3–16; James 1:27.

treatise on taking care of widows.[12] The countercultural decisions of individuals to remain single and serve the church through their singleness required the financial and social support of their entire community—yet another reminder that all holy bodies belonged to the ultimate Holy Body, the church.

Last but not least, the Christian emphasis on the importance of the well-being and holiness of all the bodies of believers was countercultural as well, as it abolished the Roman hierarchical social structure. As we noted, Greco-Roman cultural views of both food and sexuality perpetuated the power-based structure of Roman society, and the tendency of those in power to demonstrate and increase their social standing through the exercise of their power against those weaker, including slaves. Equality of all believers before Christ meant the dismantling of these structures and types of interactions for Christians in churches, homes, and the community.

Ultimately, two key concepts emerge in Paul's advice, both of which assume this equality of believers and their preciousness for God. First, Paul emphasizes the importance of keeping holy bodies for all Christians, single or married: "Do you not know that your bodies are temples of the Holy Spirit, who is in you, whom you have received from God? You are not your own; you were bought at a price. Therefore honor God with your bodies" (1 Cor. 6:19–20).

In addition to noting the importance of keeping holy bodies that are set apart for God, Paul argues for marriage as a way to keep minds free from lust that might exist otherwise. This concern with keeping both the body and the mind free from the sin of lust, which culturally was so readily acceptable, continued to occupy the Christian community after the New Testament era and is at the center of an allegorical text from the mid-second century CE, *The Shepherd of Hermas*. This text shows the impact of each individual's sins, or conversely, gradual sanctification, on the church as a whole. Its message is that holiness is communal as much as individual, and only through the cultivation of a communal holiness will the church be transformed into the Bride of Christ.

The Holiness of the Body of Christ

In *The Shepherd of Hermas*, a former slave recounts five striking visions in which he experienced the impact of believers' sins on the church in a visible way. The

---

12. Ambrose, *Concerning Widows*. For a translation, see https://www.newadvent.org/fathers/3408 .htm.

church first appears to him as a frail old woman, weighed down by the sins of individual believers. She then grows increasingly younger and more beautiful with each successive vision, finally appearing in her perfect guise as the radiant Bride of Christ. The message is clear: the sins of believers corrupt the beauty of the church, but there is hope for restoration through communal repentance and purification.[13]

The narrative structure of the text as a series of visions harkens back to philosophical dialogues in Greco-Roman literature, including such models as the Dream of Scipio episode in book 6 of Cicero's *De re publica*. There, a distinguished statesman and general, Scipio, has a vision that effectively presents Stoic cosmic philosophy to the reader. In addition, this work echoes the robust Jewish tradition of apocalyptic literature going back as far as the book of Daniel.

Adapting such long-standing pagan and Jewish models for Christian use, *The Shepherd of Hermas* opens with the narrator's vision of a former slave he once knew, Rhoda, who accuses him of impure thoughts about her. The reader quickly sees that the chief sin weighing down the church in this allegorical narrative is lust. Echoing Jesus's statements in the Sermon on the Mount, no differentiation is made between the sin of the mind (lust on which one has not acted) and the sin of the body (lust that proceeded to action). After the final vision of the church as the perfected bride, the fifth and concluding vision tells of an angel of repentance who appeared to the narrator and told him of twelve mandates and ten parables about holy living. Yes, these numbers are significant.[14]

The visible impact of sin on the church presents a striking image. But even more striking is the emphasis in this allegorical story on the importance of the sins of every single individual on the church as a whole. In a visually descriptive way, this text echoes Paul's message to the Corinthian church, that the sins of every individual affect the entire group. This message to members of early Christian communities matters just as much to us today: Christians do not live in isolation. Sinful actions and thoughts of individuals reverberate throughout the entire body. Through repentance, nevertheless, holy thoughts and actions reverberate even louder, transforming the church into the beautiful bride that she is meant to be. Culturally, our own sinful predilection, much more than for the earliest Christians, is to view ourselves as individuals rather than as part of

---

13. See Mark Grundeken, *Community Building in the Shepherd of Hermas* (Leiden: Brill, 2015).

14. For an analysis specifically of the fifth vision, see Mark Grundeken and Joseph Verheyden, "The Spirit Before the Letter: Dreams and Visions as the Legitimization of the Shepherd of Hermas: A Study of Vision 5" in Bart J. Koet, *Dreams as Divine Communication in Christianity: From Hermas to Aquinas. Studies in the History and Anthropology of Religion 3* (Leuven: Peeters, 2012), 23–56.

a whole. But just as the sins of individuals impact the community of believers, ultimately sanctification of individuals is also inextricably connected to the sanctification of their communities.

The message of sanctification reminds us that in Christianity, sin does not permanently define the sinner who repents. Rather, a Christian has a power of transformation as part of a community of fellow believers. This power of transformation, which we may take for granted, was utterly countercultural in antiquity. In the Greco-Roman world, an individual's character and personality were considered fixed, and this premise was commonly used in court of law, often bringing up proof of immoral actions dating years, even decades earlier.[15] A person who was proven to be morally bankrupt in the past could be assumed to be a rotten individual in the present and therefore likely to have committed whichever offense or crime that was brought against him now. By contrast, someone who was an upstanding citizen with exemplary character, was considered to be a good person in all circumstances. So one Athenian citizen on trial in part for adultery argued in his defense that he had performed military service and other civic duties admirably and therefore was incapable of committing the crime of which he was accused.[16]

In the world of Greco-Roman culture, the message of the *Shepherd of Hermas* about the bodies of individuals and the body of the church was distinctly countercultural. But countercultural does not always mean that it was difficult to accept. The evidence for the popularity of this text suggests that this message of the possibility of change for each individual, was one that many Christians found encouraging. Written originally in Greek, the *Shepherd* was promptly translated into Latin, Coptic, and a number of other languages spoken across the Roman Empire, including Ethiopic Ge'ez. It circulated widely from the second century on and was so widely respected that some early church fathers, including Irenaeus, considered it to be part of the canon.

In a world with fixed categories for character, the message present in *The Shepherd of Hermas* was deeply optimistic, countercultural, and profoundly revolutionary: the gospel has the power to change a person's character. A sinner, no matter how stained by cultural and personal sins, was not always going to remain a sinner. A redeemed sinner, as part of the church, could instead become a saint.

---

15. Such character witness is key, for example, in Lysias 1, Antiphon 5, and Aeschines 1. Introducing further character witness was sometimes also the job of supporting speakers, *synegoroi*. See Lene Rubinstein, *Litigation and Cooperation: Supporting Speakers in the Courts of Classical Athens* (Stuttgart: Steiner, 2000).

16. The speech in question is preserved in the work of the orator who wrote in defense of the accused, see Hyperides, *In Defense of Lycophron*.

Conclusion

In 1997, Joshua Harris's *I Kissed Dating Goodbye* became an instant bestseller and made its young author the new unofficial leader of the purity culture movement. To be sure, the movement itself had been around in some form since at least the Reagan administration, but Harris's book, along with its sequel, *Boy Meets Girl: Say Hello to Courtship*, articulated a philosophy for dating (or, rather, not dating but courting) that provided a useful blueprint for an entire generation in certain circles of evangelical Christianity.

And then in 2018, Harris issued a documentary, *I Survived "I Kissed Dating Goodbye"*, in which he interviewed many men and women who grew up in the circles that read his original books. The response was overwhelmingly negative. The documentary was effectively a catalog of myriad personal and relational traumas. Hearing this fallout blamed on his book left Harris shaken and apologetic. His remorse led to repentance, but not of a type that we see in the *Shepherd* or any ancient Christian text. Harris soon followed the denunciation of his own books and courtship philosophy by an announcement that he had separated from his wife and was seeking divorce. He no longer considers himself a Christian.[17]

As we consider this unfolding demise of purity culture and Harris's concomitant unraveling, there is a caveat to keep in mind: Are we throwing out the proverbial baby with the bathwater? Purity culture, with which Harris grew up and which he aided with his writings, created in some cases an idol out of certain types of relationships. It also undoubtedly set up many women for abusive marriages that they felt forced into and could not leave. But it also did something else that was good at its core, even if execution did not always live up to that goodness: It attempted to take a countercultural view of sexuality in the modern world. Did it fail? For many, yes. But did it aim to do something difficult and worthwhile, something that Christians struggled to do well from the earliest days of the church? Absolutely. Reflecting along these lines, Rachel Joy Welcher's book *Talking Back to Purity Culture: Rediscovering Faithful Christian Sexuality* effectively pushes back on the legalism of the movement, while refusing to compromise on biblical values.[18]

With purity culture at one extreme of the spectrum, the other extreme

---

17. A podcast interview with Harris on these developments is available as part of *Christianity Today*'s podcast series *The Rise and Fall of Mars Hill*: https://www.christianitytoday.com/ct/podcasts /rise-and-fall-of-mars-hill/joshua-harris-mars-hill-podcast-kissed-christianity-goodbye.html.

18. Rachel Joy Welcher, *Talking Back to Purity Culture: Rediscovering Faithful Christian Sexuality* (Downers Grove, IL: InterVarsity Press, 2020).

in some evangelical circles now is the delaying of marriage. Mark Regnerus's June 2020 cover story for *Christianity Today* presented a grim picture of marriage in modern American society. While in 2005, 50 percent of US men ages 25–34 were married, this number fell dramatically to just 35 percent of men in that age group in 2018. Although these numbers are higher for evangelicals, the gap between evangelicals and the rest of society is shrinking. Regnerus explained these trends in light of the emphasis on individual goals and fulfillment in life, which leads increasingly more young people to feel skeptical about the value of marriage.[19] What is particularly alarming is that many people who choose to delay marriage are also embracing the standards of the world, which see no problem with premarital sex and lead to a commodification of the bodies of believers in precisely the way that the New Testament and the early church so clearly condemned.

The embracing of the idol of self in lieu of marriage sounds bad enough as it is. Making matters worse, for many it comes along with the acceptance of cultural, and very casual, views on relationships and sexuality. That is certainly not what the early church had in mind when it advocated fiercely, through people like Paul, for the value of singles in the body of Christ. And the readily available curse that is pornography is a reminder that even for singles who are not engaged in casual physical relationships, the temptations are myriad.

The Shepherd of Hermas, with its message that even lust without action is a sin, reminds us that the church had always espoused purity as a countercultural alternative to the Roman cultural views of sexuality, which were deeply abusive. Paul's writings present that same message in response to the sexual sins in the Corinthian church. But what all of these writings, as well as the failure of the purity culture movement, remind us is that simple solutions cannot work. Or, at least, they cannot work for everyone. Paul's ideal description of singleness and marriage involves lives that are lived fruitfully for the glory of Christ. A Christian view of marriage, for Paul, never involves objectification or abuse. But no two sanctifying marriages of two sinners are likely to look the same.

Shortly before my husband and I were married, I read John Piper's *This Momentary Marriage: A Parable of Permanence*.[20] In writing this book on marriage after forty years of married life, Piper made a surprising choice to use

19. Mark Regnerus, "Can the Church Save Marriage?," *Christianity Today*, June 22, 2020, https://www.christianitytoday.com/ct/2020/july-august/marriage-save-church-declining-christians-global.html.

20. John Piper, *This Momentary Marriage: A Parable of Permanence* (Wheaton, IL: Crossway, 2009).

quotations from the works of Dietrich Bonhoeffer in opening each chapter. Why is this choice surprising? As Piper himself explained, Bonhoeffer never experienced marriage himself. Engaged at the time of his arrest for his part in an assassination plot against Hitler, he was executed shortly before what should have been his wedding day. But the death of martyrs like Bonhoeffer, Piper notes, reminds us that marriage is always momentary because life is. Marriage and sexuality, the way God imagines them, are so countercultural that we can never fully understand them in this life. But this does not mean that we should stop trying.

Cultural Christianity, especially in the Bible Belt, can entice us into assuming that we no longer need to live on mission. But the first three chapters of this book show that even in a world where Christians were a tiny minority, resisting the surrounding culture is a constant struggle. We saw how the cultural views of wealth, food, and sexuality pervaded early Christian communities and distorted the gospel in the process. In these stories, parallels to our own day are readily visible. Comfort is a modern American idol in all areas of life, and this affects our view of money. As for food, the contemporary "foodie" culture has entered the Christian world just as much as the broader society, and the jokes about Chick-fil-A as "God's chicken" show the complex connection between cultural Christianity and fast food. Last but not least, the modern media makes sure that we are bombarded with cultural messages about sexuality that are arguably more pervasive and ever-present in our lives than those encountered by the residents of the Roman Empire. We may not see phalluses on the street cobblestones, but R- and M-rated movies and television series make these themes ubiquitous. If we are that with which we fill our minds, we are all idol worshipers rivaling anyone in the Roman Empire.

The three chapters in this first section allowed us the opportunity to test-drive the methodology used in the rest of the book. What happens when we take the ancient sources at their word and assume that the concerns that the early Christians expressed about the seductive power of the surrounding Greco-Roman culture represent real problems rather than mere hypotheticals? The answer, as we saw, is striking, as this approach allowed us to see an overall thread that connects multiple patterns of sin that arose in the early Christian communities throughout the Roman Empire, as well as ways the church leaders, like Paul, attempted not always successfully to address these sins. We see a Christian community that looks surprisingly familiar, despite the stark differences from the modern world. It is a community in which cultural Christianity was the surprising norm for many believers, despite the high costs of conversion that they took on—both social and financial.

Put simply, the overall picture of cultural religion and culturally grounded sin in the early churches reminds us that people do not live in a vacuum. All people are affected by the culture around them in deeply ingrained ways that perhaps they themselves might not even be able to articulate. Living counter-culturally, as the earliest converts to Christianity discovered, was a challenge, whether they were coming from Jewish monotheism or from Greco-Roman polytheism. But what about those who converted and then decided, for whatever reason, to leave the church? It is to their stories in the context of the early church after the New Testament era that we turn next.

PART 2

Cultural Christians in the Age of Persecution

4

Trouble in Bithynia

How Cultural Sins Lead to Apostasy

AROUND 160 CE, A ROMAN PROCONSUL STATIONED IN Smyrna decided to purge the region of its growing population of Christians. Among those arrested in this persecution was the local bishop, Polycarp. Eighty-six years old at the time, he was the last living link to the apostles and the tangible world of the New Testament: as a young man, he had met the apostle John. When the proconsul ordered Polycarp to curse Jesus to regain his freedom—standard procedure in Roman trials of Christians—the elderly bishop calmly responded, "Eighty-six years have I served Him, and He has done me no wrong. How can I blaspheme my King and my Savior?"[1]

As typical in such instances, the angered proconsul ordered Polycarp's execution. Miraculously, however, the fire in which Polycarp was to be burned to death could not harm him. The executioner was then ordered to kill him with a dagger. This worked, although another miracle followed. The amount of blood that spilled from the wound that killed Polycarp flooded the same fire that could not burn him earlier, extinguishing it altogether. Polycarp died a martyr's death, preferring it to apostasy—renunciation of his faith.

---

1. An anonymous witness to the events wrote an account of these proceedings, *Martyrdom of Polycarp*, as a letter from the church in Smyrna to the church at Philomelium, both located in ancient Asia Minor and now part of Turkey. For a translation, see *The Martyrdom of Polycarp*, *New Advent*, https://www.newadvent.org/fathers/0102.htm.

Just as with many other martyrdom accounts, not everyone has taken this traditional story of Polycarp's death to be an accurate record of the actual events. But the popularity of the account is important in any case because it shows clearly that early Christians valued such heroic behavior on behalf of Christ. While the stories of famous martyrs like Polycarp glorify death over apostasy, ample surviving evidence shows that the choice that average churchgoers made in the face of persecution and death threats was not always so heroic.

Almost a century later and across the empire, in Egypt in 250 CE, in the village of Theadelphia, a mother and a daughter chose that low-resistance route. They complied with an empire-wide edict from Emperor Decius, ordering all residents of the empire to perform pagan sacrifices and obtain a certificate to that effect by a certain date. What is striking about this particular certificate is not just that the two women fulfilled the requirement, effectively renouncing their Christian faith, but that they note in the document that they have been performing pagan sacrifices all along. For them, sacrificing to the pagan gods and leaving the church was not quite so drastic a move after all.[2]

The New Testament abounds with stern warnings to converts against falling away. Jesus noted during his ministry that to have believed and subsequently rejected the faith was much worse than to have never believed at all. Such warnings were not mere theoretical discourse. The reason that the New Testament repeatedly addressed this issue in the strongest terms is precisely because it was so common. Evidence from writings of both Christians and non-Christians shows that apostasy could take a variety of shapes and have a variety of causes. The entire New Testament book of Hebrews, in particular, addresses Jewish converts to Christianity who were planning to abandon the faith, presumably to return to Judaism, which was accorded special exemptions by the Romans.[3] And a common interpretation of 1 Peter has been that persecution could lead to widespread apostasy, as some believers may be tempted to take the easy way out of the difficult situation by renouncing Christianity. The example of the Egyptian certificate of sacrifice noted above could certainly be interpreted in that light.

Though persecution was one reason for apostasy during the New Testament Era and beyond, we should not put the chief blame on it so hastily. We will

---

2. Michigan Papyrus No. 158.

3. The Emperor Augustus, for instance, issued an empire-wide decree allowing special privileges for the Jews, effectively allowing them to worship as they pleased. See Claude Eilers, "The Date of Augustus' Edict on the Jews (JOS. *AJ* 16.162–165) and the Career of C. Marcus Censorinus," *Phoenix* 58 (2004): 86–95. Of course, not all Roman rulers were this friendly—see Martin Goodman, *Rome and Jerusalem: The Clash of Ancient Civilizations* (New York: Vintage, 2008).

see later in this chapter that 1 Peter perhaps does not do that either. So why did some converts ultimately leave Christianity to revert back, in most cases, to paganism? What did apostasy mean to those who left the church, and how did believers who knew the apostates react to these events? Finally, how did early church leaders deal with this issue—in particular, how (if at all) did they attempt to love those of their flock who were eager to leave them behind? The answer to this last question, in the case of many leaders, appears to have been that they wrote letters.

Much of the New Testament consists of letters written by concerned leaders to congregations that were going through these and many other cultural sins and challenges. The testimony of these letters has much to tell us about the everyday struggles of these early believers. While it is easy to assume that the apostates were the sinners in this story, sometimes it could be their fellow churchgoers. In both cases, we see cultural Christianity at work yet again.

This chapter focuses on the nature and impact of cultural sin in producing apostasy in the early churches. Our story here follows those men and women who, following conversion, chose to leave Christianity during the New Testament era and into the early second century CE.[4] The allure of culture, we will see, sometimes proved more enticing than the countercultural community of the gospel. In this regard, this chapter is a little bit different from the other chapters in this book: instead of investigating one specific category of cultural sin, we are looking at apostasy as the result of certain types of cultural sins.

While the converts whose stories we have documented in the previous chapters seemed to embrace both the surrounding culture and the gospel, unwilling to give up either one, the stories in this chapter show that some ultimately did make the choice to leave the church. Following the threads of evidence in Christian and pagan sources, our main case study here is the history of the early Christian community in the Roman province of Bithynia-Pontus. We focus on this community for the simple reason that we have both pagan and Christian sources about it. The availability of stories from both sides allows us to tell a more detailed and nuanced story of the impact of culture on these Christians: this is a church whose numbers ebbed and flowed at times because of apostasy. And the outsider's perspective on the events comes to us from an unexpected source: a pagan Roman governor with little to no prior knowledge of Christianity.

---

4. For an authoritative academic reference on apostasy in the New Testament period, see B. J. Oropeza's three-volume magnum opus, *Apostasy in the New Testament Communities* (Eugene, OR: Wipf & Stock, 2012).

An Interview with a Roman Governor: The Bithynian Church in the Early Second Century

In the year 111 CE, Gaius Plinius Caecilius Secundus, better known to us today as Pliny the Younger, set out from Rome to the most important political post of his career. From his appointment to this post by the Senate in 111 CE to his likely death in 113 CE, Pliny was the governor of the Roman province of Bithynia-Pontus. Located in the southwestern region of the Black Sea littoral, Bithynia-Pontus was not exactly a popular tourist destination for Roman elites. In fact, the city of Tomi in Pontus was the place where the emperor Augustus exiled the disgraced poet Ovid a little over a century earlier. Ovid spent the exile writing mournful poetry bewailing his cruel fate and the horrors of the locale. Bad food, bad weather, bad company. But as far as Pliny was concerned, a governorship of any province was still nothing to sneer at.

Pliny was a superbly well-educated Roman aristocrat. His uncle was none other than the natural historian Pliny the Elder, who famously perished when he decided to sail up to take a closer look at Vesuvius mid-eruption. Death in the name of science. His nephew sensibly chose to stay back and focus on his studies that afternoon—a rare instance of homework saving lives. By 111 CE, Pliny the Younger was a career politician and public servant, with over twenty years in the Senate. But none of his previous reading or practical public service, which even included a glamorous stint supervising the sewage system upkeep for the city of Rome (no small task for a city of one million), prepared him for the challenges that he was to encounter as provincial governor.

Thankfully for historians, Pliny was a prolific letter writer, who was remarkably afraid of making a misstep that the emperor might find offensive—a sensible attitude for someone who had spent much of his political career during the rule of the notoriously paranoid Domitian (emperor from 81–96 CE). Even with less volatile emperors in charge, provincial governors knew to tread with care. Augustus once fired a provincial governor for a spelling error in a letter.[5]

Trajan (emperor from 98–117 CE) was a much kinder *princeps*, but old habits die hard. So Pliny wrote letters to Trajan about each challenge he confronted, from having to fix temples and public works in disrepair, to the question of the status of abandoned infants in the province, the staffing of prisons, and

---

5. The spelling error was substituting *ixi* for *ipsi*. See Suetonius, *Life of Augustus*, 88.

the possibility of establishing a volunteer fire brigade in the provincial capital, Nicomedia. Each time, he followed the general formula of outlining the problem, describing his own stop-gap solution and asking for the emperor's opinion on the matter. Amazingly, considering how busy the emperor of the known world was, Trajan always responded, and his replies to Pliny survive.

Arguably the most famous letter exchange between the two, and the one to which we turn now, concerns Pliny's alarmed discovery of Christians in his province in 112 CE. The story that Pliny's letter reveals, in conjunction with other evidence, is one of a church that had been in the province at that point for several decades, had faced challenges, and had largely persisted.[6] The church has also had an extremely high rate of apostasy. Pliny's letter is based on interviews with current and former Christians in his province and thus provides us with a unique opportunity to get their perspective on their struggles.

Pliny's intent in interviewing the Bithynian Christians was not to collect oral histories, of course. His intent was to conduct meticulous research and investigation to understand the situation as fully as possible. While modern historians thankfully do not use torture or intimidation tactics in interviews the way Pliny sometimes did, we are the beneficiaries of Pliny's desire to report his findings in detail to the emperor. Historians who rely on oral histories for information usually interview people and condense their findings into a report. That is what Pliny did. A careful reading of Pliny's letter to Trajan allows us, therefore, to reverse engineer Pliny's report, uncovering the original voices of Bithynia's Christians, both faithful ones and those who had fallen away. So what do we learn about the Bithynian Christians?

After the usual flattering greeting, Pliny opens his letter with an overview of his question for Trajan. He has never dealt with Christians before and thus finds the situation confusing. He is wholly ignorant of who or what Christians are, but he has apparently heard of them just enough to know that their presence in his province is cause for alarm. Even the extent to which he should be worried is unclear to him. He asks Trajan for clarification as to whether he needs to investigate particular offenses associated with the movement, what the punishment for Christians should be, and whether the penalty should take into account the age of the accused and any potential renunciation of belief. Should he treat those

---

6. For an overview of this letter as well as other documents from the period that show the different ways in which the Romans perceived and misunderstood the Christians, see Robert Wilken, *The Christians as the Romans Saw Them* (New Haven, CT: Yale University Press, 2003). For a full text of the letter exchange between Pliny and Trajan, parts of which I quote in this chapter, see https://faculty.georgetown.edu/jod/texts/pliny.html.

who are currently practicing Christians the same way as those who had been Christians at some point but left Christianity years earlier?

Pliny's lack of knowledge about Christianity and lack of previous experience with Christians reminds us just how tiny the movement was in the early second century. There appear to have been some Christians in Rome already by the days of Claudius (emperor 41–54 CE), who was the first emperor to expel Christians, most likely all of them Jewish converts, from the city.[7] Furthermore, the church in Rome was thriving in the days of Paul (who, of course, wrote a letter to the Christians in Rome) and Nero (emperor 54–68 CE).

Nero had famously blamed the Christians for the great fire of Rome in 64 CE. The apostles Paul and Peter, in fact, were executed during the subsequent persecution. Still, Christian presence in the imperial capital that was home to over one million people was clearly minuscule. Even if the movement had numbered in the thousands, the odds of Pliny's encountering Christians in Rome were low, especially after the repeated persecutions had driven the church quite literally underground. But the Bithynian Christians appear to have been bolder than their Roman brethren.

Pliny's opening questions for Trajan already give us two important clues about the Christians, past and current, that he has discovered in Bithynia. First, there is clearly a great diversity of age among them. Some are "very young," whereas others are "more mature." Second, it is clear that the group of people he interviewed included both current Christians and those who had been Christians at some point—thence Pliny's concern about whether the two categories ought to be treated differently.

We also ought to pay attention to the fact that this investigation happened at all. Who brought this matter to the diligent governor's attention? We get no direct information in the letter, but presumably the initial informers were important enough for their voices to carry some weight and force the governor to investigate. This suggests, hypothetically, a group of local magistrates or members of the imperial cult—basically, a group with some connection to the public practice of Roman religion, whose claims had to be taken seriously. Not everyone was guaranteed to have the governor's ear, so the status of those who launched the initial complaints as upstanding local citizens is likely.

Bithynia was not considered to be a sufficiently important province for a legion to be stationed there. That fact should not fool us into thinking that the governor's job there was easy. The delicate nature of the diplomatic crisis among

---

7. Suetonius, *Life of Claudius*, 25.

the locals into which Pliny stumbled here is not to be underestimated. Had Pliny simply ignored the situation, the locals who lodged the complaint about the Christians would have escalated the conflict in some way, perhaps resorting to violence of their own. And that was Rome's worst fear. Pliny's job as governor was not to figure out who was right or wrong in this situation but to keep peace and order in the province in the least expensive way possible.[8]

No Case Too Small:
The Governor Investigates

On another occasion during Pliny's time as governor, he was summoned to the city of Prusa, a little over a half-day's journey away from his seat in Nicomedia, to assist with a business that seemed, at least at first glance, less controversial than that suspicious monotheistic sect. A public bathhouse in Prusa has fallen into such a state of disrepair as to merit the governor's attention. Repairing public buildings may seem like a waste of the governor's time, but a public bathhouse had a significance in the Roman Empire far beyond what we can imagine. First, for most residents of the Roman Empire, these were the only places to wash. Only the wealthiest aristocrats could afford to build a bath in their own homes. Second, bathhouses were not just places to get clean. They were places for socialization, and many also included space for exercise. Finally, they were important symbols of Romanization. The first two types of buildings the Romans constructed in newly conquered cities were theaters and bathhouses.

Reading between the lines of Pliny's letter to Trajan on the matter, someone from the city must have complained to the governor about the sorry state of the bathhouse, and (as in the case of the Christians in the province) that someone was important enough to get the busy governor's attention. So the governor dutifully traveled to Prusa, examined the bathhouse, and concluded, as he told Trajan, that instead of trying to restore the dilapidated building, the city ought to build a new one. Might the emperor be comfortable with this plan? Yes, he would, replied Trajan, so long as this does not bankrupt the city, and as long as taxes to Rome continue to be paid on schedule.

---

8. For an overview of how provincial governors kept peace in the province, see Christopher Fuhrmann, *Policing the Roman Empire: Soldiers, Administration, and Public Order* (Oxford: Oxford University Press, 2011).

Several important trends emerge from Pliny's investigation and Trajan's response, even on this more straightforward matter. First, Pliny seems to have shared the motto of a much later fictional investigator, Encyclopedia Brown: no case too small. Second, Pliny was a detail-oriented individual who did not outsource research to others. In the case of the bathhouse in an insignificant town, he traveled there himself, examined the building, and made his own recommendations, instead of merely relying on the reports of the locals. Finally, we see that Trajan's concerns were simple and practical. He was not eager to intervene heavily but just wanted to make sure that any decision would not impact everyday business, such as collection of taxes from the province. All of these trends apply to Pliny's investigation into the Christians, but on a much larger scale than any other business he had to conduct as governor. Unlike the Prusa bathhouse, the investigation into the affair of the Christians seems to have lasted months. We now return to the governor's report.

As usual for his letters, after outlining the problem about which he is writing to Trajan, Pliny proceeds to explain what he has done so far to investigate any individuals reported to him: "I interrogated these as to whether they were Christians; those who confessed I interrogated a second and a third time, threatening them with punishment; those who persisted I ordered executed. For I had no doubt that, whatever the nature of their creed, stubbornness and inflexible obstinacy surely deserve to be punished." He adds that he sent any Roman citizens straight to Rome, as they were outside his jurisdiction—a procedure reminiscent of what happened to Paul, who used his privilege of appealing to the emperor to be sent to Rome in Acts 25:6–12. This comment is another valuable piece of evidence about the diversity of the Christian community.

Before the emperor Caracalla's citizenship decree of 212 CE granted citizenship to all freeborn residents of the Roman Empire, only about 10–20 percent of the residents of the empire were citizens. It is not surprising to hear, therefore, that not all Bithynian Christians were Roman citizens. The fact that some were, nevertheless, suggests that there were enough important individuals in the Christian community, as citizenship most commonly was granted to individuals for carrying out a significant service to the Roman state. The example of the apostle Paul is relevant here, as his father had received Roman citizenship for an unspecified favor to the empire. But the most common service that acquired citizenship as its reward was military—the citizenship diploma, granted upon successful service of twenty-five years, was a valuable carrot for recruiting noncitizen auxiliary troops into the Roman legions. Perhaps some of these retired soldiers were in the Bithynian church.

Pliny's comment about his continued threats for those who confessed to be Christians shows that he had offered them an opportunity to reject the faith at the time of questioning. As befits a traditional Roman polytheist, Pliny could not fathom why anyone would be so stubborn as to choose death instead of rejecting their beliefs. It appears that some indeed apostatized on the spot when faced with Pliny's threats while others continued to cling to their faith. This scenario of rejecting Christianity when threatened will continue to be a challenge for churches for centuries to come, as they will continue to struggle with the question of whether to readmit such members later on, and if so, on what terms. But that story is still in the future, and we will get to it in chapter 7. Our concern at the moment is with Pliny's unfolding investigation into the Bithynian church. For the initial investigation did not quite work out as Pliny would have liked.

Pliny seems to have hoped to resolve matters quickly and efficiently, and that is presumably why he did not write to Trajan initially. But the situation continued to snowball out of his control, as the next section of his letter reveals. What had started as a few isolated accusations quickly led to additional ones. Clearly, seeing that the governor was taking reports concerning Christians seriously, emboldened additional informants came forward. The culminating event in Pliny's investigation was an anonymous document that was made public, as Pliny's wording in the letter suggests, containing a lengthy list of names of purported Christians. Had the document been merely a private missive to Pliny, presumably he could have dealt with it more quietly. But the public nature of the document seems to have left him no choice but to launch a full-fledged investigation.

Before we turn to Pliny's investigation, it is appropriate to pause and think about the nature of these reports. Initially, small groups and isolated individuals submitted their reports about (presumably) individual Christians in the province. The cautious nature of these initial reports, along with Pliny's loss of ideas for how to deal with them, suggests that it has been a while since anyone had persecuted Christians in the province or investigated Christianity there. After all, Pliny likely would have known about this issue, if his immediate predecessor in the province had to deal with it.

Reconstructing the Investigation

It appears likely that the Christian community in the province had slowly been growing for a while. They were mostly left alone by the authorities but sorely resented by at least some of the locals, who lost no time in reporting Christians to the new governor. Since quite a few people in the community knew who the current or past Christians in their midst were, this suggests that the Christian community was not living in secret. In this context, it is intriguing to speculate about who may have publicized the anonymous list of Christians. One possibility may be someone who had actually been a member of the church in the past and thus did not want former friends to know that he had turned against them. Another possibility is that perhaps some Christians were in prominent positions locally, and there was fear of reporting them openly, as the informant could face adverse consequences and maybe even be prosecuted for libel. In any case, Pliny had no idea who posted this bombshell of a list, and its anonymity focused the investigation squarely on those named.

Relying on the same test as used in more official persecutions, Pliny required any of the accused who claimed that they were not Christians to perform basic Roman religious rituals: "They invoked the gods in words dictated by me, offered prayer with incense and wine to your image, which I had ordered to be brought for this purpose together with statues of the gods, and moreover cursed Christ—none of which those who are really Christians, it is said, can be forced to do." This procedure that Pliny used seems to contradict his earlier insistence that he has no previous experience dealing with Christians. But being the life-long researcher that he was, Pliny was able to find out information on how other Roman officials, presumably outside his province, had handled such investigations. As a result, he also learned some basic elements of Christian belief.

But the investigation only kept getting more complicated. Some of those accused seem to have claimed that they never were Christians. We can speculate whether they were lying or if they perhaps had visited church services at some point and simply never accepted Christ, reverting easily to their lives as Roman polytheists. Others named in the document admitted that they used to be Christians but had left Christianity, "some three years before, others many years, some as much as twenty-five years. They all worshiped your image and the statues of the gods, and cursed Christ."

The length of time since these former Christians had left the faith is striking, as we consider the anonymous informant and what this list continues to reveal about public information in the province. This is yet another clue that the Christians in Bithynia, before Pliny's arrival, enjoyed a period of freedom from persecution and thus did not hide their beliefs. As a result, other members of the community could know who used to be a Christian. Ancient cities too often functioned as *bona fide* fishbowls, where everyone knew everyone else's business. The ready flow of information for Pliny is yet one example of this phenomenon in action. Another striking point emerges: even during this period of safety, plenty of Christians who converted still left the church and presumably (as we see from their readiness to sacrifice to the Roman gods and the emperor) rejoined the traditional Roman religion.

Pliny clearly came into this investigation with a binary categorization in mind: someone is either a Christian or not. But as the responses of those he interrogated show, there was quite a gradation among the individuals reported as Christians who were not part of the church at the time of the interrogation. Some did not consider themselves to have ever been Christian, while others noted that they had been but were not any longer and strikingly provided the length of time since they had lapsed. But while Pliny does not seem to have been much concerned with their beliefs or activities, he learned additional useful information about these points from these former Christians. They argued for the harmlessness of Christians and provided the increasingly more befuddled governor with the most detailed information he was to receive about the faith:

> They asserted, however, that the sum and substance of their fault or error had been that they were accustomed to meet on a fixed day before dawn and sing responsively a hymn to Christ as to a god, and to bind themselves by oath, not to some crime, but not to commit fraud, theft, or adultery, not falsify their trust, nor to refuse to return a trust when called upon to do so. When this was over, it was their custom to depart and to assemble again to partake of food— but ordinary and innocent food.

The emphasis on the harmlessness of Christianity is important here and suggests that these former Christians were well aware of the many misunderstandings about Christianity that were circulating around the Roman world and were eager to reassure the governor of their innocence of any crimes. The specific comment about the "ordinary and innocent" nature of the food that the Christians shared as part of their meetings is especially significant, given the alarming rumors that proliferated—in particular, the idea of the Lord's Supper was especially likely to be misunderstood as ritual cannibalism. But one important detail that we still do not get from their report is this: If Christianity was wholly harmless, why did they leave the faith?

Change Is in the Air? Stories of Apostasy in the Bithynian Church

We get one hint of a change that arrived in the lives of the Christians in the province with the new governor: Pliny notes that some Christians told him that they had stopped meeting when Pliny had outlawed any large-scale gatherings in pursuance of Trajan's order. Pliny's letter about this investigation is traditionally dated to 112 CE, a year after his arrival in the province. Thus some or even most groups had presumably stopped meeting together the year before, sometime in 111 CE, when the new governor arrived and promulgated the emperor's ban on gatherings. Suspicious that this was not quite the entire truth—and it is unclear whether Pliny was expecting that the Christians did more at their meetings, or whether he questioned if they truly stopped meeting—Pliny finally tortured two female slaves who were reported to be deaconesses for additional information. To his chagrin or further confusion, he "discovered nothing else but depraved, excessive superstition."

Torturing slaves was a long-standing custom in Greek and Roman law. The assumption was that testimony obtained under torture was the most reliable, as slaves would lie otherwise. But even this last-resort method yielded Pliny no further information. Presumably, what Pliny refers to as "depraved, excessive superstition" is the deaconesses' attempts to reveal the gospel to him, even when tortured. The governor, intent on doing his job, was not interested. At that stage, feeling like his investigation was stalling, Pliny finally contacted Trajan for advice.

He concludes the letter by explaining several more reasons for asking for help. First, he notes that his investigation revealed that the number of those connected to Christianity is quite high both now and potentially in the future: "For many persons of every age, every rank, and also of both sexes are and will be endangered. For the contagion of this superstition has spread not only to the cities but also to the villages and farms." But Pliny also expresses his optimism that the growth of Christianity in the region can easily be reversed at this time, and in fact, that reversal seems to be happening already. "It is certainly quite clear that the temples, which had been almost deserted, have begun to be frequented, that the established religious rites, long neglected, are being resumed, and that from everywhere sacrificial animals are coming, for which until now very few purchasers could be found."

Pliny's concluding paragraph confirms in the strongest terms that before his arrival in the province, the local church was indeed growing steadily for some time, without any trouble from Roman authorities. As a result, the Christians, as Pliny discovered from his investigation, were an extremely diverse group of men and women of all ages and social ranks, from slaves (as the comment about deaconesses reveals) to all other ranks (as his comment about diversity of social rank shows). Attesting further to the breadth to which Christianity has permeated the province is Pliny's comment that believers could be found not only in the cities but also in the countryside.

Christianity was initially a religion that spread in cities, starting, of course, with Jerusalem.[9] Furthermore, the term *pagan* (*paganus*), which originally meant "country dweller," is a reminder that the Romans themselves were aware of the more likely persistence of the traditional Roman religion in the countryside than in the cities in Late Antiquity. Last but not least, concrete proof of the advance of Christianity in the province is Pliny's reference to the Roman temples, which appear to have been abandoned for a time but are, at the time of his writing, seeing a resurgence in activity.

Pliny's concluding point about the revival of worship in the temples of the province and the revival of the trade in sacrificial animals allows us to reconstruct a possible course of events. In 111 CE, the new governor arrived and promptly banned all large gatherings, by request of the emperor. While this was not intended to be an attack on Christians, all large-scale organizations were affected. Christian churches could no longer meet in larger groups comprising multiple households and could no longer use any public spaces for gatherings. Presumably, some members simply continued to worship together but in much smaller groups and in a less public way.[10] These are most likely the Christians who, when interrogated by the governor, refused to give up their faith and chose to die instead.

Many others, however, once banned from gathering in large groups with fellow believers, decided instead to forsake Christianity and went back to traditional Roman religion. Why? Perhaps it was the easiest thing to do. The numbers of these apostates must have been large indeed if they could make such a dramatic dent in the local sacrificial animal business! Indeed, one cannot help but wonder: Could it have been the local sacrifice suppliers who sent the anonymous denunciation to the governor? Furthermore, such apostates had no qualms, when

---

9. The classic work on the urban nature of the early church remains Wayne Meeks, *The First Urban Christians: The Social World of the Apostle Paul* (New Haven, CT: Yale University Press, 2003).

10. We do not know for certain where the Bithynian Christians met before this. House churches were common, but as Edward Adams shows, not the only possibility. See *The Earliest Christian Meeting Places: Almost Exclusively Houses?* (London: Bloomsbury, 2013).

interrogated by Pliny, about sacrificing to the emperor and the traditional Roman gods in his presence and to curse Christ to boot. For them, surely Christianity had some meaning for a time in their lives, but they easily left it behind and reverted to their old religion with no regrets.

Overall, the story that Pliny presents in his letter shows just how easily many early converts could fall away and revert to the traditional Roman religion. Also, the story shows that an empire-wide or systematic persecution was not necessary to gut a local church. Pliny did not have the last word—after all, the entire reason he wrote to Trajan was because he wanted to include his input into the situation.

The Emperor Weighs In

Once Pliny wrote his letter, it undertook the nearly three-week voyage from Nicomedia to Rome. It then likely waited in the piles of other imperial correspondence until the emperor could read it. Finally, maybe three or four months after writing his missive, Pliny received Trajan's response. It was short and sweet and must have been a surprise to the diligent no-nonsense governor. Trajan complimented Pliny on investigating the individual cases of suspected Christians, but he encouraged him not to spend his time on such investigations and not to seek Christians out. Trajan concludes his reply with a powerful warning: "Anonymously posted accusations ought to have no place in any prosecution. For this is both a dangerous kind of precedent and out of keeping with the spirit of our age."

Trajan did not seem worried about Christians, although (as noted earlier) he did forbid large-group gatherings in the province for fear that any such gatherings might turn political. We can see this fear in Trajan's response to another request from Pliny: when the governor asked permission to form volunteer fire brigades, Trajan vehemently forbade this. But Trajan's greatest concern in this letter was the dangerous precedent of anonymous accusations. The comment that such accusations are "out of keeping with the spirit of our age" is a clear reference to the rule of the utterly paranoid Emperor Domitian (emperor 81–96 CE), who imagined an assassin hiding in every corner and perhaps was justified in his suspicions—he was assassinated, after all, by his own palace staff and mourned by no one. Domitian's reign encouraged anonymous denunciations, which resulted in an extreme purge of the Roman Senate. Dozens of senators were executed on mere suspicion of treason against the emperor. The memory of Domitian's reign of terror, as well as its reliance on anonymous denunciations, was surely fresh in the minds of both Trajan and Pliny, who were both senators at the time.

Unfortunately, though, our story of the Bithynian church must stop in 112 CE. We cannot go further forward in time, although we will presently go back to the earlier history of this Christian community. But before we do so, we can still hazard a reasonable guess as to what happened following the receipt of Trajan's response. Pliny, who had already stopped much of the investigation of Christians, pending the emperor's advice, would have refused to handle any further such investigations. The denunciations would have stopped once it was clear that the governor was no longer taking on these cases. Significant damage, however, had already been done to the local Christian community, which likely felt shaken by this unexpected persecution at the hands of the new governor.

The process of rebuilding to previous levels might have taken decades. But it is important to note that the greatest damage to the local church had come not from Pliny's investigations but rather from the edict forbidding large gatherings. So the greatest wave of apostasy in the province, leading a large number of people to leave churches and go back to worshiping at the pagan temples, which had been almost entirely abandoned at that point, came simply from this initial ban on gatherings and had nothing to do with the subsequent investigation of Christians.

As we continue to reconstruct the story of the Bithynian church, we will now go backward in time and turn to a glimpse of its story in the New Testament. The evidence of Pliny's report, which mentions that some of those that he interviewed said that they had been Christians but had left the faith as long as twenty-five years ago, takes us back to the late 80s CE. We find out from the New Testament evidence that Christians had been present in Bithynia from at least the early 60s. What was the earlier history of Christians in the province then? Had apostasy always been a part of their story? Having heard from a pagan witness, Pliny, we now get the Christian side of the story from one important witness: Peter. The testimony of this witness will allow us to backtrack and fill in some gaps in the earlier story of the Bithynian church. These gaps, in turn, will prove relevant for our thinking about apostasy even today.

Back to the Beginning:
Interviewing Peter about Bithynia

We have completed our interview with a Roman governor. Now, in turn, we get to interview an apostle who wrote about the church in Bithynia as part of

1 Peter. "Interviewing" Peter, in this case, means seeking the opinion of the ultimate expert on the issue of apostasy. After all, Peter renounced knowing Jesus three times on the night of his arrest.[11] This makes him perhaps one of the most famous, as well as one of the earliest, Christian apostates ever. But his story is one that should ultimately also give us hope, for Peter became, as Jesus had predicted, one of the leaders of the early church and the author of two canonical epistles in the New Testament.

Not long before his own martyrdom in the Neronian persecution in Rome, Peter wrote a letter "to God's elect, exiles scattered throughout the provinces of Pontus, Galatia, Cappadocia, Asia and Bithynia" (1 Pet. 1:1). Paul had traveled around this region on the trip where he was ultimately not allowed to proceed into either Asia or Bithynia, although he did visit a number of other churches in the area—Galatia and Cappadocia. Just over a decade after Paul's tour of the area, we find that it is filled with churches that are experiencing a common enough set of challenges for Peter to send them a group letter instead of individual epistles.

The use of the term *diaspora* in the opening address has spurred debate about this letter's original audiences: Are the churches to which Peter wrote filled with Jewish converts? Because the term *diaspora* originally had been used to designate the exile and dispersion of Jews from Israel, that is a possibility. That said, the term could also refer more broadly to a group of like-minded people who are scattered apart, and thus can be appropriate for addressing a large group of people in several provinces. Of course, given the trouble that the Galatian church has had with Judaizers, a possible answer here is a mix of the two possibilities: there were likely some Jewish converts in the churches to whom Peter wrote, but we do not have to assume that they were the majority of the people in these churches.

The general nature of this letter is sufficient evidence that this may be a varied group of Christians by origin, despite their shared present experiences. So what led Peter to write to the churches, and what advice did Peter have for them? Just as with Pliny's letter, reading Peter's epistle closely allows us to see the real stories of real people underneath the general message. Traditionally, 1 Peter has been interpreted to refer to the suffering of Christians under state persecution.[12] Craig Keener ties it specifically to the Neronian persecution in the aftermath of the great fire at Rome in 64 CE.[13] As the analysis below will show, however, this general interpretation of the context of suffering Christians described in this

---

11. Matt. 26:69–75; Mark 14:66–72; Luke 22:54–62; John 18:15–27.
12. Karen H. Jobes, *1 Peter* (Grand Rapids: Baker Academic, 2005), 42–51.
13. Craig Keener, *The IVP Bible Background Commentary: New Testament* (Downers Grove, IL: IVP Academic, 2014), 684–85.

epistle is incomplete because it ignores the ability of culturally inspired apostasy to cause profound suffering in churches, ancient and modern.

After the opening blessing, Peter describes the blessings of salvation that his addressees have been promised and makes the following statement: "In all this you greatly rejoice, though now for a little while you may have had to suffer grief in all kinds of trials. These have come so that the proven genuineness of your faith—of greater worth than gold, which perishes even though refined by fire—may result in praise, glory and honor when Jesus Christ is revealed" (1 Pet. 1:6–7).

What are these "all kinds of trials" plaguing the letter's original audiences across the churches of Asia Minor? Presumably, the original addressees know what the trials are, and thus Peter feels no need to describe them, although we will get more overt hints shortly. Instead of describing the trials up front, Peter assures his audiences of their salvation, if they remain steadfast. He emphasizes the goal rather than the nature of these Christians' suffering, at least initially. This is our first but certainly not last hint that Peter is concerned about apostasy.

Peter spends much of the first two chapters imploring these Christians to resist the surrounding culture and commit themselves to holy living. Specific instructions that Peter notes include this exhortation: "As obedient children, do not conform to the evil desires you had when you lived in ignorance. But just as he who called you is holy, so be holy in all you do; for it is written: 'Be holy, because I am holy'" (1 Pet. 1:14–16). Peter also asks them to "rid yourselves of all malice and all deceit, hypocrisy, envy, and slander of every kind" and "to abstain from sinful desires, which wage war against your soul" (1 Pet. 2:1, 11).

Different aspects of holy living as countercultural concepts have been the focus of the previous three chapters but are worth noting here as well in connection with apostasy. Obviously, Peter would not be discussing holy living so much if it were not relevant. His emphasis implies a real connection: sin begets sin, so falling away is often packaged with other cultural sins.

The placing of specific arguments together also presents another connection: the trials through which these Christians are going have presented a real temptation to stray from living holy Christ-honoring lives. Peter mentions specific sins that he had witnessed or heard about in these churches. The list is reminiscent of the problems that Paul noted in the Corinthian church and includes the antithesis of some of the fruit of the Spirit: malice, deceit, hypocrisy, envy, and slander—meaning, disordered desires that could be dubbed passions of the mind. But in addition to these specifically named sins, Peter also includes an exhortation against "passions of the flesh," which would presumably involve acting on some of the disordered desires he had listed, such as sexual sins, and such excesses as overindulgence in food and drink.

Unlike Paul in 1 Corinthians, Peter does not name or describe specific individuals in the churches for particular sins. Yet Peter has no reason to attribute specific sins erroneously to these churches if they did not truly exist and affect these congregations. In a Greco-Roman culture whose power abuses, many of them sexual abuses to boot, were much more accepted than today, Peter's warning was yet another exhortation to resist the toxic culture. At the same time, however, the sins that Peter mentions are so remarkably commonplace, that his advice would apply just as clearly today as it did in the early 60s CE. One example, that comes to mind is the #ChurchToo movement, an outgrowth of the #MeToo movement, focusing on exposing sexual harassment and abuse in churches and parachurch ministries.

At this stage in the letter, halfway through the second chapter, Peter switches gears and exhorts Christians to be obedient subjects to all earthly authorities, specifically mentioning by name the emperor, governors, and other imperial officials and also slave masters (this last command, of course, being directed toward slaves in Christian communities). Intertwined with this command is the discussion of Jesus's suffering, "To this you were called, because Christ suffered for you, leaving you an example, that you should follow in his steps" (1 Pet. 2:21). At this stage we are finally getting to the specifics of what Peter had hinted at initially: "all kinds of trials" mentioned at the beginning of the letter involve suffering at the hands of the various levels of Roman government.

While there will be no official empire-wide persecution of Christians before the rule of Decius (emperor 249–251 CE), this does not mean that significant local persecutions did not exist. We got a hint of the scope and shape of such a persecution from Pliny's letter, and it is likely not an exaggeration to imagine a parallel situation to the one Pliny orchestrated in Bithynia, spurred by local denunciations. We can imagine similar scenarios happening on a local scale in the provinces to which Peter is writing here, including Bithynia.

But persecution at the local level could only happen if support existed for it at the local level, including informants eager to report Christians to the authorities. In such cases, the sins of malice, deceit, hypocrisy, envy, and slander suddenly acquire an added and more ominous meaning. As we noted earlier, Pliny's description of detailed denunciations of Christians, especially in the anonymous list of names, suggests the possibility of an informant from within the movement.

Christians who fall away, if led by malice or envy toward their former brothers and sisters, are poised to serve as informants, delivering Christians into the hands of the authorities. Even Christians who had not yet apostatized could be driven by envy to undermine other Christians' lives in the local church and the community. In this context, the suffering of Jesus, which Peter repeatedly brings up in the second half of the letter, seems even more relevant as a parallel to the suffering of other Christians, whose suffering came not only from the mistreatment by the Roman authorities (an expected grievance) but also from sinful treatment and betrayal by those closest to them within the Christian community.[14]

In encouraging close bonds between believers and other members of their communities, Christian and pagan, Peter briefly addresses husbands and wives early in chapter 3 of his letter before returning for the remainder of the letter to the theme of suffering for the cause of Christ. Chapter 5 briefly addresses the elders, leaders of the local churches in Asia Minor, encouraging them to lead with humility and appropriate eagerness for this great responsibility.

Peter hints that poor leadership by the elders—taking the shape of the negative qualities that Peter mentions, including excessive domineering over the flock or the abuse of power for "dishonest gain"—can be yet another cause for apostasy in the Christian community. In this case as well, modern parallels abound. Examples of pastors embroiled in scandals, whether for their own misconduct or for covering up the misconduct of others, come to mind. Underlying Peter's argument is the reality that the sins of those in power can drive more people out of churches than outright persecution.

The letter concludes with a final exhortation to all the faithful to stand firm and secure in their faith, trusting in God in the midst of suffering. Frustratingly, Peter concludes the letter in the same way that he started it—without ever acknowledging by name the kind of suffering that the Christians he is addressing are experiencing. But the hints he provides are powerful: "Be alert and of sober mind. Your enemy the devil prowls around like a roaring lion looking for someone to devour. Resist him, standing firm in the faith, because you know that the family of believers throughout the world is undergoing the same kind of sufferings" (1 Pet. 5:8–9).

This concluding warning is the most overt reference in the letter to the forces of evil that are attacking the Christian community and against which the people must watch out. But this description of the devil among the Christians is likely not a reference to official state persecutions—Peter would have described

---

14. 1 Pet. 3:13–4:11; 4:12–19.

these as external threats. Rather, he is referring to those within the community who seek to destroy it, whether through sin or through the use of the powers of Rome to attack believers.

Peter emphasizes that the kinds of suffering that the Christians of his day experienced were many and varied, but he also makes it clear that they were common to all in the universal church. And the sources of suffering that could both lead to the apostasy of others and were caused by those who had fallen away, involved mistreatment of fellow Christians by those who are in their churches or used to be a part of them, as much as the powers of Rome.

So how does this letter allow us to fill in the gaps between the planting of the Bithynian church in the early 50s CE, and the 80s CE, which is the furthest back that the Christians interviewed by Pliny in 112 CE could remember? We can do our best to fill in the gap. The intervening years were filled with conversions, as merchants in luxury goods and other traveling tradesmen and tradeswomen traveled all over the bordering provinces of Cappadocia, Galatia, Asia, and Bithynia-Pontus, sharing the gospel with any who might listen, Jews and gentiles alike. But these years were also filled with large-scale disagreements, betrayals, and apostasy in the local churches. Paul mentions one such case in 1 and 2 Timothy, as he notes that a metalworker, Alexander, abandoned his faith after a period in the faith and ultimately caused much harm to Paul and his ministry.[15] At their worst moments, Christians, current or former, used the faith as leverage against other believers, reporting them to any Roman authorities who were willing to listen. It was up to governors to decide whether to investigate and punish alleged Christians. But it was up to the local community, which included current and former believers, to decide whether they wanted to initiate the accusations to begin with.

It is significant that we cannot separate the Bithynian church from the rest of the churches that Peter addresses in his letter. Reading Pliny's report about Christians in Bithynia-Pontus, one may wonder just how similar the experience of that provincial Christian community was to those in other provinces. From Acts and 1 Peter, we get our answer: the Bithynians' experience was much more the norm than the exception—as Peter reminds his addressees, including the Bithynians, "that the family of believers throughout the world is undergoing the same kind of sufferings" (1 Pet. 5:9). Apostasy was part of their community's DNA from its earliest days and led to much suffering in the local churches,

---

15. 1 Timothy 1:19–20 and 2 Timothy 4:14, assuming these are referring to the same Alexander. But the point still applies if we have *two* apostates with the same (admittedly common) name.

playing a role even in state-sanctioned persecutions. These setbacks merely provided further divine revelation and encouragement, in the form of such New Testament texts as 1 Peter. And at each stage, some believers fell away, but even more converted, struck by the mercy of a God whose suffering provided a model for their own.

Applications and Conclusions: Apostasy in the Church Today

The story of apostasy in the Bithynian church has surprising application for us today. How many people, if attending church suddenly becomes inconvenient, whether as a result of a move, or work, or illness, simply fall away unintentionally? In the wake of the COVID-19 pandemic, in particular, losing the habit of fellowshipping with fellow Christians has caused some not to return to church, even once it was relatively safe to do so. Furthermore, the return of the Bithynian former Christians to the worship of the pagan gods in droves and of their own accord reminds us that we have been created to worship. Specifically, we have a built-in desire to worship God, but when we do not worship him, our sinful hearts readily find idols as replacements. That is what some of the Bithynian Christians did—quite literally. The gospel requires a changed life, but the pull of the old habits and idols can prove irresistible in the right circumstances, usually ones grounded in cultural structures.

Reading about such an unexpected and casual cause of apostasy is particularly convicting as we consider the impact of the COVID-19 pandemic on Christian communities. In March 2020, the explosion of the infections prompted most states in the United States to impose restrictions on large gatherings, including in churches. The move prompted a flurry of legal actions, arguing that such a ban constituted an attack on religious liberty. A few churches defied the bans, and some of them made the news for all the wrong reasons, as their gatherings became super-spreader events, killing some members or pastors. But making the situation into either an attack on religious liberty or an attack on science overlooks the much greater impact of everyday inconveniences on bringing about apostasy in believers who, in some cases, had previously been dedicated members of churches for years. And this phenomenon, in turn, forces us to consider internal rather than external forces.

One particularly pernicious force that echoes Peter's concerns in 1 Peter involves the dark history of abuses and cover-ups that came to the fore during the recent #ChurchToo movement. In the book *Jesus and John Wayne: How White Evangelicals Corrupted a Faith and Fractured a Nation*, Kristin Kobes du Mez provides the horrifying history of sexual abuse and abuse of power in churches over the course of the twentieth century. For du Mez, the culprit is a toxic masculine culture, particularly exemplified by John Wayne. But what is particularly heartbreaking in reading du Mez's book are the stories of victims who ultimately walked away from Christianity altogether because all they had experienced from their churches was pain.

Apostasy is all around us, just as it was in the early churches. As 1 Peter hints, not all instances of apostasy are solely the fault of those who fall away. Blaming the victim does not address the sin, especially in such egregious situations as spousal abuse, child abuse, or rape. But how might churches offer care especially to women in difficult situations? In what ways does women's presence in the church challenge cultural norms and thus also challenge cultural Christianity? That is the subject of the next chapter.

5

Unexpected Martyrs

Women's Challenge to Cultural Christianity in the Third-Century Church

ON A SUNNY SPRING DAY IN 203 CE, IN THE CITY OF Carthage in the Roman province of Africa, thousands of people crammed into every space available at the magnificent Roman amphitheater, jostling each other for the best seats they could get, eagerly awaiting state-sponsored entertainment that was one of the perks of living in the Roman Empire. Of course, the best seats were reserved for local officeholders and nobility. In the box of honor that day probably sat the procurator and chief Roman official in the province at that moment, Hilarian. Looking around inside the magnificent venue, he might have imagined himself in Rome. Eager to bring their brand of civilization to each territory they conquered, the Romans built impressive public baths and theaters in every major city under their control. Carthage, despite its extremely complicated relationship to Rome, was no exception.

Carthage, located in modern-day Tunisia, had a noble history that, as the Romans were bitterly aware, predated their own. Back when Rome was still a backwater, malaria-ridden village in Italy, the Carthaginians, originally a colony of Tyre in modern-day Lebanon, were already a mighty empire in their own right. Their concern was not military conquest as much as trade. Still, the Carthaginians' desire to control the Mediterranean trade routes ultimately brought them into bitter conflict with the upstart Romans, beginning in the third century BCE.

After a series of three Punic Wars, though, the Romans finally destroyed Carthage in 146 BCE, razing the city to the ground and selling its inhabitants into slavery—a brutal yet common practice in ancient warfare. In the nineteenth century, an unfounded rumor made its way into many history books—that the Romans went so far in their destruction of Carthage as to plow the earth with salt. However, a modern scholar who has critically examined this tradition concluded that at least this particular rumored atrocity should be "taken with a pinch of salt."[1]

But by 203 CE, all of this was ancient history. In the mid-first century BCE, Julius Caesar had expressed an interest in rebuilding Carthage, and Augustus carried out the plan as part of his grand empire-wide rebuilding program. Since the city was rebuilt from the ground up as a *bona fide* Roman provincial capital, it acquired some lovely baths and theaters. Its amphitheater, in particular, was a marvel of architecture that continued to fascinate visitors well into the Middle Ages, even in its ruined state. At its height, it could seat 30,000 spectators—more than the entire population of my southern town of Carrollton, Georgia. And so, on this lovely spring day in 203 CE, 30,000 or so spectators were awaiting the most popular type of entertainment, bloodshed guaranteed.

While gladiatorial games were immensely popular and were on the agenda that day as well, trained gladiators were highly expensive, as were the exotic animals they regularly fought. The Roman officials who subsidized and organized the events, therefore, regularly supplemented public games with condemned criminals. Some evidence exists that such events were specifically scheduled as a change of pace for the lunch hour. In a way, it made economic sense to use criminals in this way: since they were to be executed anyway, why not save some money and use these executions for the entertainment of the general public? Sometimes, to make the executions even more entertaining, the Romans staged them as reenactments of mythological deaths. Greek and Roman myths abounded with stories of gruesome deaths, often the result of the gods' petty grievances against humans who had offended them. But that was not essential.[2] A cheaper approach

---

1. R. T. Ridley, "To Be Taken with a Pinch of Salt: The Destruction of Carthage," *Classical Philology* 81 (1986): 140–46.

2. Kathleen Coleman, "Fatal Charades: Roman Executions Staged as Mythological Enactments," *Journal of Roman Studies* 80 (1990): 44–73.

that required less planning involved throwing condemned criminals into the arena with wild beasts who were expected to maul them. The expensive beasts, then, could be used for other matchups with gladiators later on. That day, however, the condemned criminals in question were not the usual murderers and highway robbers.

A few months earlier, a persecution of Christians in the province had begun. While some have theorized that it was ordered by the emperor Septimius Severus, it seems more likely that this was the brain child of the procurator and local officials in the province. In any case, the process was elaborate. First, it involved surveillance of suspected Christians. Eventually, they were arrested and brought before the procurator for an interrogation and trial. They were afforded the opportunity to sacrifice to the pagan gods, repent of their folly, and secure freedom. But those who persisted in confessing their Christian faith were sentenced to death in the arena. They were the lunch-hour entertainment on that day in 203 CE. We know their story because one of their number, a young noblewoman and nursing mother, kept a journal of the events and her visions while awaiting execution in prison. Following her death, someone, perhaps a deacon from the local church, preserved her journal, added a few notes by way of introduction, wrote his own description of the execution, and published the account along with a shorter journal entry from another martyr executed that day. This "Passion of the Martyrs Perpetua and Felicity" became an early Christian bestseller. It also has the honor of being the earliest Christian account written (mostly) by a woman.[3]

The spectators of that day got an excellent show if success was measured by bloodshed—as very likely it was. The animals loosed upon the defenseless Christians included a bear, a leopard, and a wild cow. The horrific mauling in the arena of two young women, the noblewoman Perpetua and her slave Felicity, gave pause to the hardened and bloodthirsty Roman audiences, noted the anonymous narrator who added his account of the execution to Perpetua's journal. Felicity appeared especially vulnerable, as she had given birth not twenty-four hours earlier and thus still looked pregnant. But once the moment was over, the crowd swiftly forgot and focused on the entertainment that continued for the rest of the

---

3. Detailed book-length studies of Perpetua and her story include Thomas J. Heffernan, *The Passion of Perpetua and Felicity* (Oxford: Oxford University Press, 2012); and Barbara K. Gold, *Perpetua: Athlete of God* (Oxford: Oxford University Press, 2018). For an accessible introduction to North African Christianity, with a special focus on Carthage, see David L. Eastman, *Early North African Christianity* (Grand Rapids: Baker Academic, 2021).

day. If not for the Christians, who preserved Perpetua's passion account and popularized it over the next century as a harbinger of the coming victory of Christ over the evils of the present world, this execution would have been just another day at the theater.

Both the content of Perpetua's journal and the sheer fact that it exists exemplify the differences between the cultural values of the Roman world and those of Christianity. While the cultural heroes of the Roman world had always been powerful military commanders and emperors, Christianity promoted heroes of the faith who looked very different from the Roman ideal—weak, female, and possibly even enslaved, as was the case with Felicity. The Romans who opposed Christianity as the ultimate enemy of Rome may not have understood the beliefs of the Christians, but they did get something right: the Christian values truly were incompatible with their own. This is not to say that Perpetua's martyrdom was not shocking for the early Christians—surely, it was.

The story of Perpetua and Felicity allows us to explore the ways the misogyny of Roman society, which saw women's value as wholly connected to their childbearing, posed difficult questions for women who converted to Christianity and, as a result, for the church at large.[4] Put simply, conversion of women from all ranks of society, from the noble and free to enslaved, challenged Roman culture and therefore also posed a unique challenge to cultural Christianity. The response of the church ultimately involved acknowledging women's unique place in Roman society and the church and a willingness to move beyond the confines of traditional Roman culture for women. By defining itself as the family of all believers, especially the family that cared for single women of all ages, the church allowed a life choice of singleness for women that was deeply countercultural. With this life choice came a recognition of women's worth as powerful prayer warriors and, in the case of women martyrs, faith heroes for all believers.

---

4. For an examination of a related issue—the shifting standards of sexuality from the Roman world to Christianity—see Kyle Harper, *From Shame to Sin: The Christian Transformation of Sexual Morality in Late Antiquity* (Cambridge, MA: Harvard University Press, 2013). For an overview of Roman women more generally, see Eve D'Ambra, *Roman Women* (Cambridge: Cambridge University Press, 2007); and for a more readable alternative, Holly Beers, *A Week in the Life of a Greco-Roman Woman* (Downers Grove, IL: IVP Academic, 2019). For women in early Christianity more specifically, see Lynn Cohick, *Women in the World of the Earliest Christians: Illuminating Ancient Ways of Life* (Grand Rapids: Baker Academic, 2009); and Lynn Cohick and Amy Brown Hughes, *Christian Women in the Patristic World: Their Influence, Authority, and Legacy in the Second through Fifth Centuries* (Grand Rapids: Baker Academic, 2017). Finally, for a fascinating story of other roles that early Christian women took in their communities, see Nicola Denzey Lewis, *The Bone Gatherers: The Lost Worlds of Early Christian Women* (Boston: Beacon, 2007).

The Lives of Freeborn Women in the Roman World: Perpetua

Early Roman history is shrouded in myth and legend. Although we may question the existence of the motherly she-wolf or the fratricidal twins she nursed, we know that in the mid-fifth century BCE, the Romans passed their earliest law code. Inscribed on twelve bronze tablets, it was creatively called the Twelve Tables. Table V dealt with inheritance and guardianship and had this to say about women: "Women, even though they are of full age, [because of their levity of mind] shall be under guardianship . . . except Vestal Virgins, who . . . shall be free from guardianship."[5]

The view that women had a "levity of mind" that made them incapable of managing their own affairs was deeply ingrained in Roman attitudes toward them and persists in subsequent writings. In a court speech he delivered four hundred years after the Twelve Tables, Cicero noted matter-of-factly that "our ancestors determined that all women, on account of the inferiority of their understanding, should be under the protection of trustees."[6] So Roman women were supposed to be under the guardianship of a male relative for the entirety of their lives—first under guardianship of their father and then a husband. If a woman was widowed or divorced, she (and her dowry, which was her property) reverted to her father's guardianship. If the father was deceased, an older brother or another male relative was supposed to take responsibility.

Guardianship had implications beyond the management of property. Like in all other ancient Mediterranean societies, Roman women could not be full citizens. Paradoxically, the main significance of some women for society was that they could give birth to citizens. Indeed, this work of bearing children was expressly mentioned in the Roman definition of marriage.[7] In writing on the subject, Cicero used the intriguing term *coniunctio*, whose Greek equivalent, *koinonia*, became a key term for the early church and is commonly rendered as

---

5. For the full text of the Twelve Tables, see *The Twelve Tables*, *Avalon Project*, https://avalon.law .yale.edu/ancient/twelve_tables.asp. I bracketed in the translation the phrase "levity of mind," which although sometimes interpolated into translations of the Twelve Tables (such as this translation), may have been added from the much later Gaius, *Institutes* 1.144. Still, the concept of denigrating women's intellectual ability is well attested in the Roman Republic, including in Cicero's comments cited below.

6. Cicero, *For Lucius Murena* 27, trans. C. D. Younge, for *Perseus Project*, https://www.perseus .tufts.edu/hopper/text?doc=Cic.+Mur.+27&fromdoc=Perseus%3Atext%3A1999.02.0019.

7. Some examples of sources that mention these aspects of marriage include Cicero, *De Officiis* 1.54 and *De Finibus* 5.65, and Aulus Gellius, *Attic Nights* 1.6.2.

"fellowship" in English. According to Cicero, children facilitate the fellowship that brings the household together through their parents' love for them from birth.[8] Infertility, by contrast, was common cause for divorce among aristocrats.

This significance of bearing children was specifically attached to freeborn and legally wed women. The emperor Augustus, concerned over the falling aristocratic birthrates, instituted a law that included both carrot and stick incentives for aristocratic men and women to get married and produce legitimate children.[9] In particular, freeborn women who gave birth to three children were exempt from the requirement of guardianship. Perhaps Augustus felt that this was an appropriate reward for those who survived the most dangerous activity for women in the premodern world three times.[10]

Vibia Perpetua was born sometime around 180 CE to a noble family in Roman Carthage. Most residents of the city at this time were descended from the native African tribes to the south, but they may also have had some traces of the original Carthaginians, who were descended from the Phoenicians. Perpetua, like most other locals, probably did not look white. It is not clear if her family already had Roman citizenship. Some but not all noble families did. In 212 CE, the emperor Caracalla would extend Roman citizenship to all free residents of the empire at the time, but that would be a decade after Perpetua's death. Regardless of her family's citizenship status, we can be sure that her upbringing was privileged for its time.

Of course, health threats always loomed, and while Roman demography is a tricky science, the estimates that different scholars present, though highly varied, are invariably grim.[11] Possibly 50 percent of Roman children did not

---

8. For a history of Cicero's own marriage and family life, see Susan Treggiari, *Terentia, Tullia, and Publilia: The Women of Cicero's Family* (London: Routledge, 2007).

9. For legal sources connected to Augustus' marriage legislation, see Regia Academica Italica, *Acta Divi Augusti* (Rome, 1945), 166–98. A short series of related documents on the legislation are collected in Naphthali Lewis and Meyer Reinhold, eds., *Roman Civilization*, vol. 1, *Selected Readings: The Republic and the Augustan Age* (New York: Columbia University Press, 1990), 604–7. The best modern studies of Roman marriage and family life before Late Antiquity are Susan Treggiari, *Roman Marriage: Iusti Coniuges from the Time of Cicero to the Time of Ulpian* (Oxford: Clarendon, 1991); and Jane Gardner, *Family and Familia in Roman Law and Life* (Oxford: Clarendon, 1998). For a case study of the life and marriage of one particular aristocratic woman in the era immediately before Augustus's rise to power, see Susan Treggiari, *Servilia and Her Family* (Oxford: Oxford University Press, 2019).

10. This initiative failed, as I explained in "How (Not) to Drive Up the National Birthrate: A Cautionary Tale from the Roman World, and an Under-Explored Pro-Life Answer," *Anxious Bench* (blog), November 3, 2021, https://www.patheos.com/blogs/anxiousbench/2021/11/how -not-to-drive-up-the-national-birthrate-a-cautionary-tale-from-the-roman-world-and-an-under -explored-pro-life-answer/.

11. Bioarchaeology has been helpful here. See Alessandra Sperduti, Luca Bondioli, Oliver E. Craig, Tracy Prowse, and Peter Garnsey, "Bones, Teeth, and History" in *The Science of Roman History:*

live to age ten or (a more optimistic estimate) fifteen. Surviving the first year alone was a major milestone in the premodern world, with some estimates suggesting that as many as 35 percent of infants died in the first month, and the more optimistic ones stating the same figure for the first year.[12] But Perpetua defied the odds. She was born around the end of a major pandemic that swept through the empire—the Antonine Plague, which was most likely smallpox. That pandemic, in fact, may have carried off one of her two brothers. One of the visions she describes in her journal is about her brother Dinocrates, who died at age seven and had horrible ulcers on his face at the time of death. Could it have been smallpox?

As was appropriate for a noble girl, Perpetua was likely educated at home. Weaving surely was included in the curriculum as the traditional skill for Roman women. Indeed, Augustus, the first emperor, used to brag that his wife, daughters, and granddaughters made his clothing themselves.[13] This doesn't quite square with the image of Livia the poison queen that we otherwise get from the historians Tacitus and Cassius Dio, but presumably Augustus knew Livia's better side, or at least invented one for propaganda.[14] In addition to weaving, Perpetua's well-composed and thoughtful journal shows that she received excellent rhetorical education. Women's literacy in the ancient world was not guaranteed, but an aristocratic woman would have received the best education possible, all with an eye to securing a good marriage.[15]

In her late teens, she was indeed married off, presumably to another local

---

Biology, Climate, and the Future of the Past, ed. Walter Scheidel (Princeton, NJ: Princeton University Press, 2018), 123–73.

12. The most significant studies on the topic have relied on a combination of evidence from burials and epitaphs. See Christian Laes, *Children in the Roman Empire: Outsiders Within* (Cambridge: Cambridge University Press, 2011); Maureen Carroll, *Infancy and Earliest Childhood in the Roman World: 'A Fragment of Time'* (Oxford: Oxford University Press, 2018); Jacopo Tabolli, ed., *From Invisible to Visible: New Methods and Data for the Archaeology of Infant and Child Burials in Pre-Roman Italy and Beyond*, Studies in Mediterranean Archaeology 149 (Uppsala: Astrom, 2018); and Kyle Harper, *The Fate of Rome: Climate, Disease, and the End of an Empire* (Princeton, NJ: Princeton University Press, 2017), 72–91.

13. Suetonius, *Life of Augustus*, 73.

14. Both Tacitus (Annals 1.5) and Cassius Dio (55.22.2) accuse Livia of poisoning Augustus with fresh figs.

15. See Marguerite Deslauriers, "Women, Education, and Philosophy," in *A Companion to Women in the Ancient World*, ed. Sharon James and Sheila Dillon (Hoboken, NJ: Wiley-Blackwell, 2012), 343–53. This theme also comes through powerfully in the biographies of prominent Roman women in the Oxford University Press series Women in Antiquity. See in particular the biography of Perpetua in this series: Barbara Gold, *Perpetua: Athlete of God* (Oxford: Oxford University Press, 2018), 103–20. Education of aristocratic women in all parts of the Roman Empire and its neighboring territories is also prominent in Edward Watts, *Hypatia: The Life and Legend of an Ancient Philosopher* (Oxford: Oxford University Press, 2017); Nathaniel Andrade, *Zenobia: Shooting Star of*

noble, and gave birth to a son. Yet again she survived a health risk, as did her child. She was well on course to fulfilling her prescribed duties as a Roman matron. But then she discovered Christianity. By the time she opens her journal, her husband is gone. She never mentions him. Furthermore, she is back to living in her father's home instead of her husband's. The most obvious conclusion is that her husband objected to her conversion and considered it a scandal worthy of divorce. Perhaps he even made the argument for keeping her dowry instead of paying it back to her father—a rarity that could only occur if the divorce was demonstrably the wife's fault.[16] But Perpetua's story is not just her own. It is intimately intertwined with that of another young woman who did not leave any writings of her own.

The Parallel Life of an Enslaved Woman: Felicity

Around the time of Perpetua's birth, another girl was born and ultimately grew up to be an enslaved woman in Perpetua's family home in Carthage. Her enslaved name was Felicitas (or Felicity in English). We know much less about her origins. She may have been born into slavery in Carthage or elsewhere in the empire. She may have been one of the many thousands of captives taken during Marcus Aurelius's military campaigns across the Danube (which concluded in 180 CE) or in another war and sold into slavery in the Roman empire afterward.

Taking captives and selling them into slavery was common practice in ancient warfare, and not only in the Roman Empire. If this was indeed Felicity's fate, she was quite young at the time of capture and suffered forcible separation from her birth family and homeland. When she arrived in Carthage, she would have been considered exotic: if she came from the Danube regions, she had light skin and possibly fair hair and blue eyes. Her appearance would

---

Palmyra (Oxford: Oxford University Press, 2018); and Duane Roller, *Cleopatra's Daughter and Other Royal Women of the Augustan Era* (Oxford: Oxford University Press, 2018).

16. Another possibility is that Perpetua's husband died, and that is why, for instance, she was allowed to keep custody of her child. I believe, however, given the many details offered about Perpetua's life up front, her status as an honorable widow would have been mentioned if this had been the case. The conspicuous absence of any mention of her husband, other than to note that Perpetua had once been honorably wed, suggests that the marriage did not end in a way that either Perpetua or the original editor thought appropriate to mention. This lends credence to my theory that the marriage ended in a way that reflected poorly on Perpetua, at least in the Roman worldview.

have marked her as a foreigner, but slavery in the ancient world was most likely not racially based.[17]

Her name, Felicitas, was common for enslaved women. Meaning "luck," the term appears on the coins of Antoninus Pius, Marcus Aurelius's adoptive father and predecessor as emperor, in reference to the empire's military success. The term was also associated with fertility, so it also appears in a suggestive inscription (with a phallus for good luck and to ward off evil) on a plaque set up at a bakery in Pompeii—*Hic habitat felicitas* ("Luck dwells here"). On a side note, one cannot help but feel kinship with those ancient bakers who too felt that baked goods require luck to achieve perfection.

Felicity's name, with its associations of fertility, suggests the possibility that in addition to her expected role as an all-purpose servant in the household, she was also a breeding slave. We know that at some point in her life, she arrived in the home of Perpetua and her family in Carthage. And we know that at some point, like Perpetua, she too discovered Christianity. Did she introduce Perpetua to the faith, or did Perpetua introduce her? Or did someone else introduce both? We simply do not know. We do know that Felicity was pregnant at the time of her arrest and gave birth in prison the night before her martyrdom. Who fathered this child? Again, we do not know, but Perpetua's father, as head of the household with absolute power over all in his house, is the most likely contender.

By choosing a martyr's death, Perpetua and Felicity interrupted the default life story that the Roman Empire had in mind for them. It is worth considering: What might their lives have looked like had they not converted? In the case of Perpetua, she likely would have remained married to her husband or would have remarried, and she would have had more children. Each childbirth would have carried a risk of death for her, but perhaps she would have continued to defy the odds and survive. Since men in Roman society were typically older than women at the time of first marriage, she likely would have been widowed at some point in her thirties or forties. But as an aristocratic woman, she would have had the resources to support herself in old age. If she had born three children, she would have even had that rare luxury—the right to manage her own property without a male guardian.[18]

In the case of Felicity, had she lived, she would have continued in her role as

---

17. Some new research, however, is complicating this long-standing assumption in the field. In particular, see Sarah Debrew, *Untangling Blackness in Greek Antiquity* (Cambridge: Cambridge University Press, 2022).

18. A great resource for those interested in the bigger picture of Roman law in Late Antiquity, including those legal issues pertaining to women and their place in society, is Ralph Mathisen, *Law, Society, and Authority in Late Antiquity* (Oxford: Oxford University Press, 2001).

an enslaved servant and possibly breeder, giving birth to additional children who would have inherited her enslaved status. Unlike the American South, Romans greatly valued slaves born in the house and were not likely to sell them. So at least she would have been able to see her children grow up—assuming, of course, that they survived infancy and childhood. Once she turned thirty years of age, she would have been eligible for manumission. In that best-case scenario, and especially if she had particular skills, she could have either started on a business venture of her own or assisted her former masters in some way. In the worst-case scenario, if she were freed because she had outlived her usefulness to the household, her status in society would have been akin to childless widows.

The role of widows throughout the ancient world was uniformly precarious, with the possible exception of aristocratic widows who had property to support themselves. The Old Testament book of Ruth revolves around the challenges these widows faced, living on the edge of starvation and mistreatment. While God ultimately provided for Ruth and Naomi, their story abounds with uncomfortable near misses that are worth considering because these disasters could happen to any poor women in the Roman Empire.

After Naomi is widowed and both of her married sons die, she rightly acknowledges the most practical solution for her daughters-in-law: they can return to their fathers' homes, and their fathers would arrange new marriages for them. Ruth refuses to abandon Naomi, however, which means that Ruth gives up her security out of covenant love for Naomi. Let us consider what the alternative would have been if Ruth left Naomi. As a childless widow with no relatives left to care for her, Naomi most likely would have starved to death. Yes, the Mosaic law technically provided for the destitute, such as by extending the opportunity for those in her situation to gather leftover grain from the fields at harvest. But this was not a realistic way to get food for the entire year. Furthermore, we see that it was Ruth alone who went to glean in the fields, suggesting that perhaps Naomi was too weak and frail to do so herself.

In the case of Ruth, we see nearly averted disaster, even in her happiness. She was able to find a new husband, Boaz, and everything works out well for her and Naomi. But what if Boaz had not wanted to marry her? By Jewish law, as suggested in Ruth 4:13–17, Ruth's son was considered to be the child of Naomi rather than of Boaz, so any hesitation on the part of Boaz would have been understandable![19] But had that scenario prevailed, Ruth and Naomi's circumstances

---

19. See Carolyn Custis James, *The Gospel of Ruth: Loving God Enough to Break the Rules* (Grand Rapids: Zondervan Academic, 2011).

would have only deteriorated over time, as Ruth could only be considered as a potential wife for the duration of her childbearing years, and those are likely few at this point. Besides, Ruth's childless status from her first marriage would have been interpreted as proof of her infertility. After all, ancient societies blamed women rather than men for all incidences of infertility. A childless woman who had previously been married would have had a particularly difficult time finding a new spouse. This could have been an even greater deterrent to Ruth's remarriage than her scandalous Moabite origins.

Before Boaz offers to marry Ruth, we suddenly learn of a closer kinsman, who had first choice of this marriage. When asked, the man declines. That we never heard of this kinsman before shows that he simply did not care about providing for his destitute relatives. While he would have been happy to inherit some property, he was not sufficiently interested in it to marry the woman attached to it. In a small village, surely this kinsman knew that his relative, Naomi, had returned to the area with her widowed daughter-in-law. Yet he never offered assistance or acknowledged his duty as the closest kinsman.

In a world where women had to rely on a male relative to provide for them, the existence of relatives was no guarantee of their support. But the lack of relatives was a death sentence. As the widowed single mother told the prophet Elijah on another occasion, once she and her son ate the last of the grain and oil that was left in her home, they would die.[20] She was not exaggerating. The virtual absence of such stories from the Roman Empire is not a sign of improved care and provision for vulnerable women. Rather, this silence highlights all the more the Roman view that women had no worth for the empire, aside from the children they bore. By this standard, single women and childless widows were the most worthless of all, and potentially a threat to society. A late second-century Roman writer, Apuleius, describes such women almost uniformly throughout his novel *The Metamorphoses* (better known as *The Golden Ass*, a title Augustine gave it later on), as dangerous witches, liable to trap and harm men who happen to fall into their clutches.[21] The hapless protagonist of Apuleius's novel was only all too familiar with such dangers: his girlfriend accidentally turned him into a donkey by smearing the wrong ointment over his body.

The repeated references to caring for widows in the New Testament, including childless widows specifically, remind us of something that we might take for granted, as we live in a society that allows the choice of singlehood. Christians

---

20. 1 Kings 17:7–16.

21. For a translation of the novel, see P. G. Walsh, *Apuleius: The Golden Ass* (Oxford: Oxford University Press, 1995).

were the first group in the history of the world to value women of all life choices and circumstances, whether single, married with children, married and childless, or widowed. This inclusion of all women in the church required confronting difficult questions about the nature of sin incurred through the actions of others. Ultimately, women's unique circumstances, carried over as baggage from Roman and ancient Mediterranean culture, required the church to acknowledge the ways women pushed these boundaries of culture to serve them well. For male cultural Christians, the presence of women in the church ultimately served as a call to resist Roman culture.

Perpetua's Journal

Right around the time of Jesus's ministry, the Roman historian Valerius Maximus published his *Memorable Acts and Sayings of the Ancient Romans*. One of the more sensational stories he includes concerns a poor father, who was sentenced to die by starvation. Unable to stand by and do nothing, his daughter, who was a nursing mother, secretly nursed him on her visits to prison. But the secret finally came out. The guards, surprised that the man was still alive after a while, spied on the daughter's visit. As a result, the daughter's devotion to her father was celebrated, and the father was released. The story fascinated the Romans, and a painting of it was prominently displayed in the temple to Pietas (piety). The message is clear: the best Roman daughter would not only obey her father but would risk her life to save his.

The only thing that Perpetua and Valerius Maximus's heroine had in common was that they were nursing mothers. In contrast to the daughter glorified in Valerius Maximus's story, Perpetua would never have been considered an example of Roman piety. Her story, which revolved around disobedience to the authority of her husband and father, challenged the Roman norms of expected behavior for women. At the same time, however, her story also challenged many of the values outlined for women in the New Testament. After all, the obedience of children to parents and obedience of wives to husbands is highlighted multiple times.[22] While the supremacy of Christ's authority over all was understood, women's disobedience to male relatives and state officials for the cause of Christ posed unique challenges for those women, challenges that pushed the definition

---

22. Commands for children to obey their parents include Eph. 6:1–3 and Col. 3:20. Commands for wives to obey their husbands include Eph. 5:22–24; Col. 3:18–19; and 1 Cor. 11:3.

of sin. Perpetua appears to have felt this acutely and highlighted those moments of potentially sinful disobedience in her diary.

Perpetua structures her journal account into three distinct episodes, punctuated by three visions. In each of the three episodes, her father appeals to her to reject Christianity, and she refuses. The second episode also includes the narrative of her formal trial by the procurator, Hilarian, the highest-ranking Roman official at the time. In even stronger terms than her father, Hilarian asks Perpetua to reject her faith, but she refuses. As male authority figures repeatedly threaten her and command her to reject Christianity, her visions confirm to Perpetua that even though she has chosen a difficult path, it is the right one.

Following her brother's advice, Perpetua asks for her first vision from God to learn whether she would be released from prison or martyred for her faith. In the first vision, Saturus, who will eventually be martyred together with her, ascends ahead of her on a ladder, and they arrive in a garden. They are greeted by a shepherd clad in white and surrounded by a large crowd. The shepherd warmly greets Perpetua and gives her a refreshing curd from sheep's milk. She correctly interprets this vision to mean that she will be martyred.

Both the vision and the context for it are spectacular in a number of ways. Strikingly, Perpetua's brother and Perpetua herself recognize her power in this situation: she asks for a vision, and it is given to her. Saturus, however, protects her to the best of his ability, even during the vision when he steps ahead of her onto what looks like a dangerous ladder. Additionally, the glimpse of heaven in her vision shows the ultimate family of believers with Christ, who described himself as the good shepherd and was commonly portrayed as a good shepherd carrying a lamb in early Christian art. The comfort that Perpetua gets from this vision comes from the certainty that she has in her identity and in the community into which she will be accepted upon martyrdom.

Perpetua's brother Dinocrates is the subject of her second vision, which takes place after her trial and sentencing. Dinocrates died at age seven and had horrific ulcers on his face at the time of death, possibly from smallpox. In the first half of Perpetua's vision, he is suffering in squalor in a dark place, is hot and thirsty, and looks as deformed as he did when he died. His thirst plagues him especially. While a fount with water is next to him, he is unable to reach the water. After Perpetua prays for his salvation, she sees Dinocrates again but now healed, dressed in clean clothing, and able to access freely a fount with water. The meaning of the vision is clear: through Perpetua's interceding prayers, he has been saved.

In her final vision, Pomponius, one of the two deacons who have been ministering to her in prison, leads her to an amphitheater, where she miraculously transforms into a man and fights an Egyptian in gladiatorial contest. Perpetua wins the fight because of her ability to fly and fight the Egyptian from the air. She receives the applause of the audience and a victor's crown. This final vision assures her of the spiritual victory that she will attain, while the victor's crown presages her martyrdom. At that point, she concludes her journal noting that it is the night before her execution, and it is now up to someone else to write the account of the event itself.

Perpetua's journal raises a number of challenging and uncomfortable questions both for her and for the church. At the most obvious level, her repeated disobedience to her father and the state authorities challenged both Roman law and various commands in the New Testament. All in all, Perpetua has disobeyed three different men with authority over her: her husband (who, if my theory is correct, subsequently divorced her), her father (who appealed to her time and time again), and the representatives of the Roman state. Since men were not subject to their fathers' authority in adulthood to the same extent as women, a male convert in her position would only have been guilty of disobedience to the Roman state. Technically, *patria potestas*, the father's absolute authority over his children, extended over his sons as well up until his death. That said, the pressure that adult men would have felt was more cultural, whereas women's entire lives were lived under a comprehensive control of male guardians. In addition, Roman women were often still in their teens at the time of marriage, whereas men married closer to age thirty. This meant that men were likely to be freed from their father's authority either before or soon after marriage.

But the hints of possible sin in Perpetua's journal extend further. The anonymous editor was clearly worried that her lack of discussion of her husband could lead to assumptions of sexual immorality by the readers. The anonymous editor's introduction to the journal notes at the beginning that Perpetua had been legally wed. Perpetua herself never mentions this husband who had likely divorced her. The editor's implied concern is that a woman who so easily disobeys all authority figures in the matter of her faith could be judged harshly by the readers and assumed to have disobeyed in other areas of her life. The editor is trying to forecast the concerns that readers would have brought to the document and attempts to portray Perpetua in the most positive light possible. But the editor's comments only highlight further the difficulty of the task.

Looming over the entire narrative in the eyes of the Roman readers (and we need to remember that the Christians were Romans as well) is the uncomfortable question of Perpetua's abrogation of her responsibilities as a mother. By choosing to die in martyrdom, she leaves her son to be raised by her parents. Felicity's conduct is even more shocking: according to the anonymous editor's comment at the end of the document, she prayed before the execution that she would give birth in time. Pregnant women could not be executed, and she did not want to delay the execution. By giving birth the day before the games, she felt that her prayers were granted. But this only would have astounded the readers more: What kind of mother gives up her baby less than twenty-four hours after birth, just so she could die for her faith? Bubbling just underneath is the question: Is this kind of martyrdom true heroism, or are these examples of behavior that the church must condemn, just as the pagans would have?[23]

That the decisions Perpetua and Felicity made were not seen as natural for women in the Roman world is suggested in Perpetua's final vision: in that vision, she became a man and fought another gladiator in the arena. Her actions and choices, as she herself was aware, would have been natural for men, even if dishonorable—no respectable Roman would have fought in the arena. The vast majority of martyrdom accounts before Perpetua told of the martyrdom of men. It appears that even Perpetua herself realized that her identity as a woman, therefore, impacted the expected narrative. Why did she write this journal, and what did it accomplish?[24]

We can only guess Perpetua's motives, but it seems that she truly wanted her story to survive in her own words. The few narratives about earlier women martyrs, of whom Thecla may have been the most famous, were not authored by the martyrs themselves. They generally presented the saints as one-dimensionally saintly. The apocryphal *Acts of Paul and Thecla*, furthermore, belonged squarely in the genre of the novel and greatly romanticized its subjects.

In light of the misrepresentation and fictionalizing of previous women martyrs, Perpetua's motivation in writing her own account may have been simply to tell her own story, even as she surely realized how shocking her agency in writing it would be. As an educated Roman woman, she knew that women rarely wrote works for public dissemination. In the few cases when they did, they did not write something like she wrote. We only know of a few women authors from ancient Rome, compared to the number of male authors, and most of these women wrote

---

23. For a discussion of these complex questions and ways in which different martyrdom accounts attempted to respond to them, see Candida Moss, *Ancient Christian Martyrdom: Diverse Practices, Theologies, and Traditions* (New Haven, CT: Yale University Press, 2012).

24. For a consideration of the bigger question of authorship in early Christianity, see Derek Krueger, *Writing and Holiness: The Practice of Authorship in the Early Christian East* (Philadelphia: University of Pennsylvania Press, 2004).

poetry.[25] Furthermore, only the work of one Roman woman author predating Perpetua survives in a state of reasonable completeness—the six short love elegies of Sulpicia, who wrote in the first century CE. But some scholars have questioned whether Sulpicia ever existed since her poetry survived as part of the collection of another poet, Tibullus. Her poetry is rather explicit for a young Roman woman, leading to even more questions.

Perpetua must have known that her account would be controversial and groundbreaking for many reasons, including the fact that she wrote it herself. But her desire to preserve the truth outweighed any fear that she may have had of breaking tradition. To see what her story accomplished takes us now from Perpetua's own thoughts and words and into the meetings of local church leaders in Carthage shortly after her execution.

The Church Responds

Just a small scroll, crumpled and rolled up awkwardly. Maybe stuffed into a visitor's tunic to smuggle it out of the prison. It would have been easy for this journal to disappear. Since Perpetua wrote it in prison, the journal's initial survival was entirely up to the two deacons, Tertius and Pomponius. They (as she tells us) visited her regularly and cared for her at a time when her family and friends had abandoned her. Presumably, these deacons brought her writing materials upon her request. After she finished the journal the night before her death, she likely entrusted it to them, and this left the decision in their hands: What to do with this unusual document?

The answer to this question did not rest with the deacons alone. After Perpetua gave the journal to Tertius and Pomponius, they likely circulated it among the elders of the local church and discussed the best course of action together. Their decision to publish the document is striking. It reflects the interest in circulating, studying, and discussing communally written texts that has been a key feature of Christianity from the beginning.[26]

---

25. For an authoritative list of women authors of antiquity, see Joel Christensen, "An Impressive List of Female Authors from Antiquity," August 1, 2016, https://sententiaeantiquae.com/2016/08/01/an-impressive-list-of-female-authors-from-antiquity/.

26. For this rise of the culture of literacy that was so integral to Christianity, see Anthony Grafton and Megan Williams, *Christianity and the Transformation of the Book: Origen, Eusebius, and the Library of Caesarea* (Cambridge, MA: Belknap, 2006); Richard Bauckham, *The Gospels for All Christians: Rethinking the Gospel Audiences* (Grand Rapids: Eerdmans, 1997); and David Smith, *The Epistles for All Christians: Epistolary Literature, Circulation, and the Gospels for All Christians* (Leiden: Brill, 2020).

The anonymous Christian editor who added the description of the martyrdom to the journal prior to publication, noted just how uncomfortable the execution itself made the Roman audiences. It seems likely that he is speaking for himself and the local Christian community as well. And if the brutal execution of two young women made audiences uncomfortable, that discomfort was likely nothing compared with the discomfort the local church leaders, likely all of them men, experienced when they first read Perpetua's journal. How did the local church interpret Perpetua's account, and how did they react to it? Finally, what can we tell from these reactions about the Christian community's view of women as saints and sinners?

We already know that two deacons had been assigned to minister to Perpetua in prison, and they knew her well. She has only positive things to say about their support for her. When they decided to take her journal to the local church leadership, they must have been prepared to advocate for its significance. This meant, in particular, convincing the foremost intellectual leader of the Christian community at the time, who has been known to speak out against other documents about women martyrs.

One of the local church leaders, and possibly an elder at this time, was the local celebrity apologist and one of the most prolific writers for the church not only of his age, but all of antiquity—Tertullian. Tertullian was notoriously prickly and opinionated, and had very particular views about women's behavior, especially in the church. Around this time, he published a very passionate denunciation of the *Acts of Paul and Thecla*, accusing the work's presentation of Thecla to be contradictory to biblical teachings of women's roles in the church. To be fair, many stories in the novel, such as the account of Thecla's baptism of herself in a vat of seals in the arena, were bizarre by any standard, ancient or modern, and probably not representative of what anyone, man or woman, was ever likely to re-create. Tertullian was opposed to more than Thecla's self-baptism, however. He took much greater issue with her public preaching and teaching.

But if Tertius and Pomponius were worried about Tertullian's reaction, they were soon reassured. Perpetua's journal must have passed Tertullian's test of orthodoxy, since it was approved for publication. Once Tertullian and other local church leaders had approved it, they had to discuss the logistics of preparing the document for publication.

The version of the document that we know suggests that they rejected the option of publishing the journal "as is" and decided that it needed three particular additions before publication. First, some notes needed to be added to the document by way of preface. Second, an account of Perpetua's actual martyrdom needed to be included by way of conclusion. And third, someone in the group of leaders presumably suggested that it would be appropriate to include a short journal of visions by another individual who was martyred with Perpetua, Saturus. There were at least two likely arguments in favor of including Saturus's account in the publication. First, he was martyred at the same time as Perpetua, so his account fit with hers. Second, perhaps some of the church leaders felt that publishing a controversial journal by a woman would seem slightly less controversial if Saturus's account were also included.

A final decision had to be made: Who would take on the task of editing Perpetua's journal and preparing it for publication according to the agreed-upon specifications? Surely Tertullian, as the leading local Christian writer, was given the right of first refusal for the task. We know from a brief reference that he makes to Perpetua in his treatise *On the Soul* as "a most heroic martyr" that he admired her.[27] It is possible that he indeed accepted the task of editing her journal, although I think it unlikely for one simple reason: someone like Tertullian, who always signed his name to his writings, would surely have noted that he was the editor of the document, especially since the task involved writing an introduction and the description of the martyrdom itself at the end. It seems more likely that Tertullian turned down this opportunity, and someone else, perhaps one of the two deacons who knew Perpetua well, took on the responsibility of editing her journal as one final act of care for her.

So Perpetua's journal was published. But the story does not end there. Over the next half century, Carthage was the site of publication of multiple treatises on women's dress and behavior. While modern scholars have been quick to attribute these texts to the misogyny of individuals like Tertullian, I argue that they show, rather, the church's desire to recognize women's unique struggles in Roman society and, as a result, within the church.[28] In this regard, it is not an exaggeration to see these texts as the church's response to Perpetua, and this response is actually encouraging, as it shows the church's acceptance of the call to embrace countercultural expectations for women.

Over the course of his writing career, Tertullian published two treatises on women's clothing: *On the Veiling of Virgins* and *On the Dress of Women*. In addition, he wrote a related treatise *On Modesty*. He also wrote two books on matters

---

27. Tertullian, *De Anima* (*On the Soul*), 55. For a translation, see https://www.tertullian.org/anf/anf03/anf03-22.htm#P3041_1098102.

28. For an examination of these texts and women's clothing in the context of Roman and Christian culture, see Kristi Upson-Saia, *Early Christian Dress: Gender, Virtue, and Authority* (London: Routledge, 2011).

related to marriage, which address women's issues as well: *On Monogamy* and *To His Wife*. His biggest fan and intellectual successor, Cyprian, who would serve as bishop of Carthage from 248/9 to 258 CE, would go on to write a treatise *On the Dress of Virgins*. This body of literature, new to the church, aimed to address the kinds of challenges that were unique to women in Roman society and carried into the church.

While bits and pieces of Tertullian's and Cyprian's treatises are easy to excerpt as part of arguments for their misogyny, this body of work, taken as a whole, displays consistently a language of provision and care. These works reflect the church self-staging as the parent of women converts, whether young or old, married or single, replacing traditional Roman guardianship with the fatherhood of the church. And so these treatises acknowledge Perpetua and Felicity's greatest challenge: women in the Roman world had no right over their own bodies, much less any significant life decisions. Clothing, in particular, served to mark women's social class in a way that reflected on their families. The sin of disobedience to their Roman guardians and government authorities, of which women converts were guilty by default, would be erased or at least mitigated through the church's intersession as their new family. Clothing was simply the surface level at which this care was manifested.

Through denouncing ostentatious Roman dress, Tertullian and Cyprian provided women converts the freedom to depart from the Roman expectations of them, which included strict standards regulating appearance, the requirement to get married and have children, and the requirement to worship the Roman gods.[29] Instead of constraining women's bodies, Tertullian and Cyprian aimed to facilitate the creation of a new category—sacred virgins, women converts who decided not to marry and instead dedicated their lives to serving the church through prayer. The acknowledgement of singleness as a viable option for women believers allowed the church to value women for more than simply their child-bearing. Furthermore, the uniform standards of dress helped to erase social categories, encouraging the equality of believers in the church, just as we see modeled by Perpetua and Felicity, a noblewoman and her slave, who were martyred together as equals. The application of the same standards also translated to defining sin and sinner in the same way for men and women—no action should be a sin for women, but not for men. These standards permeate Cyprian's expectations of behavior for Christians during persecution.

---

29. Nadya Williams, "Wild Girls in the Carthaginian Church? Cyprian's *De Habitu Virginum*," *Vigiliae Christianae* (May 12, 2022): 1–20.

Yet there is a shadow of the old discomfort left regarding Perpetua and her authorship of her own story. We see it in a marked absence: the absence of any mention of Perpetua by Cyprian, who was born right around the time of her martyrdom, and whose family likely knew that of Perpetua. Why does Cyprian, a well-regarded bishop who cared deeply about providing for women in the church, never mention Perpetua? It seems like mentioning her example would have been especially apt, as he was counseling his flock about persecutions. We cannot know for certain, but one possible explanation is his ambivalent attitude toward martyrdom in general. While Perpetua saw only two options in her situation—to forsake the church or to become a martyr—Cyprian saw a third option. Perhaps, he would have said, she should have escaped, gone into hiding, and lived quietly and happily with her son. But where is the heroism in that?

It is a joke among ancient historians that the study of every topic about the ancient world ought to begin with Homer. And Perpetua's story brings to mind Homer's Achilles. The "Best of the Achaeans," this hero of the Greek army that besieged Troy was famously given a choice by the gods. He could either live a long life in peace and obscurity, or he could fight in the Trojan War and die young, achieving immortal glory. Perpetua, the path-breaking writer of her own journey to martyrdom, would likely have appreciated this comparison.

Conclusion

The story of Perpetua and her journal allows us to reconstruct some of the debates that took place in one late antique Christian center in the third century, as the early church sought to serve women of all social ranks and life situations more effectively. Had Ruth and Naomi been Christian women in third-century Carthage, perhaps their lives would have been far less precarious and would not have depended on remarriage. To our twenty-first-century sensibilities, this narrative may seem anticlimactic, but we ought to remember just how counter-cultural and revolutionary the church's answer was for its time.

Yet many of the challenges that women in the church had to confront in the third century CE have proven surprisingly persistent and attest to the challenge of resisting the gendered aspect of cultural Christianity. The church today continues to have a particularly difficult time serving single women of all ages, albeit for different reasons than in the Roman Empire. As the number of single Christian women far exceeds the number of single Christian men, not all women who are single in the church today have chosen their singleness. Then there is another category of single women in the church today who did not exist in the New Testament but who need a caring community—single mothers, whether divorced or never married. This latter category, in particular, are the modern-day Ruths and Naomis—women who are considered scandalous and who are statistically more likely to live in poverty. What remains unchanged, however, is the church's call to minister to all believers. This ministry involves seeing every believer's worth through God's eyes rather than our own. After all, Perpetua and Felicity did not look like the customary and expected faith heroes at first glance.

At the same time, the story of Perpetua and Felicity challenges us today to consider systemic injustices of not only gender but also race in our society and the church. The martyrdom of Perpetua and Felicity, a noble freedwoman and her enslaved fellow martyr, emphasizes the revolutionary role of early Christianity as the great equalizer in a world that was strictly hierarchical. We see this not only in these women's interactions with each other but also in their treatment by the Roman authorities. Ultimately, Perpetua and Felicity's social status and racial identity did not matter in the eyes of the Roman procurator who decided on their fate, but their faith did.

In our society today, in churches as much as in the surrounding world, racial disparities continue to exist between women in all walks of life. Women of color are more likely than white women to deliver premature babies, to die in childbirth, and to live in poverty. Yet it is often conservative Christians who argue against government social programs that might provide these women with better healthcare or other modes of assistance. Perpetua's story should continue to make us deeply uncomfortable because her questions continue to demand answers from us and point out our complicity in structural—and cultural—sins of our age in the process.

Another surprising connection to the debates about women in the early church involves modern conversations in Christian circles about women's dress and modesty. These conversations are quite different from what they looked like in the third century. Instead of focusing on how clothing provides a way for women to distance themselves from the domination of the world and culture over their bodies and souls, the conversation today is more likely to focus on ways in which women's dress causes men to sin. There is a certain irony in this modern discourse that casts women as complicit in the sins of others rather than viewing them, as the Church Fathers did, as spiritual equals of men and thus worthwhile members of the local churches.

Furthermore, treatises and sermons on women's clothing, of the sort that Tertullian and Cyprian produced, seem directly relevant today, as periodic critiques of women's clothing as immodest circulate in evangelical circles. In spring 2022, for instance, "leggings-gate" made rounds on social media. This was the result of a podcast by Owen Strachan, a pastor and theology professor, who criticized leggings as the kind of immodest clothing designed to lead men astray. Such statements are part of a long-standing pattern over the course of the twentieth and twenty-first century that has placed responsibility for men's sexual sins on women in a manner that is obviously unbiblical and dangerous.

One danger of such teaching can be seen in the aftermath of the release of the Southern Baptist Convention report on sex abuse in churches: blaming women for sins done against them had been not only part of cover-up strategies but also a way to avoid providing essential pastoral care for those women who needed it most. The early church fathers' care-centered teaching, by contrast, that women should choose their attire with an eye toward glorifying God and ensuring that God can recognize them in it, is as humbling and liberating to hear now as it likely was for early converts in the third century.

The story of Perpetua and her journal shows in action the early church's countercultural model of care for women through the family of God. This is only one part, however, of the greater context of the church's mission to care for not only its members but also those living in the same communities, embracing a countercultural ethic of love and provision. As it happens, Cyprian, who had written one of the texts about women's clothing and, by implication, their place as members of the church, had spent his ministry thinking and writing about how to care for the diverse needs of Christians and pagans alike. And reflecting on this topic afforded him plenty of opportunity to observe cultural and countercultural behaviors among his flock. It is to his views on the cultural sin of idolizing self-care that we turn next.

6

When Sharing and Caring Disappear

The Problem of Self-Care in the Age of Crisis

SOMETIME IN THE 250S CE IN THEBES, EGYPT (MODERN-DAY city of Luxor), a number of people were buried in an unusual manner in the tomb complex of Harwa. Burned *en masse*, the bodies were hastily covered with lime and buried in a pit. The tomb, which had been continuously in use up to that point since the seventh century BCE, was never used again. What could possibly explain this unusual burial and then the disuse of the tomb thereafter? The hint lies in the use of lime—antiquity's best disinfectant. Those in charge of the burial were, quite simply, afraid for their lives, and what they feared was a horrific plague, whose victims were the last to be buried in the tomb.[1] But this plague's arrival must have felt like just one more hit in a series of many troubles for the unfortunate residents.

The third century was a time of unprecedented upheaval in the Roman Empire. Between the assassination of the emperor Alexander Severus in 235 CE and the consolidation of power by Diocletian in 284 CE, the empire had at

---

1. Owen Jarus, "Remains of 'End of World' Epidemic Found in Egypt," *Live Science*, June 16, 2014, https://www.livescience.com/46335-remains-of-ancient-egypt-epidemic-found.html.

least twenty-six officially recognized emperors. Most were "barrack" emperors, elevated to power by a proclamation of their own soldiers. They subsequently spent their rule trying to consolidate power, often not succeeding entirely. Some ruled for less than three weeks, and all spent their rule fearing an assassin's strike that invariably came, sooner for some and later for others. The official count of twenty-six does not even factor in the regional claimants to power, such as Queen Zenobia of Palmyra, who made a significant but ultimately unsuccessful bid for the empire.[2] To say that there was alarming political and military instability during the third century would be an understatement, and we can only imagine how this stress impacted the residents of the empire, who often could not be sure who exactly was in charge of the empire at the given moment.

This internal instability was accompanied by pressures on the frontiers, as various neighbors or quasi-allies of Rome, especially to the north and east, tried to take advantage of this moment to reclaim territories. Hadrian's Wall in Britain, for instance, seems to have experienced increased pressure from the late second century on, leading to a reconfiguration of forces stationed at the forts along the walls.[3] Also, after two centuries of slow debasement of coinage, which began with the emperor Caligula (39–41 CE), a financial crisis finally came to a head. The rampant inflation in the empire exacerbated the already severe social and financial inequalities. Then a new and previously unknown plague arrived in the empire ca. 250 CE and circulated in waves for two full decades—that is the plague that scared so greatly the inhabitants of Thebes who burned the bodies in the monument at Harwa. This devastating plague, added to the other pressures, proved catastrophic.

It is no wonder that historians refer to the period from 235 to 284 CE as the Third-Century Crisis. It is a testament to the remarkable resiliency of the Roman Empire as a political entity that it managed to survive and rebuild afterward. Still, the empire that emerged from the crisis did not look the same, and the late third century and the early fourth century were, arguably, the period of the greatest change and restructuring in the Roman world since the days of Augustus, the first emperor. But the Third-Century Crisis affected Christians even more than the rest of the empire's residents. While sporadic persecutions existed before the mid-third century, as we saw in the last chapter, this period saw the first empire-wide persecutions.

---

2. For a biography of Zenobia and her short-lived but no less impactful bid for power, see Nathaniel Andrade, *Zenobia: Shooting Star of Palmyra* (Oxford: Oxford University Press, 2021).

3. See Adrian Goldsworthy's book on the history of the wall: *Hadrian's Wall* (New York: Basic, 2018).

The persecution under the Emperor Decius in 250 CE required all residents of the empire to sacrifice to the Roman gods by a certain date. Only Jews, long granted special recognition as living outside the Roman religion, were exempt. Then in 257 CE, the Emperor Valerian undertook another empire-wide persecution, specifically targeting clergy. For Christians, living in communities already devastated by all of the other challenges of the period, including a pandemic, the stress during the decade of the 250s must have been astounding. So how did the church handle this stress? What cultural sins manifested themselves most clearly during this time of crisis, and how well did Christians resist those sins? These questions form the subject of this chapter, as we consider the case study of one church, whose pastor wrote extensively on the cultural sin of self-care at the expense of caring for others in this age of crisis.

These questions are of relevance for our own age as well, as we are living through a series of overlapping crises ourselves: the COVID-19 pandemic just keeps going, the brutal Russian invasion of Ukraine in February 2022 had unleashed fears of a world war and an economic crisis, and religious and political tensions in the US are mounting as a result of intensifying culture wars. "Jesus is coming soon. Are you ready?"—a church sign down the street from my house asks. The third-century church was as divided as the church today in its feelings about this question.

An Archive of a Church during Crisis

Cyprian's decade as a bishop of Carthage overlaps with this period of empire-wide crisis. Born to a well-to-do Carthaginian family in the early third century, right around the time of Perpetua and Felicity's martyrdom, he converted to Christianity in middle age and was fast-tracked into leadership. Appointed bishop of Carthage in 249 CE, he served in that post until his own martyrdom during Valerian's persecution in 258 CE.[4]

His extensive writings during his decade in ministry reveal a question that duly occupied the Christians of the period and elicited a variety of responses: Is self-care a sin in an environment of constant crisis and stress on all sides? Responses in the Christian community varied. Some tried to keep a low profile during persecutions. Others went so far as to offer the required pagan sacrifices

---

4. For a biography that situates Cyprian in his social, cultural, and religious contexts, see Allen Brent, *Cyprian and Roman Carthage* (Cambridge: Cambridge University Press, 2010).

to save their lives. Cyprian himself went into hiding for about a year during the Decian persecution, arguing that this was the best course of action he could take to deflect persecution from his community.[5]

On the other end of the spectrum, as Cyprian himself tells us, were ardent believers who worried that circumstances beyond their control, such as the plague, would rob them of the glorious martyr's death to which they aspired. For them, self-care meant refusing to care for the sick and dying in order to save themselves for martyrdom. Meanwhile, the crises engulfing the empire ensured that the number of the hungry, poor, sick, widowed, and orphaned within and outside the church was growing.

Cyprian's ministry focused on turning Christians back to care for each other and others financially, physically, and with prayer in this time of need. But such redirection of resources from the self to the community, already present in Acts 4, did not come any more naturally to Christians living through the Third-Century Crisis than it does to us today.

Creating a Christian Framework of One-Anothering

Have you ever thought about why it bothers us so much to witness others suffering? Why do we feel a moral obligation to help others, whether by volunteering in soup kitchens, donating to charities, or assisting financially or physically with disaster relief after a hurricane or a tornado? You might actually have never even thought about it because this moral stance is such an ingrained part of our worldview, regardless even of religious belief. Yet this idea should not be taken for granted. Seeing suffering of all kinds certainly did not bother people in the ancient world, who exposed unwanted babies to die or be enslaved and watched gladiatorial games in which enslaved men fought to the death.

Some forms of suffering, in other words, were normalized as entertainment—indeed, as mentioned in the last chapter, Roman executions were regularly staged as reenactments of mythological tales involving gruesome deaths. Mourning the suffering of others and feeling compassion for such suffering are only possible if we accept Jesus's view of the preciousness of humanity.[6] Abandoning others

---

5. Cyprian, *Epistles* 20.

6. See Dane Ortlund, *Gentle and Lowly: The Heart of Christ for Sinners and Sufferers* (Wheaton, IL: Crossway: 2020).

in their times of need could only be seen as sinful in a framework that says all life is precious because it is made in the image of God. As we unpack this idea further, let us first consider the structure of Roman society and its safety net (or lack thereof).

In the last chapter, we considered the "building block" of Roman society—the *familia*, which consisted of the head of household, *paterfamilias*, along with his immediate family, his slaves (if he was wealthy enough to own slaves), and even freed former slaves. When we think of Roman community beyond the family unit, we should imagine myriad households connected through the bonds of patron-client relationships. Of course, we saw that women like Perpetua challenged the culture of the Greco-Roman world by refusing to obey the head of household, claiming the authority of Christ over them as supreme.

In our consideration of Ananias and Sapphira in chapter 1, we looked at their self-fashioning as Greco-Roman community benefactors. The model of euergetism that motivated them had a parallel in the patronage system ingrained in Roman society. Wealthy leaders in the community—meaning those who could afford to pay for public works in their towns, stage plays and other entertainment for the public at their own expense, and perhaps even hold a public office locally or in Rome—were patrons.

As patrons, they were available to assist clients, those below them in the social pyramid. Those clients, in turn, could function as patrons to others lower than them in the socioeconomic structure and so on. Most people in the Roman world had at least someone to whom they could go to beg for a favor or support. In turn, these clients were expected to show up and provide a public display of power for their patrons if the latter had to attend court or another public event. For especially prominent public figures, the size of their retinue that turned out to support them on public occasions was yet another source of prestige and confirmation of their *auctoritas*, or public clout.

If we look for a public safety net in the Roman Empire, the system of Roman households and the patron-client network is the closest that we can find aside from the free or state-subsidized grain handouts for the urban poor, especially in the city of Rome. But this was not a system for care. It was, rather, a system designed to reinforce social structures and emphasize the power of some over others. In this traditional Roman framework, the patron had a general obligation to assist the client, but any assistance was always in the context of making the patron look good in the process. It was conditional, and it was not guaranteed. At a time of crisis, if the patron himself was suffering or faced a threat if he helped, refusal to help must have been common.

Let us consider this example of a narrowly averted disaster for one minor Roman aristocrat in the Late Republic. In 81–80 BCE, Sextus Roscius, a Roman citizen and scion of a wealthy family from Umbria, faced a triple blow. His father was mysteriously murdered one evening in Rome after attending a dinner. Next, an unscrupulous freedman of the dictator Sulla illegally conspired to requisition the family estate of the Roscii by adding their property to the list of the properties of those who were enemies of the state. Since Sulla's earlier decree of proscriptions had allowed the confiscation of the properties of enemies of the state, the freedman seized upon this opportunity, although the deadline for the declaration of public enemies under this decree had at this point already passed. Adding an ultimate insult to injury, the same unscrupulous freedman accused the young Roscius of killing his own father, possibly acting together with two of the latter's relatives.

Parricide was, for Romans, arguably the worst crime imaginable. If convicted, Roscius faced a brutal execution: parricides were sewn in a leather sack with a dog, a rooster, a viper, and a monkey, and cast into the Tiber. If acquitted of killing his father, he still would have faced an uphill legal battle for getting back his family's estate. And, of course, he was presumably still grieving the loss of his father (that is, if we believe that he was not the killer).

One key element in this situation made it unlikely that anyone would have wanted to help Roscius: his opponent, Chrysogonus, was a freedman of Sulla, the most powerful man in the Roman Republic at the time and one who had just completed a round of state-sanctioned purges of suspected enemies. It is not surprising, therefore, that none of Roscius's relatives or fellow-townsmen came to his aid in this case. Despite his relatively high social status, the safety net failed him entirely in his pursuit of justice. His only luck was that a then-unknown lawyer, Cicero, undertook his case and managed to present such a convincing argument about Chrysogonus's corruption and plotting that he won. We know about the case only because Cicero subsequently published his winning courtroom speech, *Pro Roscio*. Cicero went on to build a spectacularly successful career as a lawyer and politician in the late Roman Republic before losing his own life in another round of proscriptions in 43 BCE, but that is a story for another time.

It is difficult to overemphasize just how close Roscius came to losing his life as well as his property. Aside from an unknown upstart lawyer who risked taking on his case for entirely selfish reasons (Cicero rightly estimated that winning such a scandalous case could be his ticket to fame), no one came to Roscius's aid—no relatives, no patrons or clients, and no local friends of his family that someone from his background surely had.

Considering that this was the level of uncertainty that even the well-to-do sometimes faced in the Roman world, imagine the exponentially greater likelihood of facing crises with no assistance for the unnamed multitudes of the urban poor, from whom so many of the early Christians were converted.[7] And lest you think that such troubles were the feature of the Roman Republic alone, let us consider another example, this one from the late second century CE and thus only sixty or so years removed from Cyprian's day.

In the late second century CE, the North African philosopher and rhetorician Apuleius wrote a novel, *The Golden Ass*. This work of fiction, which is the only novel in Latin to survive in its entirety, is considered by historians today to be one of the best literary primary sources that we have for everyday life in the provinces of the Roman Empire. The fictional narrator is a young man traveling around the Greek-speaking provinces, starting out in Thessaly, best known already in antiquity for witchcraft. Over the course of the book, he falls into repeated mishaps himself and witnesses the mishaps of others. Accidentally turned into a donkey, he spends much of the novel in that guise.

In his donkey form, he is repeatedly stolen, sold, beaten, and mistreated in a variety of ways, as he experiences life in the underbelly of the mighty empire. The world he describes is one filled with constant anxiety and utterly lacking in social structures of support, especially for outsiders. Robbers rule the roads, and when agents of the empire appear, they are no better than the robbers. On the one occasion when a Roman centurion runs into an impoverished market gardener with his donkey, his prize possession, the centurion requisitions the donkey from the gardener in a scenario that swiftly turns violent and ultimately costs the gardener his life.

In effect, the novel raises the question: What did most of the residents of distant corners of the Roman Empire gain from living in this mighty empire? The answer appears to be: not much. Living on the edge of starvation, most residents only saw Rome as yet another agent of abuse. The state had zero obligation to take care of its residents and only saw slight obligation to take care of its citizens—the latter simply received some perks, such as the right to appeal directly to the emperor, as Paul famously did in Acts 25. Furthermore, most citizens simply did not think that they had to take care of anyone in trouble. If someone was suffering, maybe it was their bad fortune—perhaps literally the goddess Fortuna, to whom the narrator in *The Golden Ass* refers multiple times.

---

7. The foundational study of the lives of the urban Christians remains Wayne Meeks, *The First Urban Christians: The Social World of the Apostle Paul* (New Haven, CT: Yale University Press, 2003).

If the person suffering was of a much lower social status, especially if the individual was a slave, a widow, or someone disreputable in Roman society, then their suffering was simply of no consequence.

In contrast to this worldview, heartlessness or turning a blind eye to the suffering of brethren at a time of crisis was a sin within the Christian framework because of the fundamentally different perspective of humanity that Christianity presented. For Christians, all humanity was valuable for two reasons. First, all people are made in the image of God. Second, Jesus had come to save humanity, considering all people sufficiently valuable to give his own life for them. This valuing of fellow men and women meant that, as Paul describes in Philemon—a letter about Onesimus, a runaway slave who converted to Christianity—every Christian was first and foremost a fellow brother. And this had an impact on the level of obligation that one should feel for others.

The sociologist Rodney Stark made the intriguing argument that the growth of Christianity during the third century, this age of crisis, was the direct result of the Christians' better care for each other at a time when such care was needed.[8] Not only was it the reason why Christians were able to weather the storms of the age, but it was also a powerful witness that they bore to the Romans around them. While others around them only focused on survival, the Christians went out of their way to take care of all people in their communities, pagans and Christians alike.

But as the story of the Carthaginian church shows, the Christians at a time of crisis were still sinful people, just as Christians in any society in crisis or not. This radically countercultural view of humanity that the Christians adopted was not an easy guarantee against the sin of heartlessness. After all, it is one thing to believe in the value of all humanity. It is another to live out such a radical message every day in one's own actions. Cyprian's writings show the sinful struggles of his community, but they also reveal the power of a pastor to call his people to godly action. In effect, the bishop became a new kind of patron for his community, one who not only cared for his people but led them to take care of each other.[9]

---

8. Rodney Stark, *The Rise of Christianity: A Sociologist Reconsiders History* (Princeton: Princeton University Press, 1996), 73–94.

9. Charles Bobertz has argued that we should see Cyprian as a patron in the Christian community, in the tradition of the Greco-Roman euergetism; see "Patronage Networks and the Study of Ancient Christianity," *Studia Patristica* 24 (1991): 20–27; and "Patronal Letters of Commendation: Cyprian's Epistulae 38–40," *Studia Patristica* 24 (1991): 252–59.

Things Money Can Buy:
Almsgiving and the Care of the Poor

Church budgets in a typical church today are a thing of science. With the goal of transparency and accountability, a typical church provides a regular giving report to its members, showing them both how much money is coming in and how it is spent. Indeed, to retain their tax-exempt status, churches are required to make such regular reports to all members of the congregation.

This seeming obsession with money is ultimately a testament to how our society is structured: fiscal responsibility is an essential feature of a healthy organization of any kind, and this includes churches. A healthy church that manages its finances well is able to take care of its building, pay its pastoral staff, and ultimately, is able to do works of benevolence for the needy of the congregation and beyond. But how do churches encourage members to give generously, self-sacrificially, and joyfully? The challenging task that modern pastors have to perform, in encouraging their members to give out of love for others, is one that has been the purview of church leaders from the earliest times. While money cannot buy happiness, it can ensure survival and support for Christians and community members in need, who rely on the church as their safety net.

One of the topics that appears most often in Cyprian's writings is the use of money by the church for the benefit of the needy in a variety of situations. As noted above, the Third-Century Crisis increased the potential for even the well-to-do to fall into trouble for a variety of reasons. Cyprian's letters, in almost every single one of which he mentions the need for continued financial support of those who are suffering, provide us with a broad picture of the range of situations with which the bishop had to assist his flock. But in addition to the letters, early in his pastoral ministry, Cyprian wrote the treatise *On Works and Alms*.[10]

The Christian framework of one-anothering that Cyprian set out for his community and the broader North African church, to which this treatise circulated, was directly rooted in the Christian view of human personhood. Embedded in this treatise is also an overview of ways in which the believers in the Carthaginian church were falling short. Cyprian shows that even believers struggled with fears that made them feel conflicting emotions. While believing

---

10. One of the best studies of this treatise remains Geoffrey Dunn, "The White Crown of Works: Cyprian's Early Pastoral Ministry of Almsgiving in Carthage," *Church History* 73 (2004): 715–40. For an overview of Cyprian's early pastoral career more broadly, see Mattias Gassman, "Cyprian's Early Career in the Church of Carthage," *Journal of Ecclesiastical History* 70 (2019): 1–17.

in Christ and his sacrifices on their behalf, they still wanted to place their security in their own wealth and felt a profound fear over giving any of it to others.
Cyprian confronts these conflicting emotions in his treatise.

On Works and Alms thematically falls into three parts, and is structured
like a sandwich, with the first and third part providing biblically grounded theological reasoning and the middle part confronting the Carthaginian sinners
about their fears of giving. The first part, chapters 1–8, provides an overview
of God's blessings for the believers and his calling the believers into a relationship with himself and with each other. Cyprian provides examples from both the
Old Testament and the New Testament of individuals whose faith led them to
provide for others kindly and extravagantly. The culminating example is the tax
collector Zacchaeus, whose conversion is marked by his declaration that he will
give half of his possessions to the poor and will repay four-fold anything that he
had defrauded from others as part of his work collecting taxes. Chapters 9–16
turn to confronting the local believers directly, naming the varied fears that lead
them to not give to others or take care of them. Finally, chapters 17–26 conclude
the treatise with a list of admonitions from the Bible, showing examples of both
inspiring generosity and reasons for belief in God's provision for generous givers.

While the theological portions of the "sandwich" are predictable in their
orthodox teaching, the meat in the middle of the "sandwich" is key for us to
examine more closely now. For the middle portion allows us to get to know the
sinners in Cyprian's local church intimately through the eyes of their bishop.

The main fear that Cyprian identifies, from which the sinful fears of giving emerge, is the fear that if they start giving generously, they will use up all
of their wealth and would themselves be reduced to poverty.[11] This fear is one
that was more complex in the ancient world than today, as Cyprian's discussion
of the concept of patrimony shows. While most of us did not inherit wealth or
an estate from parents, which we feel obligated to keep intact and pass on to our
own children à la constantly cash-strapped and stressed aristocrats of *Downton
Abbey*, anyone with even minor land holdings in the ancient world would have
felt that pressure.

Just think of the rich young ruler who was unable to follow Jesus because he
had a large estate that he did not feel allowed to give away.[12] To use up all of one's
estate and have nothing left to pass on to one's children was not only a source of
economic distress in the present but also a source of considerable shame for the

---

11. Cyprian, *On Works and Alms* 9–10. All references and quotations from this work in this chapter
are from this translation: https://www.ewtn.com/catholicism/library/works-and-alms-12550.

12. This story appears in Matt. 19:16–30; Mark 10:17–31; and Luke 18:18–30.

family. But Cyprian reminds his flock that generosity is not profligacy. Using one's wealth on others is a wise investment in God's kingdom. Contrary to the pagan world's values, hoarding wealth is not a virtue. Rather, in the Christian worldview, the rich man who does not give generously is put to shame by the generosity of widows.[13]

Furthermore, the sinful fear of giving leads to related sins, Cyprian notes. Not giving is both a symptom of a lack of faith and an encouragement for such weak faith to grow yet weaker. As Cyprian poignantly asks about such individuals, "What is a faithless heart doing in a home of faith?"[14] In addition to a lack of faith, not giving displays avarice, and Cyprian accuses such individuals of being captives to their own money.[15] Finally, one's vision is distorted by lack of giving: someone who is afraid of giving is unable to do any good works for the church (thence the connection between works and alms in the treatise's title) because such a person effectively trains himself to not be able to see the needs of others.[16]

This last point leads Cyprian to advise those who are rich and are not giving to refrain from participating in the Lord's Feast, as their heart does not make them fit to celebrate it. Such table-fencing advice is rare for Cyprian and shows his view about the seriousness of not giving. Cyprian reminds his flock that Christianity is all about sacrifice—ultimately, the sacrifice of Jesus but also the everyday sacrifices of believers for each other. It appears that the wealthy were especially likely, despite having wealth, to be unwilling to give. They are the ones to whom Cyprian's strongest language in the treatise is directed.

In many ways, this document served as the declaration of vision for Cyprian's ministry. In making it clear to the Carthaginian Christians that they must not be afraid to give to others and that generously giving to others truly is God's will for them, Cyprian set the course for the remainder of his ministry.

Countercultural Networks of Care

Cyprian's influence in caring well for his own flock can be seen in the way other bishops rely on him to help resolve challenging situations involving congregational care. In a letter to another bishop, Eucratius, Cyprian is responding to a concern that Eucratius sent his way. A new convert in Eucratius's congregation

---

13. Cyprian, *On Works and Alms* 15.
14. Cyprian, *On Works and Alms* 12.
15. Cyprian, *On Works and Alms* 13.
16. Cyprian, *On Works and Alms* 15.

came from a particularly scandalous profession in the Roman world: acting. After conversion, presumably unable to think of another way to support himself, the actor has begun teaching acting to others, thoroughly worrying his bishop. Scandalized and concerned, Eucratius wrote to Cyprian, asking what he should do about this situation.

Before we consider Cyprian's response, it is important to note that certain professions in the Roman world were considered categorically disreputable.[17] Individuals employed in these fields, which included acting, were considered to be on the fringes of society and subject to a number of social ostracism measures. How should the church deal with someone like this? Eucratius may well have expected Cyprian to respond that it was perfectly acceptable to expel someone like that from the congregation, although maybe not. Eucratius genuinely seems to have been flummoxed by this situation.

Cyprian's response begins with acknowledging the scandalous nature of the former actor's past and present behavior. He agrees that just as acting is scandalous in the eyes of the pagan world, there are reasons to view this profession as contrary to the gospel as well.[18] But Cyprian then spends the second half of his letter getting to a problem that Eucratius had not identified: the actor, as is common for someone from a disreputable profession, has no safety network. If he abandons his profession entirely, he has no source of income. Cyprian states, therefore, that the local church is obligated to support him financially for the time being, offering his own resources if needed.[19]

This compassionate response is striking for its practical understanding of the complexities of the situation. Is the actor acting the way that he is because he is a disreputable person who does not know how to behave? Or is he in dire financial straits because the only career that he has ever had is now closed to him, and he is unable to find another? Cyprian leans toward the latter. Furthermore, Cyprian does not impose the former actor on Eucratius and his church's resources, which may be meager, but offers help from his own coffers.

We do not know how this situation was resolved. It is possible that the actor did end up being supported by Cyprian. Even if he was not, the ease with which Cyprian offers his own money as a safety net for this new convert, whom he has never met, is remarkably typical of his ministry. Such a giving attitude, especially

---

17. See Sarah Bond, *Trade and Taboo: Disreputable Professions in the Roman Mediterranean* (Ann Arbor: University of Michigan Press, 2016), 10. Examples of disreputable professions include actors, musicians, those employed in the mortuary trade, and tanners.

18. Cyprian, *Epistle* 2.1.2.

19. Cyprian, *Epistle* 2.2.3.

toward a convert from a scandalous background, should be convicting to us today as well if we wonder if some new Christians' previously sinful lives have placed them beyond the possibility of God's redemption. Cyprian realized in this situation something that others did not: what looked like a scandal with spiritual ramifications could have simply been a lack of money to pay the bills.

On another occasion, Cyprian had to address a crisis that involved literally redeeming members from several churches in Numidia. This story provides us with further evidence not only about Cyprian's generosity and his encouragement for his congregation to give but also about his role in leading giving campaigns to benefit Christians outside his local church.

Cyprian's Carthage was a well-established Roman city in the province of Africa. Located on the shore on the farthest northernmost point of the continent, it was far enough removed from the troubles that plagued residents of the province who lived further south. Things were considerably less secure in Numidia, located to the southwest. A variety of nomadic tribes patrolled the region, and occasionally made raids into Roman territory, taking advantage of the absence of a legion in the area from 238 CE to 253. Inscriptional evidence suggests a particularly high level of nomadic raids and attacks during the 240s and 250s.[20] Christians were not spared this trouble.

At some point in the 250s, eight Numidian bishops wrote to Cyprian, asking for financial assistance. A sizeable group of Numidian Christians has been captured in a particularly bold raid and carried off into captivity. The raiders planned to make a profit by selling the captives into slavery but presumably were also open to acquiring the same profit by allowing the captives to be ransomed back.

Cyprian's response can be divided into halves. In the first half of his letter, he provides a theological analysis for the valuing of these captives, explaining why their suffering is significant and should be of concern for all Christians. Cyprian emphatically states that Christians should count the suffering of their brethren as their own. He was especially concerned about the women who had been captured since they faced certain sexual abuse and rape during the captivity and were likely to be sold to brothels if not ransomed back. Furthermore, all baptized Christians have Christ indwelling them, so "we ought to behold Christ in our

20. Graeme Clarke, *The Letters of St. Cyprian of Carthage*, vol. 3 (New York: Newman, 1986), 278–79.

captive brethren and we ought to redeem Him from the peril of captivity who has redeemed us from the peril of death."[21]

In transitioning to the second half of his letter, Cyprian says, "Such were the painful thoughts and reflections which your letter prompted amongst our brethren here."[22] This comment makes it clear what happened: upon the receipt of the Numidian bishops' letter, Cyprian assembled his church, perhaps calling an emergency meeting, and read the news to them. It is likely that he proceeded to present theologically grounded reasons to his flock for doing all they can to help the Numidian Christians.

The inclusion of so many carefully thought out reasons for helping the captive Christians suggests that Cyprian did not take the financial support of his congregation for granted but worked hard to convince those with the ability to give that this support was essential. While he did not have to include these reasons in his response to the Numidian bishops, Cyprian often did include theological justifications for his actions. In this case, such reasoning was likely on his mind from presenting it to his flock. After all, a large fundraising campaign is not easy to organize, and it can be especially difficult to convince people to give a large amount of money on short notice.

The results of Cyprian's appeal to his community are striking. While the Carthaginian Christians could be hesitant to give on some occasions, Cyprian was able to raise one hundred thousand sesterces in cash. Just how much was this? A typical day-laborer earned 30 sesterces a month. This sum was the pay of almost 278 laborers for a year.[23] Even for wealthy givers, of whom there probably were some in the Carthaginian church, this was still a lot of money to raise on short notice. This sum, sent with Cyprian's letter, came not only from the Carthaginian clergy and laity but also from any visiting members from other churches, who perhaps were in the area for a regional meeting.

Cyprian's repeated reminders to both Christian clergy and laity in many other letters to keep on giving, and especially to keep supporting the widows and the poor, show that the sin of self-focus and the concomitant fear of giving money for others, lest one have nothing left for one's own needs, was always near.[24] But the bishop's leadership and theological teaching continued to equip the flock to overcome this sin time and again.

---

21. Cyprian, *Epistle* 62.1–2. All translations from the Epistles are from Graeme Clarke's translation and commentary.

22. Cyprian, *Epistle* 62.3.1.

23. Clarke, *The Letters of St. Cyprian of Carthage*, 284–85.

24. Examples of letters that mention giving, even if in passing, include *Epistles* 5, 7, 8, 10, 12, and 13.

Things Money Cannot Buy:
Comforting Others in a Pandemic

Somewhere in Ethiopia in 249 CE, a vicious and highly contagious virus jumped from an infected ape or bat onto a human host and began its devastating journey northward. It arrived in Alexandria that same year and presumably made its way to Cyprian's Carthage soon after. By 251 CE, it was in Rome. From there it had easy access to spread everywhere, using the established reliable networks of travel and trade. After all, wherever humans go, viruses travel along. An incubation period of just a few days would have meant that someone could have boarded a ship feeling healthy and died of the plague by the end of the journey, having infected many others on board in the intervening period.

Glimpses in the written and archaeological sources show that this plague continued to circulate throughout the Roman Empire and beyond for the next twenty years. Spread through bodily fluids, the disease was especially dangerous for caretakers of the sick. It was also more deadly than anything else the empire had experienced up until that time—approximately 50–70 percent of those who contracted the illness died. The few survivors usually acquired immunity, but the plague struck in waves, hitting the same areas time and time again, mostly in the winter. Survivors were often maimed for life. While densely populated urban areas were an easier target, rural regions were not spared. It simply took the virus longer to get there. In his analysis of the evidence for this plague in the context of the history of Roman climate and disease, Kyle Harper made a convincing argument that the symptoms described by various ancient witnesses, including Cyprian, are most consistent with filoviruses, suggesting something like Ebola or very similar to it as the best candidate for this plague.[25]

This "age-defining crisis," as Harper has dubbed it, arrived at a time when the empire was already facing so many other crises. It created additional suffering for Cyprian's community, Christian and pagan alike. While many other crises Cyprian had to resolve could be solved with the aid of money, this was a crisis in which money could not help, at least not directly. This is not to say that giving was not required. Caring for others in a contagious pandemic spread through close contact required giving of the highest order—potentially, the giving of one's life. This meant that the pandemic brought forth an additional layer of sinful

---

25. The information presented here about the history of this plague comes from Harper, *The Fate of Rome*, 137–144.

attitudes in the church. As leader of his community, Cyprian had to address these attitudes, and he did so in a treatise that likely began its life as a sermon, *On Mortality*.[26] Ironically, Cyprian's writing about this plague would eventually lead historians to name it after him, the Plague of Cyprian.

Similar to his approach in *On Works and Alms*, in *On Mortality* Cyprian identifies the sins of which he judges his community to be guilty in attitudes related to the plague. He then provides theological antidotes to resolve them. Perhaps because this format worked especially well for public delivery to people he knew well, Cyprian structured much of this treatise as a sort of "Q and A," directly identifying particular questions and concerns about the plague in his congregation. Although he originally delivered it in person to the Carthaginian church, Cyprian almost certainly circulated the written version of the document to other churches.

Just as with *On Works and Alms*, Cyprian identifies one specific underlying fear, which leads to other questions and concerns that his flock have about the plague. The fear is a logical one: death. As we ourselves got to see in 2020, fearing death from a deadly pandemic is a natural human reaction. Seeing this fear in the Carthaginian congregation, however, is yet another sign of how serious the disease was. The Romans were not healthy people—far from it, in fact. Infant mortality was commonplace, and death from various diseases could attack people at any time, ensuring that only the lucky few made it to old age. Thus the extreme fear that the pandemic elicited shows just how much more serious this threat was than anything else to which the residents of the Roman Empire were accustomed.[27] But while many Christians in Carthage shared this fear of death from the pandemic, their reasons for it varied dramatically, as Cyprian's sermon makes clear.

The first question Cyprian considers is: Why does this plague attack the Christians just as much as the pagans?[28] This question, which seems to arise from believers who are less secure in their faith, reminds us of the allure of prosperity gospel for converts of all periods. It is tempting to believe that conversion to Christianity will provide the cure from all earthly evils. It appears that some Carthaginian Christians believed just that. In fighting bad theology with good

---

26. For an analysis of Cyprian's pastoral ministry specifically in light of this pandemic, see Nadya Williams, "Pastoring Through a Pandemic: Cyprian and the Carthaginian Church in the Mid-Third Century," *Fides et Historia* 53 (2021): 1–14.

27. For an overview of the typical disease ecology of the Roman Empire, see Harper, *The Fate of Rome*, 65–91. Through a combination of archaeological and written records, Harper demonstrates that the Romans were much sicklier and shorter-lived, on average, than has been generally assumed.

28. Cyprian, *On Mortality* 8.

theology, Cyprian responds with a passionate explanation of the benefits of faith, specifically emphasizing that these benefits look forward to the life to come rather than just this one. In this life, Cyprian notes, Christians share the same evils as non-Christians. But the difference lies in what they can expect afterward. The knowledge of God's eternal promises should equip Christians for dealing with the difficulties of this life: "This, in short, is the difference between us and others who know not God, that in misfortune they complain and murmur, while adversity does not call us away from the truth of virtue and faith, but strengthens us by its suffering."[29]

It is not coincidental that in this context of explaining how the awareness of the afterlife should comfort Christians and equip them for the present suffering, Cyprian provides the most detailed and horrifying description of the plague in all of his writing. The illness initially manifested with diarrhea and vomiting, along with a horrific fever. Hemorrhaging from the eyes followed and some limbs could become completely incapacitated. Finally, not only were the patients left very weak from the other symptoms of the disease, but the survivors could be left deaf or blind for life.[30]

It is one thing to read a list of symptoms and progression of a disease in a clinical setting. It is quite another to hear it presented to an audience that is in the midst of crisis. What did this sermon, a call to countercultural living and caring, call Christians to do and feel?

Speaking Truth to Power in a Pandemic

This vivid description of the disease served to do something powerful especially for the original audience of Cyprian's sermon. The frank description of the symptoms reminded people of the deeply personal impact of the plague on their community. It showed them, furthermore, just how intimately familiar their bishop was with the plague. Reading this description, it is difficult not to wonder if Cyprian did not learn these things from visiting the many sick in the local Christian community and trying to comfort them and their loved ones in the midst of their suffering, as he was also trying to do for the entire community at once with this very sermon.

In reading this sermon, I am tempted to think that even though Cyprian

---

29. Cyprian, *On Mortality* 13. For a complete translation, from which all quotations of this work in this chapter derive, see https://www.newadvent.org/fathers/050707.htm.

30. Cyprian, *On Mortality* 14.

retired into hiding for a time during the Decian persecution, he did not hide from this disease but instead ministered to his people both individually and, as this sermon shows, collectively. Why? As Cyprian says at the end of his description of the course of the disease, suffering all of this, just as any suffering in this life, "contributes to the proof of faith." Cyprian was the leader to whom the community turned for encouragement. He modeled financial giving to his community, leading his people to overcome their sinful fear of giving during a time of crisis. Likewise, during the plague, he shared his community's suffering in every way he could, leading the people to overcome their fear of caring for others during the pandemic. This meant understanding the very different questions that the members of his church had about the plague.

While the first question that Cyprian addressed in the treatise is one that may have come from less secure believers, whose faith was easily shaken or whose theological understanding was less established, the second question came from a group at the opposite end of the spectrum. These Christians were afraid of death in the plague because it would deprive them of the death to which they aspired. Their question was, therefore: What if the plague should deprive them of the glorious death in martyrdom for which they had been preparing all along?[31]

As we have noted in other contexts already, prestige in the Greco-Roman world was visual. Public recognition was everything, and so was competition for excellence. Over a thousand years after the Homeric epics were finalized, the values of competitive excellence presented in them still dominated the imagination of the residents of the Mediterranean world. In the Homeric epics, the heroes were all after one prize, first and foremost, and it was not Helen or the victory of their side in the Trojan War. Rather, the ultimate prize that every hero pursued was public recognition as the best of all the heroes. And while Homeric excellence and the Roman ideal of *virtus*, courage, were both military, the rise of Christianity and its creation of martyrs as the new culture heroes allowed for another type of competition—the competition for the most impressive martyr.

So it appears that some aspiring martyrs in the Carthaginian church were pursuing martyrdom like the Homeric heroes had pursued the title of the best of the Achaeans. But martyrdom was not a sport, as Cyprian repeatedly reminded his flock in his letters. In fact, avoiding a public and distracting martyrdom was Cyprian's own goal in going into hiding for about a year at the beginning of

---

31. Cyprian, *On Mortality* 17.

Decius's persecution. Pursuing martyrdom for the selfish reason of craving personal glory was ironically a sin. The only right reason for martyrdom should be the same as for any other activity—to give glory to God alone.

Cyprian's response to the group of believers wrestling with this question is as kind and pastoral as his response to the first group. In neither case does he rebuke or berate. He turns, instead, to explaining God's sovereignty as key to dispelling fear. In this case, Cyprian notes that God is in control of every Christian's time and mode of death. Thus, a fear that one might be deprived of martyrdom is, effectively, a selfish fear that stems, ironically, from a lack of faith in God's sovereignty over all things.[32]

The final question that Cyprian considers in the sermon has to do with implications from the first two: What is the appropriate attitude of Christians toward death from this plague? Related to it is the implied question: What are the implications of the trust in God's sovereignty for the community as a whole and for each individual's behavior toward the rest? In introducing this final section of the sermon, it is no accident that Cyprian opens with a reminder of the Lord's Prayer: If Christians fully believed it, would they not accept God's plans for them each day, whatever they may be?[33]

Cyprian's reference to the Lord's Prayer is appropriate and highlights the sins to which all believers, from Cyprian's day to today, are prone. Even while asking God for our daily bread, we are tempted to fix all our problems ourselves instead of relying on God. Furthermore, even as we pray that God's will be done, we secretly hope that it will match our own. Cyprian reminds his people that our obedience to God's will applies even in such situations as these, when he may be calling on Christians to die at a time and in a manner that they did not expect. This obedience has implications for Christians in caring fearlessly for others right now. If the believers do not have to fear death, as Cyprian repeatedly notes, then they should not fear taking care of the sick in the middle of the plague. For such a death from the plague would be yet another way of martyrdom—a death beautiful and glorious because it was self-sacrificial for others.[34]

Ultimately, through his responses to questions from the congregation, Cyprian's pastoral heart comes across especially strongly in *On Mortality*. He recognizes that his people are afraid, saddened, and discouraged in the midst of a deadly pandemic that was happening simultaneously with all the other crises

---

32. Cyprian, *On Mortality* 17.
33. Cyprian, *On Mortality* 18.
34. Cyprian, *On Mortality* 26.

of the age. His aim in this sermon is, therefore, to comfort and console.[35] But instead of providing empty comfort, he provides comfort that is rooted in the gospel. And interwoven throughout his responses to different fears is a discussion of spiritual warfare. The end of the world is near, the enemies of Christ prowl, and this plague is merely another sign of the spiritual battles that rage. Yet for Christians, there is no reason to fear because they know how the story ends. The end will be truly glorious—why fear death, if it means an eternity with God?[36]

Conclusion

Continuing to follow his own advice in modeling Christlike behavior for his congregation, Cyprian was martyred in the persecution of Valerian in 258 CE. The pandemic that he described continued to rage throughout the Roman Empire for at least another decade after his death, subsiding mysteriously around 270 CE. But Cyprian's pastoral ministry provides us with insights into a historical mystery: In the midst of all the crises of the third century, culminating with a deadly pandemic and two empire-wide persecutions, how and why did Christianity grow to encompass from less than 1 percent of the Roman Empire's residents in 200 CE to 16 percent in 313 CE?[37]

The answer takes us back to the cultural differences between the Roman and Christian ideas of a safety net. As noted at the beginning of this chapter, because the Romans did not consider all people equally valuable, there was no safety net aside from personal family ties and patronage networks. But these were no guarantee of assistance. As the sociologist Rodney Stark has argued, the Christians' distinctly countercultural approach to caring for others in the midst of crisis was the reason for the explosion in the rate of conversion over the course of the third century, even as persecutions intensified. Cyprian's pastoral ministry gives

---

35. See J. H. D. Scourfield, "The *De Mortalitate* of Cyprian: Consolation and Context," *Vigiliae Christianae* 50 (1996): 12–41 for the argument that this is one of the earliest examples of the genre of Christian *consolatio*.

36. See in particular Cyprian, *On Mortality* 22 and 26.

37. The work of Rodney Stark is particularly useful to read in considering these questions, Rodney Stark, *The Rise of Christianity: A Sociologist Reconsiders History* (Princeton: Princeton University Press, 1996), 13–21. Also, see Thomas Kidd's analysis of this growth: Thomas Kidd, "How Many Christians Were There in 200 A.D.?" *The Gospel Coalition*, September 22, 2017, https://www.thegospelcoalition.org/blogs/evangelical-history/how-many-christians-were-there-in-200-a-d/; and Philip Jenkins's thoughts, to which Kidd is responding: Philip Jenkins, "How Many Christians?" *Anxious Bench*, September 22, 2017, https://www.patheos.com/blogs/anxiousbench/2017/09/how-many-christians/.

a concrete example in support of Stark's theories, as it shows the Christian model of social care in practice.

Ministering to a large urban church with a diverse local population and strong ties to other churches throughout the broader region, Cyprian made it his duty to minister to all in need, drawing no distinction between Christian and pagan, Carthaginian or not. Such a remarkable model of care for others was not easy to achieve, as Cyprian's writings show, and its success is testament to the power of the gospel as well as the importance of local pastors. The impulse of the Christians in his church in a time of crisis was to focus inward, but Cyprian's work as a pastor centered on helping his flock see the beauty of ministering to one another and not fearing either the loss of property that might occur if they give generously or the loss of life that might occur if they care actively for the sick.

Reading *On Mortality* as the world struggles to recover from the devastating COVID-19 pandemic is more than a little eerie. In the US alone, the number of victims of the plague has surpassed one million. In 2021, there were more deaths than births in my neighboring state of Alabama, a first in its history. Just as in Cyprian's Carthage, this pandemic presented a serious challenge to pastors, who had to make loving decisions for their churches and their flock. How to meet safely? How to help those whose faith is weaker or those who have lost their loved ones or jobs? How to care for one another in a time of crisis, especially when getting together could literally prove deadly? In addition, adherence to or flaunting of such safety measures as social distancing and mask-wearing swiftly became politicized. As a friend in another congregation reported, his church auditorium had become divided into two sections, with the mask-wearers sitting on the left side of the auditorium and those who refused to wear masks sitting on the right. The irony of the implied political statement was not lost on my friend. All the while, just as in Cyprian's Carthage, the pandemic has not discriminated based on political or religious views and has targeted all those it could get.[38]

Cyprian's example of openly acknowledging fears in a way that is convicting yet deeply pastoral sets a good model for all Christians today. Yes, many of our fears in times of crisis can stem from sins, and proper theology can help us fight these sins and fears. At the same time, however, people are created for companionship. Caring for others is a powerful weapon for addressing sins that might

---

38. Although it is worth noting this study that argues that since Republicans were more likely to be opposed to safety and disease spread mitigation measures, they were more likely to die from the disease: Aria Bendix, "Covid Deaths Are Higher among Republicans than Democrats, Mounting Evidence Shows," October 6, 2022, *NBC News*, https://www.nbcnews.com/health/health-news/covid-death-rates-higher-republicans-democrats-why-rcna50883.

fester in isolation, and thankfully, in the age of technology, one-anothering during a deadly pandemic does not have to happen in person. Comforting words can be spoken by phone or via a text message just as well as through a papyrus scroll.

So the story of the Carthaginian church and its bishop's leadership of his flock through selfish desires to commit sins of omission of care for others has much larger repercussions for us, as we think about the obligations of Christians today to care for one another and for the larger community, locally and globally. While our structural networks of care through the government seem strong on paper—strong enough, in fact, that many Christians in this country cry out against social welfare programs as an excessive burden on the taxpayers!—the reality is much more complex.

Sociologist Jessica Calarco said in a viral Tweet in 2020, "Other countries have social safety nets. The U.S. has women." While, as Calarco herself has noted, this is an oversimplification of the burden that crises such as the COVID-19 pandemic have placed on women, there is significant truth to this statement. But nuancing this statement is not the point here. Rather, Calarco's observation should be convicting to the church today, precisely because this answer leaves out the church. During the pandemic of the mid-third century CE, by contrast, someone could easily have said, "Other countries have no social safety nets, but the Roman world has Christians."

Cyprian's pastoral ministry in Carthage showed us some concrete glimpses of a countercultural social safety net in action. This safety net required the leadership talents of a caring bishop and the assistance of deacons and elders in both his local church and the leaders of churches throughout the region. And it required, of course, Christians to overcome their sinful desire to turn away from the needy at this time of extreme need for all and to give sacrificially instead. Through this process, at least some of these pagans likely ended up seeing the beauty of the gospel and joining the church themselves.

Some churches today may see this story in their congregations and local communities, but this is not the universal story of the church today. The stories of reluctant sinners turning into self-sacrificial givers should inspire us and encourage us toward what could still be our own story today. What might this look like in our churches? I see encouraging examples in my own church and its mission to love children and families in foster care.

Several years ago, the pastoral staff of my church made a conscious decision to embrace foster care and adoption as our church's central mission and began to look for concrete ways to care for orphans in our community. At that time, only four families in the entire county were certified to foster, but the need significantly exceeded available foster homes. Our pastor, himself an adoptive father, wondered: Could we be the hands and feet of Jesus to our community in this way? The church encouraged those families and individuals in the church who were willing and able to become certified as foster families, established a prayer and weekly meal-train support network for these foster families, and hosted annual simulcast training conferences on trauma-informed parenting.

Seeing this ministry in action has been personally encouraging and reminds me of the purposeful leadership in caring for others that Cyprian's ministry in Carthage exemplified. This example highlights also the significance of recognizing even small ways in which Christians can give and help. Furthermore, the stories of how the church grew through ministering to others during much worse challenges than we face provide a reminder that retreating into our own sinfulness is never the gospel-led answer, no matter how tempting it may be.

PART 3

Cultural Christians
in the
Age of Constantine
and Beyond

7

"Are You Washed in the Blood?"

Sectarian Violence among Cultural Christians

SOMETIME IN 347/8 CE, THE CITY OF CARTHAGE, WHICH had been no stranger to persecutions and scenes of martyrdom, as we saw in chapters 5 and 6, witnessed yet another such scene. Two martyrs, Maximian and Isaac, were arrested, brutally tortured, and publicly executed for their faith. Although some features of their passion account seem very familiar and echo earlier such writings, there is something distinctly new here. In this story, instead of asking who is being martyred and why, the key starting question is *when?*

One of the expected features of Late Antique passion accounts is a gruesomely graphic description of the martyr's execution. Respecting the audience's expectations, the author of *The Passion of Maximian and Isaac* spares no possible detail in his description of the prolonged tortures that the two martyrs experienced prior to their deaths. The story does not end there, however. Instead, the account concludes with a miracle, whereby the bodies of the two martyrs, when thrown into the sea, were carried back ashore to receive honorable burial from the Christian community. Clearly, the author, Macrobius, had a greater point to convey than simply commemorating these martyrs. He concludes his account with a passionate exhortation to his readers to be inspired by the examples of these worthy martyrs and many others like them and to hurry to embrace similar martyrdom eagerly for themselves. Run, don't walk to your death, he urges.

Macrobius's pleas to his audience to not fear death but run as fast as they can toward martyrdom for the church may not seem quite so unusual for martyr accounts—although most of them generally do stop short of encouraging absolutely everyone else to actively seek martyrdom—until we consider its historical context.[1] Writing ca. 347–48 CE, Macrobius lived in the post-Constantinian Roman Empire, an environment that was significantly friendlier to Christians than much of previous Roman history. Persecution of Christians ended with Constantine, after all, although it is worth remembering that persecution of Jews continued. Furthermore, Constantius II, a son of Constantine, and emperor during the period when Macrobius was writing, went so far as to ban pagan sacrifices.

It may rightly seem surprising, therefore, that it is in the fourth century, a world in which the Christians were gradually squeezing out the pagans from places of prominence in the political realm, that we see a new body of martyrdom accounts pop up—the martyrdom stories of the Donatist sect. These passion accounts, generally more graphic in their descriptions of anti-Christian violence than the earlier martyrdom accounts of the pre-Constantinian Roman Empire, should make us deeply uncomfortable. After all, the violence against these martyrs was committed by other devout Christians of a different sect.

In other words, the removal of state-sanctioned persecutions of Christians as a whole resulted not in the growth of the church as a unified body, triumphantly celebrating its success in acquiring legitimacy and all its perks. Rather, the consequence was the solidification of divisions in the church. This resulted in a new type of persecution—those of one faction of Christians against another, based on theological disagreements that, both sides felt, were a matter of salvation. For one side, the Donatists, this made them worth dying over.

The three chapters in this final part of the book center around this question: How did the transformation of Christianity—from a persecuted minority, then to a favored minority, and eventually to the favored majority—impact the existence of cultural Christians in the church? Each chapter will consider a different piece of the question. The answer involves new forms of cultural Christianity that

---

1. For an overview of martyrdom in the early church, see Candida Moss, *Ancient Christian Martyrdom: Diverse Practices, Theologies, and Traditions* (New Haven, CT: Yale University Press, 2012); and *The Other Christs: Imitating Jesus in Ancient Christian Ideologies of Martyrdom* (Oxford: Oxford University Press, 2012).

were not possible when the Christians were a persecuted minority. This chapter considers as its main case study the Donatist controversy in the churches of Late Antique North Africa as a manifestation of one of the most uncomfortable challenges in the post-Constantinian church: sectarian strife and Christian-on-Christian violence.

In some ways, the Donatists were not unique. The Nicene controversy against the Arians was violent as well. More generally, the ancient world had a casual level of embedded violence that should shock us. Watching gladiatorial games and executions for entertainment required a significant tolerance of violence in society. What makes the Donatists a useful focus for this chapter, however, is the sheer volume of materials that they left, glorifying their martyrs and the significant persecution against them. Ironically, these martyrdom accounts merely emphasize the degree to which this sectarian violence was ultimately a symptom of cultural Christianity.

In using the Donatist controversy as our gateway into studying Christian violence against other Christians, we can ask difficult and timeless questions about pursuing the unity of the church and the ways cultural Christianity can prevent such unity. What are the theological problems with Christian-on-Christian violence? What are the causes of such violence, and what kinds of divisions in the church could lead to it?

Before we get to the Donatists and the questions and warnings that they still have for us today, we need to understand the complex historical background that shaped their story. This background includes the church's transformation from a minority that was persecuted into one that was favored by the state. We also need to understand the new involvement of the emperor in the church, which changed the dynamics of church leadership and arguably amplified strife and violence in the body in ways that seemed unexpected and surprising at the time.

From a Persecuted Minority to a Favored Minority: The Rise of the First Christian Emperor

By the time of Macrobius's life, the very real and very bloody war between the Donatist Christians and the rest of the church in North Africa had been the status quo for a full generation. But how did this division happen, and why did it happen just as Christianity achieved the status of a favored minority after centuries of persecution and discrimination? The answer, in a word, is Constantine.

As we noted in the last two chapters, the third century was particularly challenging for the Roman Empire, and the empire that emerged at the end of the Third-Century Crisis looked rather different than before. Coming to power in 284 CE, the emperor Diocletian realized an important truth that the conflict had revealed: a single emperor in charge of the entire empire was much too vulnerable, a sitting duck waiting for the next assassin to come along. So in 293 CE, Diocletian established the Tetrarchy. He divided the empire into four regions and assigned a ruler to each. Two senior emperors, Diocletian himself and Maximian—each holding the title of Augustus—ruled two of the regions. Two junior emperors, Galerius and Constantius Chlorus—each holding the title of Caesar—ruled the other two.

A surviving porphyry statue of the four tetrarchs from ca. 300 CE shows them looking identical to each other. Each is wearing military garb rather than the civilian toga, suggesting the continued need for leaders to be vigilant to internal and external military threats. For Diocletian, who rose to power through the ranks of the military, the army remained key to governing. Suggestively, each of the four has a large sword on his belt, and rests one hand on its hilt, while using the other arm to awkwardly semi-hug one of the other tetrarchs. Together, the four are a column of brotherly love and unity for the sake of the empire.

The early part of Diocletian's rule included one final and brutal empire-wide persecution that particularly targeted Christians in the Roman army. Since fidelity to the emperor was confirmed each year by an oath of the soldiers, which required recognizing the emperor's divinity, or at least acknowledging the Roman pagan gods as enforcing the oath, Diocletian's concern over the degree of the Christians' loyalty is understandable. Less understandable, perhaps, is the large number of Christians in the Roman army, as they should have found the oath offensive and incompatible with their beliefs. But perhaps this is yet another example of cultural Christianity—individuals who felt that they could take the annual oath to the emperor and yet consider themselves to be Christians. We should keep in mind, at the same time, that if they converted while in the army, they would not have been able to break contract, and leaving would have been classified as desertion.[2]

By the end of the third century, as we noted in the previous chapter, it may be

---

2. Pat Southern, *The Roman Army: A Social and Institutional History* (Oxford: Oxford University Press, 2007), 148–49.

that close to 10 percent of the empire's residents were Christians, and 16 percent were estimated to be Christian in 313 CE.[3] At this point, their presence in all professions should be expected. So pervasive was the spread of Christianity that Constantius Chlorus's first wife, Helena, may have been a Christian at the time of the marriage, although Eusebius believes that she converted after Constantine.[4] Some scholars have even posited, although there is no way to prove this, that Constantius himself was a believer.[5] This would suggest the intriguing—but, again, utterly unprovable—possibility that Constantine grew up in a Christian household. But let us return to Diocletian for the moment.

Debates continue over how successful Diocletian's great experiment was. Some of his measures, such as the Edict of Maximum Prices, flopped. Anyone who has taken basic high-school economics may not be surprised to hear that, in fact, fixing the price of some goods and services (e.g., bread or haircuts) to be uniform across a vast empire with very different local economies actually would not be a great way to combat inflation.

But at the very least Diocletian managed to do something that no other emperor had done in a century: survive in power for twenty years. Then in 305 CE, Diocletian decided to do something else that no other emperor had done: to retire along with his fellow-Augustus, Maximian. The previous two Caesars were promoted to the rank of Augustus, while two new Caesars were appointed. The power transitioned smoothly, and all was well for a few months.[6]

However, Constantius Chlorus, who had recently been promoted to Augustus, died in 306 CE. His death unleashed a tangled series of civil wars, a veritable "game of thrones," defined by varied shifting alliances between current and former Tetrarchs and their sons and further complicated by marriage

---

3. Rodney Stark, *The Rise of Christianity: A Sociologist Reconsiders History* (Princeton: Princeton University Press, 1996), 13–21. See especially table 1.2 on page 13. Also see Thomas Kidd's analysis of this growth: Thomas Kidd, "How Many Christians Were There in 200 A.D.?," *The Gospel Coalition*, September 22, 2017, https://www.thegospelcoalition.org/blogs/evangelical-history/how-many-christians-were-there-in-200-a-d/; and Philip Jenkins's thoughts, to which Kidd is responding: Philip Jenkins, "How Many Christians?," *Anxious Bench*, September 22, 2017, https://www.patheos.com/blogs/anxiousbench/2017/09/how-many-christians/.

4. Eusebius, *Life of Constantine* 3.47. For a new biography of this fascinating figure, who became a Christian at some point in her life, whether earlier or later than her son, see Julia Hillner, *Helena Augusta: Mother of the Empire* (Oxford: Oxford University Press, 2022).

5. For a summary of the debates over the poorly documented but highly contentious issue of Constantius's religious views, see Mark D. Smith, "The Religion of Constantius I," *Greek, Roman, and Byzantine Studies* 38 (1997): 187–208. Smith concludes that the hypothesis in favor of Constantius's monotheism is unwarranted by the evidence.

6. See David Potter, *Constantine the Emperor* (Oxford: Oxford University Press, 2013), ch. 3–8, for an in-depth analysis of the rule of Diocletian, with special attention to his edicts and policies.

relationships among the members of the overall group. Just how complicated was this web of alliances? At the time of his death, Constantius was married to Theodora, a daughter of Maximian from his first marriage. Constantine, who was staking a claim for his father's title, married Fausta, Maximian's daughter (from a later marriage than Theodora) and Maxentius's sister, in 307 CE. Flavia Julia Constantia, one of the daughters from the union of Constantius and Theodora, would go on to marry Licinius, another contestant in the struggle for the imperial title. Family dinners had to be deeply uncomfortable. Since all of these unwilling relatives lived far from each other, in-person interactions were mercifully rare, although executions of family members, whether related by blood or marriage, were regularly on the menu.

In the end, it was Constantius's son, Constantine, who defeated Maxentius, Maximian's son, in the Battle of Milvian Bridge in Rome in 312 CE. With this victory, Constantine consolidated rule over the western part of the Roman Empire. Not until 324 CE would Constantine finally defeat Licinius and take over the rest of the empire as well. But already in 312 CE, Constantine began making important policy decisions that affected Christians, and in 313 CE, he and Licinius, the last two men standing after a prolonged civil war, passed the Edict of Milan. True, emperor Galerius's Edit of Toleration in 311 CE ended the persecution that Diocletian had started. But the new edict of Constantine and Licinius definitively ended all persecution of Christians by decriminalizing Christianity in the Roman Empire. Why did Constantine support such measures in favor of Christians? In a complicated, widely debated, and ultimately unclear way, Constantine considered himself to be one of them.

Multiple accounts survive of Constantine's initial conversion experience. As exciting as the idea of the first Christian emperor makes us, we would do well to remember that he was not baptized until he was on his deathbed. This was a common trend in his day, stemming from a logical—albeit theologically faulty—view that since baptism wiped one's sins away, it was best to save it for the moment right before death, thereby maximizing one's chances of getting into heaven. One could say, indeed, that this was another obvious symptom of cultural Christianity—a desire of sorts to have one's heavenly cake but still consume all the joys of this earth, sinful and innocent alike.

Even if Constantine did not receive Christ in baptism until the end of his life, he appears to have experienced something akin to a moment of conversion in 312 CE. According to Eusebius, Christian historian and Constantine's biggest fan, Constantine, on the eve of his battle against Maxentius, had a vision of a cross and heard a divine command declare, "In this sign, you shall conquer!"

A subsequent dream in the night confirmed this vision and Christ's blessing upon Constantine's endeavors. In the morning, Constantine asked his soldiers to put the cross on their shields, and the rest, we could say, is history.[7]

Overnight, with Constantine's victory, Christianity became the religion of the Roman emperor. Wisely diplomatic, Constantine did not mandate conversion and continued to appoint pagans to political and military leadership positions.[8] Still, perceptions mattered, and rates of conversion gradually intensified. A robust scholarly debate continues over the various elements of the miraculous story of Constantine's conversion. Disagreements abound even over its degree of impact on the church.[9] There are, nevertheless, key conclusions on which we can agree. First, Constantine publicly approved of the story that Eusebius popularized, or else it would not have been disseminated so widely and early. Second, Constantine was not afraid to get involved in the affairs of the church, working closely with some bishops and taking a deliberate stance against others. This meant a monumental shift from how the church had operated before. These changes, we will see, paved the way both for state involvement in sectarian violence and for a new type of cultural Christians.

Church Governance from the New Testament Church to the Age of Constantine

Sometime around 50 CE, the church in Thessalonica felt that all signs were pointing to the imminent return of Christ. Acting in accordance with this sentiment, the members quit their jobs, and were spending their days worshiping and eagerly awaiting Jesus's return. Their decision is an example of internal and independent church governance that the New Testament-era churches practiced. The striking rebuke that they soon received from Paul, who wrote 2 Thessalonians specifically to argue against the believers' behavior and encourage them to get

---

7. For a discussion of Constantine's use of this miracle in telling his story, see H. A. Drake, *A Century of Miracles: Christians, Pagans, Jews, and the Supernatural, 312–410 CE* (Oxford: Oxford University Press, 2017).

8. See R. M. Errington, "Constantine and the Pagans," *Greek, Roman, and Byzantine Studies* (1988): 309–18.

9. For a summary of these debates and a nuanced middle-ground argument about the significance of the event, see H. A. Drake, "The Impact of Constantine on Christianity," in *The Cambridge Companion to the Age of Constantine*, ed. Noel Lenski (Cambridge: Cambridge University Press, 2005), 111–36. Another great resource is A. Edward Siecienski's edited collection of essays by top Constantinian scholars, *Constantine: Religious Faith and Imperial Policy* (London: Routledge: 2017).

back to work, is exemplary of the outside control that leaders like Paul were able to exercise over these independent churches. As we saw in chapters 2 and 3 regarding the Corinthian church, for instance, outrageous cultural sin in individual churches ultimately resulted in outside rebuke, if no inclination for internal governance to address the sin was forthcoming.

The stories surrounding Paul's rebukes of the Corinthians and the Thessalonians exemplify in a broad sense the New Testament model of church governance. Oversight from outside seems loose and unstructured. This does not mean that it was less effective, as the obedient response from both churches demonstrates. This unofficial model of leadership and control gave way after the New Testament period to a more structured system of church councils, led by the bishop of Rome—a figure known today simply as the pope.

One of the best examples of this post-New Testament but pre-Constantinian model in action involves Cyprian, who is now quite familiar to us. Involved in a number of heated disputes over the course of his decade as bishop of Carthage, Cyprian led the annual meeting of the council of African churches. But even more of the work was done through the same medium as Paul's work: letters. Cyprian's robust surviving correspondence shows a network of bishops in constant communication with each other and with Rome, their ultimate source of authority on issues of doctrine. Through this epistolary dialogue we see the first seeds of the issues that will ultimately define the Donatist controversy.

Cyprian's decade as bishop was bookmarked by two empire-wide persecutions conducted by the emperor Decius (251–53 CE) and emperor Valerian (258 CE). During the latter persecution, Cyprian himself was martyred. But before that, the big headache for Cyprian and other bishops (in addition to the issues we considered in the previous chapter) was the question of how to treat those who lapsed during the Decian persecution but wanted to return to the church afterward. Should the church institute strict gatekeeping and not welcome back the Christians who caved in during the persecutions? What about the bishops who handed over the sacred texts but wanted to return to the church once the persecution was over? The latter question will occupy the Donatists in particular, but Cyprian's focus was more on lapsed church members, and he was an advocate of compassionately evaluating each case on its own merits.

True and genuine repentance was, for Cyprian, enough to readmit someone, man or woman, back to the body. Numerous letters survive in Cyprian's correspondence that discuss this diversity of individual cases and show that Christians who fell away but wanted to return to the church could be men and women of all ages and life stages. In his approach, which supported their reunion with the church, Cyprian clashed with Novatian, the controversial bishop of Rome (eventually declared heretic), who argued instead that once fallen away, an individual could never be readmitted to full church membership. Their readmission, he argued, would compromise the integrity of the church.

Cyprian's compassionate yet theologically grounded argument against Novatian's claim shows the priority that most local bishops placed on encouraging and growing the local churches, rather than serving as spiritual gatekeepers. Besides, Cyprian noted, Novatian's stance involved a fundamental misunderstanding of the power of Christ and, through him, the ability of the church to offer forgiveness for such grave sins. Cyprian did not go on to state, as Martin Luther will do 1,300 years later, that the Christian's whole life is repentance, but he certainly seems to have implied something similar. In a remarkably ironic twist, the Donatists, in their Novatian-like view on Christian faithfulness, will nevertheless go on to embrace Cyprian as one of their model martyrs later on. But we will return to that story later in the chapter.

Cyprian's correspondence with other bishops, including the Bishop of Rome, represents a model of church governance that Constantine's conversion will challenge. Constantine showed himself eager to be involved in difficult conversations. So his rule ushered in the era of emperor-convened councils, the most famous of which, the Council of Nicaea, resulted in the Nicene Creed.[10] The result was a new tension within the church, as well as a new layer of culture permeating the faith, in the shape of the emperor's political agenda. The role of the bishops became formalized yet challenged in the process, as they now had a new political dimension to contend with, unlike their previous place in the world, in which the empire and the emperor simply viewed them as enemies.[11] The Donatist controversy tested Constantine's new system of the emperor's involvement in church government and, perhaps as even Constantine himself would have admitted later on, showed its limits. The controversy began as a battle between two factions, Donatists and Caecilianists, over who had the right to appoint the bishop of Carthage. Continuing the Novationist beliefs that Cyprian fought so hard to stem in the previous century, the Donatists too believed that anyone who had caved in during persecution could not be restored easily to church membership. And bishops who had handed over Scriptures during persecution, in particular,

---

10. For an analysis of Constantine's heavy-handed involvement in Nicaea, see Potter, *Constantine the Emperor*, 225–38.

11. For an examination of the new role of the bishops in the post-Constantinian Church, see Claudia Rapp, *Holy Bishops in Late Antiquity: The Nature of Christian Leadership in an Age of Transition* (Berkeley: University of California Press, 2005).

could not administer the sacraments. The Donatists ended up being the majority faction in Carthage, but this did not help their cause in the emperor's eyes.

From 313 to 317 CE, Constantine corresponded with the Donatists, convened local councils, and even invited representatives of both the Donatists and their opponents to Rome for conversations. Finally, frustrated with the perceived stubbornness of the Donatists, he had them declared heretics and ordered the confiscation of their churches. Later in his rule, when dealing with the Arian controversy that led to the Council of Nicaea, Constantine was more lenient and more patient with the recalcitrant bishops on all sides. But this was later. Perhaps, as historian David Potter suggests, Constantine had learned something from his experience with the Donatists, which led to more diplomatic moves when facing sectarian controversies later on.[12]

What is clear is that in trying to restore order, Constantine showed no interest in souls. The Christian-on-Christian violence and the obsession with bloodletting reflected in the Donatist martyrdom texts was a defining mark of the Donatist controversy, and the emperor's attempts to intervene only fomented further violence. Such behavior and the emphasis on setting themselves up as martyrs makes the Donatists a particularly illustrative example of the depth of divisions in the body of Christ when there is a lack of desire for compromise.

"The Blood of the Martyrs Is the Seed of the Church"

Fifty-five years after the martyrdom of Perpetua and Felicity, on an otherwise unremarkable September day, a large crowd of Christians and some Roman officials assembled for the same reason—to witness an execution of a man condemned for his faith. In many ways, the events leading up to that September day echo remarkably the experiences of Perpetua and Felicity, although the honorand of this September day did not leave a personal account of his preparation for martyrdom.

This martyrdom account of none other than Cyprian, now a familiar figure from Chapter 6, is a jewel in the Donatist martyrdom and passion narratives. Composed sometime after Cyprian's death, probably before 314 CE, it is highly dramatic. After Cyprian's arrest, the Roman proconsul accuses him of betraying

---

12. Potter, *Constantine the Emperor*, 193–203.

and misleading the Roman people through his work as bishop. But following the pronouncement of the execution verdict, Cyprian exclaims, "Praise God!" with a chorus of Christian eyewitnesses echoing back.

In a surprising gesture, Cyprian proceeds to ask the believers present at his execution to collect twenty gold pieces to pay his executioner. There is a certain irony in this story of a bishop who spent his ministry convincing his people to give generously to the poor and the suffering, now concluding his ministry by collecting money to pay his executioner. But this is not all. Bystanders, according to this account, were eager to collect a new kind of tangible, physical souvenir immediately following the execution.

Cyprian was beheaded. Such a death results in horrific amounts of blood from the major vessels severed. The Donatist passion account notes that as the bishop's body lay on the ground, still bleeding, with the executioner presumably still standing nearby, hundreds of Christians who were present rushed up. And taking out handkerchiefs and other pieces of cloth, they dipped them in Cyprian's blood.

This scene sounds chaotic and messy and possibly repulsive to our Western sensibilities, averse to visuals of bloodshed. We can imagine hundreds of sandaled and bare feet slipping in the blood pooling on the ground, people struggling to get some of it on their handkerchiefs as souvenirs. The believers' rushing to the martyr's side right after death is also reminiscent of vultures, eager to feast on the bodies of the freshly dead. The emphasis on all that blood just seems so graphic and heightens the violence of the scene.

Brandea, as such souvenirs became known in the Middle Ages, were the earliest types of holy relics and the easiest ones to procure. Put simply, they were any textiles that had come in contact with any part of the martyr's body or a holy place. Imbued with the holiness of the person or place, they could then protect the owner and even be passed down in the family. Pilgrims easily made them. All one needed to do was rub a cloth on a tomb or a site wall or a martyr's body.

In the case of Cyprian's death, of course, we are not dealing with a typical *brandea*. Instead, we have a messy and theatrical production of many pieces of cloth dipped in the fresh, warm blood of the martyred bishop. In this regard, the mementos that the witnesses to Cyprian's execution took home with them are closer to the later Medieval relics, whose collectors relished in the tangible bits of bone from saints and martyrs. But in the context of antiquity, there is clearly something altogether unique about these mementos of Cyprian's execution. The key here is the violence of the scene.

The bloodiness of Cyprian's passion account is a defining feature of

Donatist texts. We have already encountered the similarly graphic passion of Maximian and Isaac. Let us consider now one more prominent Donatist passion account: *The Acts of the Abitinian Martyrs*. In this account of the martyrdom of Christians from the city of Abitina, the emphasis on blood is accompanied with an outright declaration that the persecution of these Christians was part of a spiritual battle over the soul of the church. The account introduces the conflict in the following terms:

> In the times of Diocletian and Maximian, the devil waged war against the Christians in this manner: he sought to burn the most holy testaments of the Lord, the divine scriptures, to destroy the basilicas of the Lord, and to prohibit the sacred rites and the most holy assemblies from celebrating in the Lord. But the army of the Lord did not accept such a monstrous order and it bristled at the sacrilegious command. Quickly it seized the arms of faith and descended into battle. This battle was to be fought not so much against human beings as against the devil.[13]

This initial account casts the persecution in cosmic terms, recalling the persecutions predicted in Revelation. But the initial description of the devil as the enemy quickly gives way to condemning those who fell away (i.e., the traitors) in equally strong terms:

> When the devil had been completely defeated and ruined and all the martyrs were filled with God's presence, bearing the palm of victory over suffering, they sealed with their own blood the verdict against the traitors and their associates, rejecting them from the communion of the Church. For it was not right that there should be martyrs and traitors in the Church of God at the same time.[14]

In glorifying the accomplishments of the martyrs in standing fast in their faith, this account as well repeatedly returns to the discussion of their blood as both a witness of the cruelty done against the martyrs, and as a source of inspiration and strength for others to persist in the faith. Already in the introductory paragraph, the text states that the martyrs "in diverse places and at various times, they poured out their most blessed blood."[15]

---

13. Maureen Tilley, *Donatist Martyr Stories: The Church in Conflict in Roman North Africa* (Liverpool: Liverpool University Press, 1996), 28–29.

14. Tilley, *Donatist Martyr Stories*, 29.

15. Tilley, *Donatist Martyr Stories*, 27.

Later in the account, during the torture of the presbyter Saturninus, the narrator notes that as he "hung on the rack anointed by the newly shed blood of the martyrs, he was incited to persist in the faith of those in whose blood he stood fast."[16] Blood again is prominent here, now described as anointing and sanctifying instruments of torture for saints to come. Of course, as we saw especially in the case of *The Passion of Maximian and Isaac*, these texts also openly exhorted other believers to aspire to such deaths.

One of North Africa's greatest theologians, Tertullian, famously wrote early in the second century CE: "The blood of the martyrs is the seed of the church."[17] We can understand Tertullian's point—because of the martyrs and the way they witnessed publicly about their faith, mass conversions resulted. Yet historians and theologians have not paid sufficient attention to Tertullian's particular phrasing.

Why the point about blood specifically? While Tertullian long predated the Donatists, such vivid phrasing reflects Roman cultural obsession with blood and violence permeating the church. These conversations about violence merely served to foment further divisions in the body of Christ. As we reflect on witnesses making *brandea* from a martyr's blood to take such mementos home and perhaps share them with others, we should imagine the blood of the martyr being treated as a seed. A powerful seed to take, share, and plant. While Tertullian focused on the harvest of converted souls, however, we cannot overlook the accompanying harvest of violence within the body that the same seeds yielded.

"There Is Pow'r in the Blood"

Like *The Passion of Maximian and Isaac* considered at the beginning of this chapter, the Donatist *Acts of Abitinian Martyrs* and the *Passion of Cyprian* glorify death by martyrdom and emphasize the violence of executions inflicted upon the Donatists by both Roman authorities (in the case of events before Constantine) and by fellow Christians (in the case of fourth-century martyrdom accounts) in a way that borders on grotesque. Why exactly do these narratives do so?

In explaining this phenomenon, Maureen Tilley, a translator of Donatist martyrdom accounts, emphasizes the long-lasting memory of local events, especially because of the difference that the Donatists relished between themselves as North Africans and the Roman government that persecuted them:

---

16. Tilley, *Donatist Martyr Stories*, 35.
17. Tertullian, *Apologeticus* L:13.

By keeping alive the memory of the martyrs, the stories accomplished several purposes: they kept alive the sense of the Donatist church as a church in touch with its roots in the pre-Constantinian persecuted Christianity; they kept alive animosity for the Catholics who persecuted them in league with the Roman government; they kept alive traditions on how to survive physical persecution; they kept alive a heritage of resistance not only to physical force but to the economic and social pressure to conform to state-sponsored Catholicism. In short, the scenes of torture served to keep Donatism alive by offering and reinforcing an alternate construal of reality.[18]

Tilley's analysis highlights the unwillingness of the Donatists to acknowledge the transition from the pre-Constantinian way of managing the affairs of the church. Emphatic that martyrdom and persecutions were a key aspect of the faith, they were unwilling to embrace a world in which they could live in unity with other Christians, whose faith the Donatists saw as weaker. As a result, when reading Donatist narratives, one feels as though it is 251 CE all over again rather than almost a century later. To quote a well-known hymn, the Donatists realized that "there is pow'r in the blood." But whose blood? It seems that by glorifying their own martyrs' blood, the Donatists claimed authenticity that other Christians, who did not suffer like they did, could not possess. Tangible souvenirs, like those collected from Cyprian's body (who, ironically, did not support the Novatianist views that manifested themselves in a new light as Donatism), only reinforced this connection.

While unusual in the context of antiquity, souvenirs of blood from saints became a common feature in late medieval Catholic worship. The story of these souvenirs, while from a much different cultural and geographical context than our direct focus in this chapter, still provides an intriguing glimpse of this feature of worship and its significance as both creating and manifesting cultural Christianity.

A Bloody Interlude

In 305 CE, during Diocletian's persecution of Christians, Januarius, the bishop of Beneventum in Italy, was arrested along with several other local Christians and sentenced to death for his faith. The Christians were thrown into an arena with

---

18. Tilley, *Donatist Martyr Stories*, xxxvi.

bears. Miraculously, the bears refused to maul them. So Januarius was beheaded instead, like Cyprian, resulting in a similarly gruesome and plentiful outpouring of blood. This is where things get interesting. Legend has it that someone collected his blood into a vial immediately afterward and took it to Naples. There it remains to this day.

Preserved in powder form in a special double reliquary, the blood of Januarius, now patron saint of Naples, miraculously liquefies on several occasions each year. Furthermore, occasions when the blood was expected to liquefy but did not have proved to be harbingers of forthcoming disaster. Januarius's blood did not liquefy during most of WWII and in December 2016 and December 2020. Catholic News Agency notes, furthermore, that "the relic also remained solid the year Naples elected a communist mayor."[19] As a faithful Christian, it appears that Januarius did not approve.

The story of Januarius's blood is striking, but while it is arguably the most famous of all blood souvenirs collected from ancient saints and martyrs, it is scarcely unique in modern Italian Catholicism. A total of 190 such blood samples are currently preserved throughout Italy. There are others, furthermore, throughout Europe. In particular, the Basilica of the Holy Blood in Bruges, Belgium, proudly displays a vial with a piece of the cloth that, legend has it, Joseph of Arimathea used to wash Jesus's body for burial after the crucifixion. The blood that has dried into the cloth liquefies on occasion, filling the vial.[20]

The bloody relics from saints are on display in churches and are used in modern Catholic worship. But the story has a twist. While all of these blood samples are purported to have been collected *in situ* from executed martyrs, the first mention of Januarius's blood and the miracle of its liquefication dates to 1389 CE, a full 1,084 years after his martyrdom. The bloody cloth relic housed in the Basilica of the Holy Blood in Bruges is one that Thierry of Alsace reportedly brought home from the Second Crusade in 1150 CE, well over 1,100 years after Jesus's crucifixion.

In other words, the bloody relics on display today are all first attested in the Middle Ages or later. They belong to a different world from Late Antiquity, but one that continues to be fascinated with the tangible and visible manifestations of holiness and desires this tangible link to the early church. These tangible relics

19. For the story about the blood of St. Januarius, see CNA Staff, "Everything You Need to Know About the Miracle of Liquefaction of the Blood of St. Januarius," *Catholic News Agency*, September 18, 2021, https://www.catholicnewsagency.com/news/249030/everything-you-need-to-know-about -the-miracle-of-liquefaction-of-the-blood-of-saint-januarius.

20. For a brief story of the vial, see "Is the Blood of Christ in Europe?," *One Life Tours*, August 26, 2015, https://onelifetours.ca/the-blood-of-christ-in-europe/.

are meant to inspire people to action: the martyrs' death is an example of just how far others were once willing to go on behalf of their faith. Might we do the same?

The Donatists' treatment of the martyrdom of Cyprian in some ways resembles this much later Medieval and even modern Catholic fascination with blood of saints and martyrs as tangible souvenirs. But this treatment of blood is not the only approach. After all, the Donatists' treatment of Cyprian's blood contrasts with the similarly bloody account of the death of Polycarp, a century and a half earlier. As we noted in chapter 4, Polycarp's death brought forth a miraculous amount of blood, which put out a (literal) fire. Yet none of the bystanders were eager to mop it up with their handkerchiefs. The language of emphasizing bloodshed in such a graphic way contrasts with otherwise gruesome earlier martyrdom accounts, such as the letters of Ignatius of Antioch, a contemporary of Polycarp, who wrote in very graphic ways about his own imagined and desired martyrdom. At the end, he got his wish. Although he desired death to be united with Christ, Ignatius still did not envision himself as worthy of becoming such a Christlike figure, nor did he dwell in such extensive detail over the outpouring of his own blood. In other words, while his martyrdom was an obsession for him, his blood was not.

These glimpses of an alternative possibility—viewing the blood of a martyr as a miraculous flow but not one that needed to be talked about at length and preserved in souvenirs—reminds us that there is something different going on with the Donatists. This difference has to do with their rootedness in the Roman culture of communal bloodshed and violence.

North African Christianity:
A History of Communal Violence

In the North African coastal city of Caesarea, there was an annual custom, called *caterva*, going back to time immemorial according to the locals. For a brief period each year, the locals would split into two enemy factions and use the allocated time to attack—wound, maim, and at times, outright kill—each other. Remarkably, it appears that the city functioned as a perfectly normal Late Antique Roman city for the remainder of the year. The city was also a significant Christian center, which Augustine visited—indeed, his work *De Doctrina Christiana* is our intriguing source for the *caterva*.

As Brent Shaw shows in his monumental study *Sacred Violence: African*

Christians and Sectarian Hatred in the Age of Augustine, historians can only ignore the impact of local culture to their own peril.[21] If we consider the local culture in more detail, we find that the extreme obsession with violence in the Donatist martyrdom accounts reflects a local culture of endemic violence. This endemic violence, as noted earlier, was not special to North Africa. It was deeply ingrained in Roman culture. But it had different local manifestations, and the *caterva* is one such example.

The annual period of ritualistic violence in Caesarea was as much a part of the city's identity by Late Antiquity as its Christian faith and its Roman citizenship. As a result, it appears that the Roman governor, although stationing troops in the city, allowed the local custom of violence to occur without intervening. Presumably, he did not see it as a threat to the stability of the empire. Brent Shaw explains the nature of this ritual:

> The custom was so deeply ingrained because it defined the people who participated in it. Every year they willfully engaged in a murderous ceremony that demonstrated to themselves, even to the point of death, who they were. Its primal causes were almost irrelevant. More significant was the long-lived history and tradition. Handed down from distant ancestors, and more immediately from fathers and grandfathers, this violent custom—a *consuetudo* as they called it—was re-enacted ceremoniously year after year because, quite simply, it was what the people of Caesarea had always done. It was irrelevant that it involved real violence, injury and suffering, and even the occasional death; or that it pitted brother against brother.[22]

When Augustine visited Caesarea in the 420s CE, he exhorted the locals to drop this custom, as ingrained as it was. In Christ, he urged, they had the strength to resist even the weight of their own history and tradition. The audience responded by breaking down in tears.

How many other cities and towns in North Africa had similar traditions, their own version of *caterva*? Shaw admits that our glimpses are few and far between. Their presence is intriguing nevertheless in reminding us of the deeply ingrained violence in the Roman world. But this particular story of localized ritualistic violence that long predated Christianization, places into

---

21. Brent Shaw, *Sacred Violence: African Christians and Sectarian Hatred in the Age of Augustine* (Cambridge: Cambridge University Press, 2011).

22. Shaw, *Sacred Violence*, 19. References to the *caterva* in the sources as *consuetudo*, an ingrained habit, highlight its nature as something done because it's always been done that way.

context the emphasis on blood in Donatist passion accounts. For individuals who had lived in cities like Caesarea, with its local custom of annual community bloodletting, bloody executions of martyrs may have seemed a naturally related concept, a sort of new and Christian version of the custom of their ancestors.

While few similar discussions survive of the structured and regularly scheduled community violence, like *caterva*, we have an overwhelming papyrological record that attests to extreme violence on a daily basis that was simply embedded and endemic in communities both before and after the advent of Christianity in the region. Strikingly, papyrologist Roger Bagnall's research on violence in ancient papyri and on the culture of localized violence in twentieth-century Egyptian villages paints a surprising picture of continuity.[23] Ancient legal records and village police reports preserved in papyri attest to regular assaults, beatings, and other kinds of violence that was simply a part of life. People who have had such violence done unto them have written (or hired scribes to write) reams and reams of papyri afterward, trying (and often failing) to obtain justice through official channels.[24]

The presence of these documents, as well as the formulaic language in them, were also a regular part of life. These too attest to the expectation that violence would occur, so there was ample language for talking about it. Everyone could expect to suffer violence at some point, so the question was not if but when. In this world, the Donatists' blood-glorifying texts fit in seamlessly. Furthermore, these petitions are a good parallel for the Donatist martyrdom accounts, as they focus specifically on the perspective of the recipients of violence rather than the perpetrators. Yet in a world where so many could expect to receive violence, surely at some point even the perpetrators would become victims.

As we consider the place of the Donatists in this culture of ever-present violence in the Roman Empire at large and in the North African landscape in particular, it is important to remember that the suffering of the Donatists was very real. So was the violence against them by the surrounding Catholic Christians. But what seems to separate the Donatists is their glorification of the violence against them. Through their own texts, the Donatists continued to glorify the violence against themselves, achieving the goal directly stated over and over again in their martyrdom accounts—that the goal of the martyrs and of

---

23. Roger Bagnall, "Official and Private Violence in Roman Egypt," *The Bulletin of the American Society of Papyrologists* 26 (1989): 201–16.

24. For this history of violence through petitions in Egyptian papyri, see Ari Bryen, *Violence in Roman Egypt: A Study in Legal Interpretation* (Philadelphia: University of Pennsylvania Press, 2013).

these martyr narratives was to create yet more martyrs. The seed of blood could only beget a harvest of more blood.

It is significant that the voice of Augustine dominates the surviving critiques of both the *caterva* and the Donatists.[25] The violence and divisions within the church bothered Augustine deeply as symbols of cultural Christianity. In asking local Christians to embrace peace instead, he reminded them that the culture they should care most about was not of the kingdom of this world.

Divisions among Christians as a Symptom of Cultural Christianity

Once upon a time, a man was marooned on an island, and he stayed there for years, all alone. When he was rescued at last, his rescuers were puzzled to find that he had put the effort into constructing three different buildings on the small island. They asked him what they were. The man explained that the first was his house, and the second was his church. The third, he added with emotion, was where he used to go to church.

This is not an actual event, of course, but this popular joke illustrates the significant division in the body of Christ today. Division and strife are so ingrained in us that even left to our own devices, we might sow them with no outside provocation. We have to laugh, or else we will cry.

In a historical and less humorous instance of division, during the American Civil War, Christians in both the Union and the Confederacy were reading the same Bible while they were killing each other over the deadly four-year conflict. As historian James Byrd has shown through a study of period sermons, they did so with a vastly different outlook to interpreting the same passages of the Bible.[26] The division, while theological, was ultimately also no less cultural.

The Donatist martyrdom accounts, and the general story of the Donatist controversy, have significant lessons to teach us today about pursuing the unity of the church in our own communities. First, the martyrdom stories we tell

---

25. In addition to Brent Shaw's discussion of Augustine and the Donatists in *Sacred Violence*, key works on Augustine's correspondence with the Donatists are Jennifer Ebbeler's *Disciplining Christians: Correction and Community in Augustine's Letters* (Oxford: Oxford University Press, 2012); and Rafał Toczko, *Crimen Obicere: Forensic Rhetoric and Augustine's Anti-Donatist Correspondence* (Göttingen: Vandenhoeck & Ruprecht, 2020).

26. James P. Byrd, *A Holy Baptism of Fire and Blood: The Bible and the American Civil War* (Oxford: Oxford University Press, 2021).

matter.[27] Glorifying violence against them became, for the Donatists, fuel for continuing to resist theological unity and to create a sort of alternate reality for themselves—a world in which they were always the persecuted minority, even as Christianity became the *de facto* religion of the empire. But second, we see the impact of Roman culture in promoting violence, including violence within the church, over theological disagreements. It is easy to blame the Donatists, but we also have to wonder: Are we continuing to misunderstand them, just as everyone else around them did?

Strikingly, the violence that the Donatists glorified in their writings was violence against themselves rather than violence that they inflicted on others. Their emphasis, therefore, was on making themselves into the symbol of true and faithful believers and martyrs, while casting the rest of the Christians around them as unbelievers. In the process, they coopted as their own earlier Christian figures such as Cyprian, who was never a Donatist. Cyprian advocated for accepting all who repented back into the church after persecutions in the mid-third century CE. Through the telling of martyrdom stories about Cyprian and others, the Donatists were able to perpetuate their version of events.

In a surprising plot twist, while modern American churches are not filled with Donatists, the belief that Christians are a persecuted minority is one that is widely disseminated within the church today. One 2017 survey found that a majority of white Protestants feel that they face significant discrimination because of their faith.[28] The administrators of the survey were surprised, furthermore, that a smaller percentage of American Muslims felt that they faced significant discrimination for their faith. The finding, especially in 2017, was particularly surprising, as then-President Donald Trump was openly hostile toward Muslims, and other data showed that Muslims faced significantly more discrimination than Christians.[29] Could this sense of feeling beleaguered and oppressed be a manifestation of cultural Christianity, in which it is easier to cast oneself as the martyr? It is in this light that we should consider one kind of souvenir that some American Christians used to collect not so very long ago.

In April 1899, Sam Hose, an African-American man, was lynched by an

---

27. This is part of the argument that Candida Moss makes in *The Myth of Persecution: How Early Christians Invented a Story of Martyrdom* (New York: HarperOne, 2014).

28. German Lopez, "Survey: White Evangelicals Think Christians Face More Discrimination than Muslims," *Vox*, March 10, 2017, https://www.vox.com/identities/2017/3/10/14881446/prri-survey-muslims-christians-discrimination.

29. "U.S. Muslims Concerned About Their Place in Society, but Continue to Believe in the American Dream," *Pew Research Center*, 07/26/2017, https://www.pewresearch.org/religion/2017/07/26/findings-from-pew-research-centers-2017-survey-of-us-muslims/.

angry mob in Newnan, Georgia, located just forty-five minutes away from my home. As part of the lynching, participants cut off parts of his body while he was still alive. They then tied him to a tree and set him on fire—again, while still alive. After his death, the angry crowds kept cutting off more parts of his body, including even the heart and the liver, as souvenirs to take home or sell. Indeed, pieces of his bones continued to be sold as souvenirs for some time.[30]

The horrific abuse that this Black man suffered at the hands of a white mob should horrify us. But there is more here that should give us pause. As violent and dehumanizing as the lynching of Sam Hose was, it is merely one of many such incidents dotting American history in the century and a half after the Civil War. In fact, this chapter in the country's history is not over yet. There have been at least eight suspected lynchings in the state of Mississippi alone since the year 2000.[31]

But what should really bring us to tears—and to our knees—as we reflect on this terrible chapter in American history is that this is, ultimately, Christian-on-Christian violence that signifies division in the church. After all, so many of those initiating this violence have been white Christians while their victims have often been Black Christians. The tendency to collect souvenirs from lynching victims afterward, ranging from body parts to professional-quality photographs to pieces of rope and clothing, is eerily reminiscent of martyrs' relics collected in antiquity and the Middle Ages. In this case, however, there is something horrifically unholy in these mementos of senseless cruelty stemming from a culture of systemic racism. To have a tangible and visible souvenir of a lynching is to commemorate this violence that has nothing to do with the true gospel.

In the book *Our Town: A Heartland Lynching, a Haunted Town, and the Hidden History of White America*, journalist Cynthia Carr explored a lynching that took place in Marion, Indiana, in 1930.[32] What made this story all the more heartbreaking for Carr, though, was her own family's connections to the event. How could her grandfather, a respectable churchgoer and pillar in the local community, have been a part of the mob visible in the photograph from the lynching, where smiling and serious witnesses pose around the victims hanging from the tree as though this were just another social outing?

---

30. For recent studies of this lynching, see Edwin Arnold, *What Virtue There Is in Fire: Cultural Memory and the Lynching of Sam Hose* (Athens, GA: University of Georgia Press, 2012); and Donald Mathews, *At the Altar of Lynching: Burning Sam Hose in the American South* (Cambridge: Cambridge University Press, 2017).

31. DeNeen L. Brown, "Lynchings in Mississippi Never Stopped," *Washington Post*, August 8, 2021, https://www.washingtonpost.com/nation/2021/08/08/modern-day-mississippi-lynchings/.

32. Cynthia Carr, *Our Town: A Heartland Lynching, a Haunted Town, and the Hidden History of White America* (New York: Crown, 2007).

The question haunted Carr throughout her research. In a broader form, she realized, this question kept haunting Marion's church community as well: How could white Christians in the community have approved and participated in this event, harming other Christians in this way? But in a foreshadowing of God's kingdom, it was Marion's churches working together who took the lead in trying to bring about a reconciliation through public repentance for the town's history of racism and vowing to forgive and work together. As we consider histories of Christian violence against other Christians, tragically common in so many shapes and in so many periods, we would do well to remember that the solution demands repentance as a starting point. As Wendell Berry's recent book suggests in its examination of the legacies of the sin of slavery in American history, such repentance may most effectively play out at the local level, with neighbors learning to reconcile and love each other despite their painful history.[33]

In addition to repentance, a recognition of the diversity of God's kingdom is in order, as that diversity may manifest itself in very different ways of worshiping and following God. While some of the Donatists were likely dark-skinned, their skin color was not the reason for their persecution in the Roman world, which had a very different concept of race.[34] Still, cultural misunderstanding was a factor in their persecution. Biblical scholar Esau McCaulley's thoughts on the significance of cultural diversity in the kingdom of God resonate here, and advise caution:

> God's eschatological vision for the reconciliation of all things in his Son requires my blackness and my neighbor's Latina identity to endure forever. . . . Therefore, inasmuch as I modulate my blackness or neglect my culture, I am placing limits on the gifts that God has given me to offer to his church and kingdom. The vision of the kingdom is incomplete without Black and Brown persons worshiping alongside white persons as part of one kingdom under the rule of one king.[35]

---

33. Wendell Berry, *The Need to Be Whole: Patriotism and the History of Prejudice* (Berkeley: Shoemaker, 2022).

34. See Sarah Derbew, *Untangling Blackness in Greek Antiquity* (Cambridge: Cambridge University Press, 2022). For translated primary sources on the topic, see Rebecca Kennedy, Sydnor Roy, and Max Goldman, *Race and Ethnicity in the Classical World: An Anthology of Primary Sources in Translation* (Indianapolis: Hackett, 2013).

35. Esau McCaulley, *Reading While Black: African American Biblical Interpretation as an Exercise in Hope* (Downers Grove, IL: IVP Academic, 2020), 116.

Heresy is a problem, but so is division, especially when it results in shedding blood from bodies made in the Father's image, just like ours. Furthermore, while our focus here has largely considered the downside of culture in potentially warping theology, we need to remember that culture can also be a rooting principle that encourages someone's faith to look different than another's. Sometimes divisions are less about good theology and more about appearances. And those kinds of divisions should worry and convict us.

8

The Altar and the Cross

Christian Nationalism in the Twilight of Empire

IN THE YEAR 29 BCE, OCTAVIAN (THEN NOT-QUITE-YET Augustus) decided to celebrate his victory over Marcus Antonius and Cleopatra, and his concomitant near-complete consolidation of power over the Roman state, in the most Roman way possible—by setting up a fancy altar to the goddess Victoria (the goddess of victory) in the Roman senate house. Presumably, immediately after the victory, he also concurred with the poet Horace's assessment about how to best celebrate the victory—*Nunc est bibendum . . .* ("Now is the time to drink")—but our concern right now is with the altar and its statue.

By this point, the particular statue Octavian chose for the altar was a seasoned Roman gal. Originally a Greek statue of the Greek goddess Nike, this was one of the spoils of war that the Romans took from Tarentum in 272 BCE during the Pyrrhic War. So Victoria had already weathered a thorough Romanization and reconfiguration of her meaning before Octavian. For another three hundred fifty years after 29 BCE, Victoria continued to stand in the Roman senate house, a beacon of the continuity of Roman greatness and victories over foes in the course of sometimes subtle yet increasingly significant changes in the empire. Emperors and plagues and disasters of all other sorts came and went, but Victoria stayed where she was. Little could Augustus or anyone who witnessed Victoria's original installation in the senate house have foreseen that a tiny movement, which was not even in existence at the time of the altar's construction, would one day prove its downfall.[1]

It is entirely possible that we would never have heard of Victoria and the altar again if not for the recasting of this altar as a very different type of symbol in the second half of the fourth century CE. While the Roman empire was only about 10 percent Christian in 300 CE, it was over 50 percent Christian by 350 CE. Also, in 330 CE, Constantine moved the capital of the empire to Byzantium, duly rechristened as Constantinople. The significance of the city of Rome thereafter became more symbolic than practical. Yet in a Rome still filled with pagan symbols, altars, and temples, the altar and statue of Victoria in the senate house unexpectedly became the centerpiece of the debates over the evolving relationship of history and religion in the Roman state. This story, furthermore, has significance for our understanding of Roman religious nationalism.

Visiting Rome in 357 CE, the emperor Constantius II, son of Constantine and an Arian Christian, ordered that the altar and statue be placed into storage. Despite his opposition to the public display of the altar and the statue, he was not willing to go so far as to destroy them. Following Constantius II's death in 361 CE, the next emperor, Julian the Apostate, restored the altar and Victoria back to their original location. Following Julian's death in 363 CE at the ripe old age of thirty-two, Christian senators began lobbying for the removal of the statue and the altar again. The next emperor, Valentinian, attempted to remain neutral in matters of religion and upheld the status quo. But in 382 CE, the emperor Gratian allowed the altar's removal yet again. Following Gratian's death—you guessed it!—new petitions came forth requesting that the next emperor, Valentinian II, restore it. Passionate arguments both in favor of restoring the altar and the statue to the senate house (from Symmachus) and against placing them back in that location (from Ambrose, Bishop of Milan) survive and show the continued presence and strength of pagan intellectual voices in the increasingly more Christian empire. Not even the emperor Theodosius I's proclamation of Christianity as the only official state religion (he even went so far as to ban the Olympic Games, ending a tradition that went back to 776 BCE, predating Romulus's founding of Rome) was enough to end this knock-down, drag-out

---

1. For a discussion of this altar, see Alan Cameron, *Last Pagans of Rome* (Oxford: Oxford University Press, 2011), 39–51.

fight over the altar of Victoria. Eugenius, who briefly took over the Western half of the Empire in 392 CE, appears to have restored the altar, which then remained in the senate house until possibly as late as 408, when it was removed again.

And then in 410 CE, the unthinkable happened. The city of Rome was sacked by Alaric's Visigoths. Even though Rome by now had not been the capital of the empire for eighty years, this sack of Rome, the first in eight hundred years, shocked all residents of the Roman Empire, throwing them into an existential crisis of identity. The event brought to the fore in a more emotional way those same questions that the debate over the altar and statue of Victoria exemplified in their core. These questions and cultural beliefs about the intricate relationship of religion and history existed from the early days of the Roman state and have been at the core of the concept of cultural religion discussed in the introduction to this book. The pagans blamed the Christians for the wrath of the gods, which, they were certain, brought about this national tragedy. Some Christians, on the other hand, blamed God for abandoning them in their hour of need.

We sometimes forget that up until that moment, Christianity had only existed in the historical context of the Roman Empire, with Rome at its helm as a symbol of power and stability unlike any other here on earth. While, as earlier chapters noted, Rome had been an oppressive colonizer for its subjects and especially for persecuted groups, such as Christians, it had been the assumed backdrop of the church for the entirety of its existence to date. And so, just as the pagans wondered if this was the end of their world, so too did the Christians. Could Christianity even exist in a world where Rome no longer was the unshaken center of power? Most important, what did it mean for Christians if God removed his favor from Rome? These questions plagued Christians across the empire, whether they were in Rome when the calamity struck or were observing the disaster from across the Mediterranean. Their questions in this time of national crisis reveal the deep roots of religious nationalism in the Roman psyche. Long predating Christianity, this Roman religious nationalism engulfed it.

Religious nationalism, especially Christian nationalism, has received much attention in the United States as of late. The dangers of Christian nationalism, in particular, have been the subject of several recent books by social scientists and historians.[2] But the idea of the United States as a nation favored by God, a sort of

---

2. Andrew Whitehead and Samuel Perry, *Taking America Back for God: Christian Nationalism in the United States* (Oxford: Oxford University Press, 2020); Philip Gorski and Samuel Perry, *The Flag and the Cross: White Christian Nationalism and the Threat to American Democracy* (Oxford: Oxford University Press, 2022); and Katherine Stewart, *The Power Worshippers: Inside the Dangerous Rise of Religious Nationalism* (London: Bloomsbury, 2022).

new Jerusalem, is nothing new and harkens back already to the time before the United States was a separate nation. Seventeenth-century Puritan colonists saw the new land as a "new Jerusalem," and "a city on a hill," favored by God as long as its inhabitants would follow divine commands.[3] For the Puritans, this was a natural way to describe Christian community that was set apart from the world. In the past several decades, however, the idea of religiously motivated nationalism has been corrupted and co-opted into political discourse in such ways as to become a distortion of the gospel.[4] But the point of this chapter is to argue that this cultural sin is not unique to us. While the modern concept of nationalism is certainly different from the Roman idealization of the city of Rome and the empire that emerged from it as uniquely favored by the gods and destined to rule the world, it is nevertheless analogous.

Based on the development of musical styles in Medieval England, musicologist Richard Taruskin has observed:

> This assertion of a local style within a universal genre may suggest the beginnings of something comparable to what we now call nationalism. . . . At this early date nationalism—or better, national consciousness—is identified with the crown, not with ethnicity, and is associated with propaganda aimed at conscripting a national army under the king's command. So far it may be viewed as merely a weaker, more abstract form of the personal loyalty one pledged to one's lord under feudalism. Nor is it easy to distinguish nationalism from imperialism: England's sense of itself as a nation had a lot to do with the efforts of the Anglo-Normans to conquer and rule their Celtic neighbors to the west and north.[5]

Taruskin's findings based on musical developments have significant ramifications for our understanding of political and religious nationalism. His analysis reveals the development of the national consciousness as the ultimate way to process group and individual identity. Such national consciousness—which in more modern periods we comfortably call "nationalism"—seems to appear so easily and organically as to have a feel of human nature. It is, after all, natural for groups

---

3. The description of the United States as a "City Upon a Hill" harkens to a 1630 sermon by John Winthrop, who will go on to become governor of Massachusetts.

4. For an overview of Christian nationalism in US history, see John Fea, *Was America Founded as a Christian Nation? A Historical Introduction* (Louisville: Westminster John Knox, 2011). Very helpful as a short primer is John Wilsey, "The Many Faces of Christian Nationalism," *Law & Liberty*, September 26, 2022, https://lawliberty.org/features/the-many-faces-of-christian-nationalism/.

5. Richard Taruskin, *Music from the Earliest Notations to the Sixteenth Century* (Oxford: Oxford University Press, 2006), 108.

to want to be better than other groups and to imagine themselves as exceptional, created and ordained to be better than the rest.

A nationalism based on belief in Roman exceptionalism was a feature of Roman religion and was also part of the worldview of many (although not all) early Christians, absorbed seamlessly by those who saw themselves as residents or even citizens of the Roman Empire. But while such nationalism can seem at first glance to be a good thing, a kind of natural pride that makes people bravely serve on behalf of their nation, making the nation into the ultimate good to which one owes everything is, of course, idolatry, as such thinking places the nation ahead of God.

In this chapter we consider the most egregious manifestation of the cultural sin of Christian nationalism in the Roman Empire—the reaction of Christians in the Roman Empire to the sack of Rome. Our best witness to the Christian reaction to the sack of 410 CE is none other than the leading theologian of his age: Augustine, bishop of Hippo. The event had a traumatic effect on Augustine, it appears, and he wrote his monumental *City of God* (the full title is *On the City of God against the Pagans*) in response. But rather than merely telling Christians how to react to the greatest tragedy of their age in the most theologically appropriate way, Augustine's *City of God* is a manifesto against Christian nationalism, which explores how to view history from a Christian perspective.

Augustine devotes much of the book to retelling previous Roman history, because the correct view of history, one that is steeped in healthy theology, is the best cure for the sin of Christian nationalism. But it is also important to remember that religious nationalism is not unique to Christianity. Patriotism can be a natural idol for any religion, including secularism and atheism. Before we turn to Augustine, therefore, we will consider further the background of the Roman religious structure that made religious nationalism possible and thus laid the foundation also for Christian nationalism in the late Roman Empire. It is no exaggeration to say that without the deeply rooted pagan religious nationalism in the Roman world, Christian nationalism would not have existed in the Roman context.

History and Religion in the Roman State: A Retrospective

Understanding the existence of Roman religious nationalism requires us to go back to the beginning of Rome and its religious structure. According to Roman legend, the city began its life as a village on the Tiber river in the mid-eighth century BCE. Malaria plagued the settlement every summer, as the locale, while having the advantage of hills for easy military defense, also came with the disadvantage of having more mosquitoes than people in the village's early days.

Expansion slowly began in the fourth century, with wars against the neighboring Latins and the Samnites. At the end of the Pyrrhic War in 275 BCE, the Romans gained control over the entire Italian Peninsula. And with their victory over Carthage in the Second Punic War (218–202 BCE), the Romans acquired a Mediterranean-wide empire. Their success in these ventures impressed and puzzled contemporaries from neighboring civilizations. The Greek historian Polybius, who spent nearly twenty years as a hostage in Rome in the mid-second century BCE, was convinced that the Romans' success was the result of their successful government as a Republic, which had checks and balances and did not allow any one individual to gain excessive power. The Romans themselves, however, had a different answer: they believed that their military success was predicated on the gods' favor.

The Roman national epic, Vergil's *Aeneid*, was composed in the Augustan Age and published in 19 BCE, but many of the ideas it contains about the divinely ordained destiny of Roman greatness likely go back centuries earlier. Specifically, the myths about Aeneas go back to at least the third century BCE, when another poet, Naevius, published an epic, *The Punic War*, that included some of the same stories and the general message of divine favor for Rome. The *Aeneid* follows a Trojan demigod hero, Aeneas, the son of a Trojan prince and the goddess of love Venus, who dramatically escapes from the burning city of Troy, leading his young son by the hand and carrying his aged father on his back. The image became iconic in Roman art as a symbol of filial piety. Aeneas also manages to lose his wife during the escape, but that was part of the gods' plans in mind for the hero, so all turns out just fine for everyone else. At any rate, the idea of Aeneas as chosen by the gods, especially by Zeus, to found a new Troy in Italy undergirds the epic and sets the foundation for Roman manifest destiny.

Moreover, legends about Aeneas and the founding of Rome are not the only ones to present this message of unique divine favor for Rome and therefore its exceptional place among all city-states of the world. According to other legends, transmitted by the Augustan-era historian Livy, the second king of Rome, Numa Pompilius, formulated the ideal of *pax deorum*—peace with the gods. The concept of *pax deorum* seems to have continued from that point on, emphasizing the key bargain: as long as Romans respected the gods and worshiped them appropriately, the state would remain undefeated. On the flip side, however, any defeat indicated divine displeasure.

Military defeat or any other state-wide disaster required the work of experts—the members of the various priestly colleges—to ascertain the cause of the divine wrath and the appropriate course of action to expiate for it. Then in cases of particularly horrific disasters, such as dramatic military defeat, the Sibylline Books of prophecy were consulted for assistance. Expiation measures could range from sacrifices to certain gods, to rituals for the purification of the city, to the construction of a new temple for a particular deity. Following two particularly devastating military defeats, the Sibylline Books required the Romans to bury alive two Greeks and two Gauls in the Forum Boarium (Cattle Market). These were the only times when the Romans diverged from their general distaste for human sacrifice. Although these desperate measures were periodically needed to expiate for military defeats elsewhere, the city of Rome itself would not be captured again until 410 CE after the infamous Gallic sack of Rome in 397 BCE—a particularly shameful episode in Roman history, which imbued the Romans with fear and hatred of the Gauls for generations to come.[6]

Rome's subsequent history shows that Polybius was wrong in attributing Rome's success to its form of government. Roman success in conquering and subsequently maintaining an empire continued unabated long after its Republican form of government collapsed in the late first century BCE. For Romans, the proof of the success of *pax deorum* in making and keeping their empire great was in the proverbial pudding.

Remarkably, Christians, just like the Romans, seemed to buy into the idea of divine favor for the Roman Empire, setting the stage for a new cultural sin. This is why when the city of Rome was sacked by the Goths in 410 CE, the outcry and shock of Roman Christians, whose religion was now the official state religion, was just as powerful as that of their pagan neighbors. The pagans were struggling to understand how the Roman Empire could survive in a world without Rome and were blaming the Christians for what they viewed as evidence of violation of *pax deorum*. The Christians, in the meanwhile, were stunned that God could allow this disaster to occur and were struggling to envision the survival of Christianity in a world without Rome.

The reactions of both groups to the events of 410 CE show the strong feeling of religious nationalism. For both groups, both the cause of their religious

---

6. For a study of the Roman processing of defeat during the Roman Republic, see Jessica Clark, *Triumph in Defeat: Military Loss and the Roman Republic* (Oxford: Oxford University Press, 2014).

nationalism and their coping mechanism in processing the trauma and shock of the sack of Rome were to cling to their respective vision of history. In other words, the debate of pagans and Christians over how to understand the sack of Rome correctly—and whom to blame for this disaster—was at its core a debate over the correct telling of Roman history. Ultimately, by providing a Christ-centered consolation through a revised history of Rome, Augustine both confronted the cultural Christians around him in their sin and attempted to remove it. Before we consider how exactly Augustine did this, it is helpful to consider briefly some representative manifestations of the Roman pagan religious nationalism in the same period. As these examples show, not everyone took the direct approach in criticizing others in the state and blaming them for the disaster. For some other writers from this period, it appears that denial was not just a river in Egypt.

Two Dates with the Ghost of Glory Past

In the year 416 CE, a Gallic aristocrat, Rutilius Namatianus, undertook a sea voyage home to southern Gaul from Rome, where he had briefly held the distinguished post of *praefectus urbis*, prefect of Rome, one of the most prestigious political posts at the time. With what could be construed as an overinflated view of his own importance, Rutilius wrote an epic poem about his journey, *A Voyage Home to Gaul*. Invoking Rome as a goddess early on in the work, Rutilius (who appears to have remained a lifelong pagan in an increasingly Christian world) speaks of the eternal city and its empire as the pinnacle of all creation. It is blessed by all the gods and is a blessing to all mankind. Its many military achievements are legendary, and its temples still gleam proudly, a reminder of the victories that the gods have formerly bestowed on Rome and promising many more to come.

Rutilius leaves the glorious city overcome with emotion over all that it stands for, but finds consolation in telling (in appropriately elegiac verse, formerly reserved for love poetry) of the beauties of the coastline that his ship hugs on its journey home. The Roman Empire is still a wonder to behold, even as there are hints of decline—"from precedents we discern that towns can die," he notes upon visiting the coastal Etruscan town of Populonia.

The poem is artistically beautiful but rather saccharine in content, as one considers the realities of Rutilius's day. First, his waxing poetic about the eternal city ignores its diminished importance over the course of the previous century and a half. Constantine had moved the capital of the empire to Constantinople almost a century earlier. But even earlier than that, during the rule of Diocletian and the Tetrarchy in the late third century, the capital of the Western half of the empire was moved from Rome to Mediolanum (modern-day Milan). And in 402 CE, during Rutilius's lifetime, the regional capital moved once again, this time from Mediolanum to Ravenna. But second, mentioned obliquely, only in the few brief and acerbic remarks about the wicked Goths, is the most important event of Rutilius's lifetime: the horrific sack of Rome by the Goths in 410 CE.

What was it like for Rutilius to be prefect of Rome just a few years after a violent and devastating sack of the city? Traces of destruction were still visible everywhere, and rebuilding was ongoing. Trauma for the residents was significant. Many chose to leave. Refugees from Rome, whose number of residents exceeded one million for much of the period from the Age of Augustus on, fled to other parts of the empire. Augustine's North Africa was a particularly popular destination. All of this means that Rutilius was governing a city that was, in many ways, a shell of its former self—much less populated, poorer, and stunned.

None of this is visible, however, in Rutilius's mini epic. The only hint of enduring trouble lies in his decision to sail to Gaul from Rome instead of traveling overland. As he points out, the roads are still not safe because of roving Goths. When reading Rutilius, unless one knows the context in which he lived and wrote, one might imagine that Rome was still the untouched and unrivaled capital of the empire, as blessed by the gods as it always has been.

But Rutilius was not alone in his conscious rewriting of the present to offer a vision of timeless Roman greatness. Writing about a decade before the sack of Rome, Claudian was aware of the coming danger. He wrote his own epic about the conflict, *The Gothic War*, although he did not live to see the sack of Rome. However, his most famous poem, "The Old Man of Verona," shows a similar manipulation of history as that seen in Rutilius's epic.[7]

The hero of Claudian's poem is a farmer who has lived the entirety of his long life on the same farm. Born in this very farmhouse, he lives there still. In fact, the poem's title is a bit of a misnomer: although Verona is just down the road from his farm, it might as well be as far as India to our hero, says Claudian. So attached is this farmer to his farm as to have never traveled even to that nearby city. But, asserts Claudian, this farmer is happier than those who have chosen other professions. He is certainly happier than soldiers or tradesmen who travel to far-off lands.

Tombstones for Roman soldiers in military towns across the empire show that Claudian is not merely being hypothetical. Standard information on tombstones

---

7. Nadya Williams, "Once Upon a Time Near Verona: Is the Rootedness of the Farmer a Christian or a Pagan Ideal?," *Plough*, July 25, 2022, https://www.plough.com/en/topics/culture/literature/once-upon-a-time-near-verona.

for military personnel includes the city of their birth. So we know that Verona and other towns in northern Italy had been popular recruitment grounds for Roman legions since the early empire. Once recruited, these farmers-turned-legionaries traveled to far-off lands, and never returned. The Romans had a policy of stationing recruits far from home, so the recruits from Verona were likely to end up in Britain or the Germanic frontier. Once they finished their twenty-five years of service, they could live out their retirement in the town that had grown up around the military fort where they had served. But, again, this farmer rejects such opportunities in favor of staying put. Even more striking, though, is Claudian's comment that this farmer marks the year not by names of consuls but by seasons of crops. Politics, in other words, have no meaning for him. No emperors are mentioned. His farm is a timeless bubble of Roman Republican values.

Reading Rutilius's epic, one would never know that the sack of Rome had occurred or that Rome was no longer the capital of the empire. Likewise, reading Claudian's poem, one would never know that the Roman Republic, in which the consuls were the chief political leaders, ever gave way to the empire and emperors. The agricultural ideal presented in the poem recalls such Roman heroes as Cincinnatus, a leader from the early Republic who gave up a dictatorship and returned to his farm to live in peace. It also brings to mind Vergil's *Georgics*, another idealized and timeless glorification of agriculture in poetry, written in the age of Augustus as part of the official state propaganda about the return to the Golden Age that the First Citizen's rule epitomized.

The poems of both Rutilius and Claudian are, ultimately, imaginary dates with the ghosts of Rome's glories past, and that is precisely what makes them such valuable witnesses to pagan religious nationalism. We see an attachment to the greatness of Rome, to the point of denying any changes that ever occurred in the political structure. The myth of *Roma aeterna* does not recognize that Rome is no longer the capital. Instead, the attachment to this myth merely seeks out culprits for any damage to its idol. But if Rutilius Namatianus and Claudian are not revealing directly what they knew of the events of the early fifth century, Augustine, by contrast, devotes the entire first book of *City of God* to documenting these experiences.

A City Sacked: Interviewing Survivors

Early in Vergil's *Aeneid*, the hero of the epic dramatically tells Dido, the queen of Carthage, on whose shores he was shipwrecked, the events of the sack of Troy, which he witnessed himself before his secret flight from the city. The culminating scene of Aeneas's account is an event that highlights the disruption of all civilized norms inherent in the violent capture of a city—the savage slaughter of the king of Troy, Priam. Achilles's son, Neoptolemus, infiltrates the royal palace where the aged king lived. He proceeds to kill one of the king's sons in front of him. Then he drags the king himself to the altar of Jupiter. Usurping the rituals normally used for animal sacrifice, Neoptolemus murders the king there, fouling the altar with his blood.

Vergil certainly intended this narrative to be horrifically shocking. There is no honor in slaughtering a defenseless old man in his own home, and on an altar, no less. Yet audiences familiar with the Greek version of the myths surrounding the sack of Troy would have remembered the many other atrocities that occurred when the Greeks captured and sacked the city. These included the killing of all men, including Hector's infant son, who was thrown off the city walls. Those who survived did not fare better. The retellings of the myths in Greek tragedy emphasize the capture and rape of the Trojan women, who were subsequently sold into slavery. But in this case, myths were not mere myths.

The sack of ancient cities was always a violent and horrific event. While the fall of some cities became more famous than others—such as the sack of Melos told by Thucydides or the capture of Jerusalem by Titus—the expectation was generally the same. In any captured city, the conquerors would kill all or most adult males. They would then sell all survivors, mostly women and children, into slavery. The rape of girls and women was common in the process. In fact, evidence exists that it was a common military strategy.[8] Furthermore, although at other times people could expect safety when sheltering at the altars or temples of gods, this practice was not guaranteed to be respected during the sack of a city, as the slaughter of Priam at an altar shows.

Book 1 of Augustine's *City of God* is devoted to Augustine's summary of the experiences of the survivors of the sack of Rome and responses to survivors' complaints about their own fate and the fate of those who did not make it out of Rome alive to tell the story. Since many of the survivors poured into North Africa, including Augustine's city of Hippo Regius, the bishop likely took the opportunity to interview the survivors. Although Augustine was not the warm and caring pastor in the mold of Cyprian, he did take his duties to his flock

---

8. Kathy Gaca has written extensively on this concept of systematic rape and enslavement (also known as andrapodization) of war captives. See in particular Gaca, "The Andrapodizing of War Captives in Greek Historical Memory," *Transactions of the American Philological Association* 140 (2010): 117–61.

seriously. His writings suggest that he understood the need to listen to refugees and counsel them about their trauma, especially as it deeply shook their faith. So what kinds of stories did these survivors tell him? Just how typical was the sack of Rome of 410 CE?[9]

Chaos and violence ruled when the city was initially breached and overrun. The conquerors' treatment of pagans and Christians was equally harsh. The Goths were not known for their gentleness, and many civilians were slaughtered. In addition, survivors told Augustine stories of widespread rape of women, including some virgins who had taken vows for the church. In the aftermath of such violation, some women committed suicide, a consequence that troubled Augustine more than any other.

The suffering of all who were in the city of Rome at the time of the sack was significant. Many were captured by the Goths and sold into slavery. Others lost much or all of their property when their wealth was carried off by the conquerors. Stories abounded of people who had hidden possessions and were then tortured by the Goths until, overcome with unbearable pain and agony, they revealed the hiding places. Some refused to reveal their treasures and were killed. Others, who had no hidden treasures to reveal, were tortured nevertheless, as the Goths did not believe their claims of poverty. The Goths' greed, it appears from the stories the survivors told Augustine, knew no bounds.

For those Romans who were unharmed themselves in the sack but lost loved ones, there was yet the pain of not being able to mourn or bury their relatives, whose bodies were desecrated and never returned to families for burial. Last but not least, once the Goths receded and left the sacked shell of a city behind, famine moved in and consumed at least as many victims as the initial sack and slaughter. It is no wonder that so many fled in the months that followed. Rome, overpopulated since at least the first century CE, had always depended on an organized system of food supply from across the empire. Ships laden with grain sailed in a steady stream from Alexandria to Rome for almost half a millennium. Once the violent sack disrupted that supply and emptied the city's food stores, Rome's high population became a liability instead of a strength.

Since Aeneas, the hero of the *Aeneid*, fled Troy as it was being sacked by the Greeks and went on to become the ancestor of the founders of Rome, it seems appropriate that the account of the sack of Troy in the *Aeneid* was on Augustine's mind as the obvious comparison to the sack of Rome by the Goths.

---

9. For an intriguing narrative of the fall of Rome from the perspective of the Goths and Alaric, see Douglas Boin, *Alaric the Goth: An Outsider's History of the Fall of Rome* (New York: Norton, 2020).

This comparison brought out an important uniqueness in the sack of Rome. Yes, many of the standard atrocities, including rape and slaughter of women and other noncombatants did happen during the sack of Rome. Yet the Goths, who were themselves Christians (albeit of the Arian variety, which the Council of Nicaea had declared heretical), spared the Romans who hid in Christian places of worship. So Augustine emphasizes that all the horrors that happened during the Gothic sack of Rome were utterly normal, but the acts of clemency and sparing of those hiding in Christian churches were miraculous:

> But what was novel, was that savage barbarians showed themselves in so gentle a guise, that the largest churches were chosen and set apart for the purpose of being filled with the people to whom quarter was given, and that in them none were slain, from them none forcibly dragged; that into them many were led by their relenting enemies to be set at liberty, and that from them none were led into slavery by merciless foes.[10]

The sparing of those who chose to hide in churches is, in Augustine's view, an example of God working to show mercy. Furthermore, the safety that both pagans and Christians who hid in churches were able to find in the process is a reminder that throughout all previous Roman history, God has always shown favor and mercy to both the good and the wicked. One could never earn God's mercy, but it has always been a free gift to some. This concept of God's presence in previous Roman history proves central to Augustine's response to the lamentations of the traumatized survivors. Those Christians who suffered through the sack of Rome ought to model themselves on the example of Job, urged Augustine. But they needed to rethink their view of God's role in the history of Rome. The eternal city is the city of God, not Rome, the city they have idolized here on earth.[11]

Augustine Responds

Sometime in the early 350s CE, around the same time that Augustine was born in North Africa to a family with more aspirations than wealth, one of the wealthiest and most noble families in the Roman Empire welcomed a son. Pontius

---

10. Augustine, *City of God* 1.7, trans. Marcus Dods (Peabody, MA: Hendrickson, 2011).
11. Peter Brown's biography of Augustine is excellent grounding for Augustine's intellectual and theological life story: *Augustine of Hippo: A Biography* (Berkeley: University of California Press, 2013).

Meropius Paulinus had blood that was the bluest shade of blue and a family with land holdings all over modern-day France, Spain, and Italy. If there were a list of "top ten richest Roman families" of the period, this family would have been somewhere near the top of the list, competing for the top spot with close relatives, such as Melania the Elder. In proper Roman fashion, Paulinus's family used their wealth to launch their son into politics. The family's spectacular wealth and influence is a reminder of the continued influence of pagans in the Roman world long after the age of Constantine.

But Paulinus's political career, fast-tracked at first, suddenly stalled after the assassination of the emperor Gratian in 383 CE. Imperial transitions, especially violent ones, habitually upended the political careers of previous favorites, as each emperor wanted to advance those he considered loyal to himself alone. Retreating abruptly from politics, Paulinus spent some time studying with Ambrose of Milan, whose teaching was instrumental in the conversion of Augustine. Paulinus then married a Christian woman and was baptized. After the couple lost their only child, a daughter, mere days after her birth, they gave away their possessions and resolved to live out the rest of their lives in service to God. Shortly before the sack of Rome by the Goths, Paulinus was named bishop of Nola in southern Italy. He then had the misfortune of living through the sack of Nola by the Goths, which appears to have been similar to the sack of Rome in its brutality. We sometimes forget, after all, that the Goths did not have Rome as their only target. They pillaged their way through Italy.

For Christians throughout the Roman Empire, Paulinus was little short of a sensation during his lifetime—a philanthropist who had given away not just some of his wealth, but absolutely all of it. One of the few such stories from Late Antique Christianity that was even more extreme was that of Melania the Elder, the fabulously rich relative of Paulinus, who herself had given away all of her formidable fortune to become a Desert Mother.

Augustine knew Paulinus personally and interviewed him about the sack of Nola. Paulinus, whom Augustine mentions in book 1 of *City of God*, was for Augustine a model of how to react to the savage treatment by the Goths because Paulinus was genuinely resigned to God in all things. Long before the sack, he had already given away his massive wealth and thus had no material concerns to fret over when Nola was sacked. Having lived a life of service to God and his local community before the sack, he continued in his mission as though the sack never happened. The grieving survivors of the sack of Rome would do well, therefore, to model their pattern of thought after individuals like Paulinus and, of course, Job, the ultimate biblical model of suffering. So what kinds of wisdom did Augustine present for the traumatized survivors of the sack of Rome, and how did he respond to their specific concerns?

In addition to presenting Paulinus and Job as models for God-honoring suffering, Augustine also provided specific responses to the particular traumas that he learned from his interviews with survivors of the sack of Rome. First and foremost, as noted above, Augustine emphasizes the sparing of those pagans and Christians who hid in churches as nothing short of miraculous. It is striking, Augustine notes, that pagans who hid in churches were spared by the Goths along with the Christians. This is a reminder of God's favor to both groups.

To highlight the exceptional nature of God's favor, Augustine uses previous Roman history, citing Vergil's *Aeneid*, the poetry of Horace, and a speech of Caesar from Sallust's *Catilinarian Conspiracy*, listing the customary horrors awaiting any individuals living in a conquered city. Hiding in the temple of Juno, who was the queen of the gods, did nothing to spare the Trojans during the sack of Troy. By contrast, "these churches of Christ were chosen even by the savage barbarians as the fit scenes for humility and mercy."[12] And as Caesar's speech shows, even the most talented commanders in previous Roman history could not restrain their troops from ravaging a conquered city. Clearly, the sparing of churches and those who hid in them during the sack of Rome was the work of God and his direct provision for the people.

This is part of Augustine's answer to those who complained that God abandoned them or wondered why God did not spare the Christians from suffering. Instead of thinking that God abandoned them, they should compare and contrast the sack of Rome with other such events in history, and the difference will show God's active involvement on their behalf. In addition, Augustine reminds them not to blame God for their misfortune; instead, think of the example of Job, who experienced suffering not because God abandoned him but precisely because God had called him to suffer.

The substance of Augustine's response, especially his repeated references to Job as a model for seeing suffering as a calling through such events as the sack of Rome, readily resembles Cyprian's response a century and a half earlier to the suffering of his flock at the time of another crisis—the double hit of pandemic and persecution. This is no coincidence. Both bishops were models of theological orthodoxy in their discussions of Christian suffering. But the similarity of their responses also suggests a similarity of mindset in the late Roman Christian communities at times of suffering. The nature of the crisis changed, but the believers'

---

12. Augustine, *City of God* 1.4.

sinful processing of it remained the same, visible especially in the question of why Christians suffer the same things as the pagans around them.

And yet, as Augustine notes, the religious identity of the enemies was not so different from that of some of their victims. After all, the Goths were Christian, and that is why they spared those who sought asylum in churches. So why were they so utterly brutal to the residents of Rome, and how did they reconcile their faith with their actions? In reading Augustine's rebuke for those who mourned the loss of loved ones or property or freedom or bodily purity, one wonders if it truly was wrong for them to mourn such losses and bemoan their faith. Was it wrong of them to ask God why he allowed such misfortunes to happen to them? Even Job mourned the loss of his family, wealth, and health, even as he continued to cling to his belief in God's goodness and faithfulness.

Ultimately, Augustine's emphasis on the correct way to mourn suggests his own trauma at processing the sack of Rome and what the city stood for even for him. In other words, the sin of idolizing safety, wealth, and personal well-being, all of which were connected to the prosperity of Rome and the empire, may have been his own sin too, just as much as it was the sin of the survivors who escaped. In preaching to others, Augustine could have been preaching the truth to himself as well. It is possible, after all, to know what is true yet recognize a sinful reaction within oneself.

As we read Augustine with our own knowledge of the events that were to follow, it is striking to reflect that at the end of his life, the elderly bishop would find himself in the same position as the unfortunate refugees to whom he ministered. The Vandals invaded North Africa, and laid siege to Augustine's town of Hippo Regius in 430 CE. Augustine, who died during the siege, at least did not live to see the city occupied and ravaged in much the same way as Rome in 410 CE. But he likely did spend his final days praying for the safety of his flock.

Theologically Sound History as the Antidote to Christian Nationalism

"The glorious city of God is my theme in this work. . . . I have undertaken its defense against those who prefer their own gods to the Founder of this city . . . as the plan of this work we have undertaken requires, and as occasion offers, we must speak also of the earthly city, which, though it be mistress of the nations, is itself ruled by its lust of rule."[13] So wrote Augustine in the prologue to the *City of God*, thus introducing his distinctly Christian philosophy of history. This view of history, he hoped, would be both the perfect antidote and the consolation for both pagans and Christians who mourned the sack of Rome.

While Augustine's analysis of the sack of Rome is largely limited to book 1, which we considered above, the rest of *City of God* expands on that analysis. Augustine uses Roman history to show that everything Rome and the symbols of its superiority, such as the altar and statue of Victory discussed at the beginning of this chapter, stand for has always been a myth. Blinded by their pagan beliefs, earlier Romans simply did not realize this. Furthermore, copying blindly the religious nationalism of their pagan neighbors, those Christians who felt their world shatter with the sack of Rome needed that same antidote: the consolation of Christian history. That is precisely what Augustine goes on to provide in the remainder of his book.

It is difficult to overemphasize the difference in Augustine's historical outlook not just from previous Greek and Roman historians but also from Christian ones, such as Eusebius. Most previous pagan Roman historians began their works with the founding of Rome and brought their narrative to their own day. The most famous Roman history, that of Livy, was actually titled *Ab Urbe Condita*— "From the Founding of the City." Both Luke in writing Acts and, later, Eusebius in writing *The History of the Church* challenged that model by beginning their respective works with the founding of the church, thus emphasizing the significance of the church as a separate kingdom with its own history that is worth documenting. Pagan and Christian writers alike simply brought the narrative of their historical works to their own day, stopping there. Augustine was not satisfied with this model because it left out the most important part of the story—its conclusion.

While previous historians, pagan and Christian alike, wrote their histories as retrospectives on the past, explaining how the unfolding events led to the present situation, Augustine treated his history of Rome in *City of God* as future oriented. Using the sack of Rome as his starting point, his narrative of previous Roman history was not meant to explain the present but to point to the future and explain why that future matters much more than the sinful past of the Roman state, or its mournful present after the sack of Rome. In that future, there is no earthly Rome, but the city of God shines eternally bright. In this regard, Augustine's historical philosophy is pastoral and echoes such earlier pastoral consolations as

---

13. Augustine, *City of God*, prologue.

Cyprian's reminders to his flock: the painful present is but momentary, but glorious eternity with God is the Christians' reward.

Instead of longing for eternity, many Romans, both pagans and Christians, were idealizing the Roman past. The sack of Rome, therefore, merely made them long for that indeterminate time in the past where, for instance, Claudian's "Old Man of Verona" resides. If only one could turn back the clock and live in that age, during the height of the Pax Romana! Yet Augustine's narrative of Roman history seeks to disabuse his audiences of idealizing that past by exposing its significant flaws. We cannot unpack the complexities of Augustine's argument in its entirety, but representative examples will suffice.

As we saw earlier, one of the main arguments that the pagans used to blame the Christians for the sack of Rome is that the Christians' abandonment of the pagan gods violated the *pax deorum*, a quid-pro-quo, bargain-oriented peace with the gods on which Roman religion had been built. In response to this argument, Augustine provides an exhaustive review of disasters in Roman history before the birth of Christianity. "Those evils which alone are dreaded by the heathen— famine, pestilence, war, pillage, captivity, massacre" show that the pagan gods have not protected the Romans as much as they might think they had.[14] It is hypocritical, Augustine notes, for the pagans to blame the Christian God for their misfortune now, whereas in their earlier history they repeatedly did not blame the Christians for other disasters. That said, the worst disaster of all, thinks Augustine, has been something that the Romans never really acknowledged: the utter corruption of the Roman character through vice of all kinds, including vice encouraged directly by Roman religion through religious festivals.

For Augustine, merely proving that the Christians are not to blame for the collapse of the empire is not enough. In books 4–5, he goes on to argue that the success of the Roman Empire, which the pagans have touted as evidence of their divine privilege, is precisely because of God's will to make it prosper. First, earlier Romans were more virtuous and perhaps merited such favor, even though they did not believe in God. More important, as Augustine unpacks in the rest of *City of God* through a survey of not only Roman history but also the entirety of the history covered in the Bible, God is sovereign over all history, although sometimes we can only try to guess how and why he worked through particular events at particular times. Our knowledge right now is undoubtedly limited. Yet the beauty of the city of God that awaits us lies in part in the secure knowledge that everything will work out at the end. Current history should frighten us less if

---

14. Augustine, *City of God*, 3.1.

we know how it will end. Or, rather, as Augustine's discussion of hell in book 21 notes, our own reactions to current history might frighten us more in light of the coming judgment. Augustine concludes in book 22 that the saints can look forward to an eternal Sabbath of rest with God. "There we shall rest and see, see and love, love and praise."[15]

Conclusion

In rewriting Roman history in *City of God*, Augustine encourages us, just as he seems to have been encouraging himself, to confront a question that turned out to be deeply countercultural: What does it mean to approach history first and foremost as a Christian rather than a resident of any earthly state? To answer this question, he makes a complex and compelling argument for not idolizing the history of the greatest empire his world had ever known. Rather, he proposes that sometimes it is acceptable to let it all burn down—as indeed it did in the hands of the Goths in 410 CE.

Augustine was not trying to say that Rome did not matter. Rome and its history certainly mattered a lot to him, as the plethora of historical references and quotes from many Roman historical writers show. Although he believed it mattered a lot, he wanted to convict those who believed that it mattered most. For Augustine there was a difference between placing value on something as important and placing value on it as the most important—a distinction that matters as we think of Christian nationalism today as well.

Ultimately, as Augustine reminds us, theologically sound writing of history requires acknowledging God's working through history, and that changes the narrative. This message, Augustine thought, would comfort both pagans and Christians who were living through the collapse of an empire and were trying to process that trauma. This message, though, is even more necessary than ever for Americans today, as debates over the correct telling of US history abound. At the time of this writing, multiple states are considering bills that will have an impact on the teaching of American history in public schools and universities.

The questions under debate are, without a doubt, challenging. Was America founded as a Christian nation? How do we recognize the horrific sins perpetrated against so many groups of people as part of American history? Should we publicly discuss these sins and teach about them in public schools and universities, or is it

---

15. Augustine, *City of God*, 22.30.

better to leave them in the past, as some suggest? How do we talk about historical trauma, such as that stemming from the institution of slavery, and recognize its ramifications on our society and churches to this day? And perhaps most important, what happens if we refuse to talk about such painful topics as systemic structural racism and focus entirely on presenting American history positively? Where does this kind of idolatry of a nation's past take Christians?[16]

The debate over these questions is unfolding largely between some politicians and members of the public, who have made these questions into a political shibboleth, rather than professional historians, secular and Christian alike, who overwhelmingly agree on the importance of teaching history honestly and openly.[17] The range of possible answers among those who have turned this issue into a political battleground echoes Augustine's concerns quite closely. Just as the faith of Roman Christians who idolized Rome was shaken by the city's fall to the Goths, so does the earlier idolatry of America shake the faith of some Christians, who have come to see the flaws in the nation's history. At the same time, other Christians have found the idol of nationalism to be so deeply rooted as to refuse to recognize any flaws in the nation's past at all.

Numerous American historians and theologians have written on these issues in ways that are convicting and, in some cases, deeply pastoral. Here are several recent examples. In *Was America Founded as a Christian Nation?*, John Fea provides an overview of the arguments on both sides of the debate but recognizes, just as Augustine did, the importance of thinking historically for being able to understand the problems latent in the very question in the book's title. Our identity as Christians should lie in God and thus should not be connected to idolizing the nation's history as Christian. Ours is not the city of God.

Different philosophies of history and thinking historically likewise play a role in John Wilsey's consideration of American Christian nationalism specifically through a study of American exceptionalism: a belief present since the days of the Puritans that God was working particularly special plans through

---

16. For a thoughtful and poignant response to such legislations, see John Fea, "An Open Letter to American History Teachers: Stop Teaching Critical Race Theory," *Current*, May 28, 2021, https://currentpub.com/2021/05/28/an-open-letter-to-american-history-teachers-stop-teaching-critical-race-theory/. For particulars on such proposals in my own current home state of Georgia, please see Nadya Williams, "National Sins and Gag Orders," *Current*, March 3, 2022, https://currentpub.com/2022/03/03/national-sins-and-gag-orders/.

17. For an example of a politically and theologically conservative Christian historian's honest assessment of the sins in American history and the importance of that honest assessment in providing hope for the future, see Wilfred McClay's textbook survey of American history for middle school and high school ages, *Land of Hope: An Invitation to the Great American Story* (New York: Encounter, 2019).

America. Deeply critical of the idea of America as a Christian nation, Wilsey also explains the dangers of such distortion of both history and the gospel for our understanding of God's role in history.[18] Such distortions bear a remarkable resemblance to the ways pagan Romans thought about Roman exceptionalism as a state favored by the gods and destined to a greatness unlike any other.

Christian nationalism and the desire to control a certain telling of American history go hand in hand, as Fea and Wilsey show. In addition, few have done as much as Jemar Tisby to bring attention to the consequences of not address-ing historical trauma. Ignoring trauma stemming from systemic racism in American churches across centuries has only resulted in more sin. In *The Color of Compromise*, Tisby provides a moving and painful history that confronts the idolatry of America's past by some and calls for repentance before reconcil-iation.[19] The history he presents shows in practice the danger of idolizing the nation's history instead of seeking truth.

In *Reading While Black*, Esau McCaulley picks up Tisby's message from a pastoral angle, as he documents the ways in which injustices of the past have affected an African American reading of the Scriptures.[20] The burden of history has been heavy, and by denying its weight, some evangelicals have preferred the idolatry of their nation's past over seeking justice and repentance now.

Last, in *We the Fallen People*, Tracy McKenzie urges Christians to view previous and current American history specifically through the lens of original sin. If we admit that we are a deeply fallen people rather than heretically believ-ing that we are good, it will perhaps make it easier to admit to the horrific sins present in our nation's history. The admission of sin is a necessary prerequisite for acknowledging the need for the correct response to American history: the need for genuine and sorrowful repentance.[21] Augustine would have agreed wholeheartedly.

Overall, calls for repentance, collective and individual, are a common thread in recent publications that critique Christian nationalism in America. Yet at the time of this writing, thirty-seven states are considering bills that would outlaw

---

18. John D. Wilsey, *American Exceptionalism and Civil Religion: Reassessing the History of an Idea* (Downers Grove, IL: IVP Academic, 2015); and *One Nation Under God? An Evangelical Critique of Christian America* (Eugene, OR: Pickwick, 2014).

19. Jemar Tisby, *The Color of Compromise: The Truth About the American Church's Complicity in Racism* (Grand Rapids: Zondervan, 2019).

20. Esau McCaulley, *Reading While Black: African American Biblical Interpretation as an Exercise in Hope* (Downers Grove, IL: IVP Academic, 2020).

21. Tracy McKenzie, *We the Fallen People: The Founders and the Future of American Democracy* (Downers Grove, IL: IVP Academic, 2021).

or significantly restrict teaching in public schools and universities that there is still structural racism in this country. At the other end of the spectrum, a number of churches, such as First Presbyterian Church in Augusta, Georgia, and Historic First Presbyterian Church in Montgomery, Alabama, have chosen to repent openly and publicly of their historic racism.[22] The sorrowful admission of "the sins of our fathers" that churches have had to acknowledge remind us what Augustine believed all along: theologically sound history, just like a theologically sound sermon, should comfort the afflicted and afflict the comfortable. If we truly look toward the "glorious city of God," religious nationalism has no place in our worldview.

---

22. Thabiti Anyabwile, "A Burden Removed: A Biblical Path for Removing the Racism of Our Forefathers," *The Gospel Coalition*, November 18, 2019, https://www.thegospelcoalition.org/blogs/thabiti-anyabwile/burden-removed-biblical-path-removing-racism-forefathers/.

9

The Siren Call
of the Desert

*Why Running Away from
the Church Cannot Solve the
Problem of Cultural Sin*

SOMETIME IN THE MID-280S CE, EARLY IN THE REIGN OF
Emperor Diocletian, a Christian ascetic who had spent much of his life up until
that point quietly organizing monastic communities in Egypt, decided to break
contact with society altogether. This ascetic, Antony, moved into an abandoned
Roman fort by the Nile to pursue holiness alone. It is ironically appropriate that
he chose an abandoned fort as his place of refuge, but not for the reasons that he
thought. Various pilgrims and others who were likewise fascinated with the idea
of running away from society and moving into the desert began trickling into
the vicinity of his fort, effectively surrounding the shut-away saint. In his fort,
Antony was increasingly under siege from like-minded quitters. Perhaps he put
an extra bar on the gate.

Rumors about him continued to spread unabated until one day, twenty years
after he had disappeared inside the fort, a crowd of pilgrims in search of a miracle
broke in. They were amazed to find the ascetic, Antony, looking miraculously

youthful and beautiful, unaltered in his appearance from twenty years of confinement, malnutrition, and daily battles with demons.

When Athanasius, bishop of Alexandria, published his *Life of Antony* in 360 CE, a mere four years after Antony's death, it became an instant bestseller. It inspired an entire new subgenre of hagiography: the lives of desert saints. But people did not want to read only about Antony. Many who learned about him wanted to see Antony, or even *to be* Antony. The Egyptian desert, in a surprising plot twist, became filled with sightseers and with other aspiring saints over the next century, as the monastic movement and the ascetic movement both experienced significant growth. As Athanasius said poignantly, the desert became a city.

Strikingly, the movement appears to have been remarkably inclusive of women—or, rather, women ascetics made sure to include themselves in this movement, sometimes choosing to live entirely alone, and at other times, in monastic communities, sometimes cross-dressing as men to be allowed to join. One of the most spectacular stories is that of Mary of Egypt, whose biography would go on to fascinate generations of readers beyond antiquity—indeed, I first encountered her story in a survey of Medieval French literature in college. Born in Egypt in the mid-fourth century, she ran away from home at age twelve, right at the cusp of marriageable age. Renouncing all societal expectations, she instead spent the next seventeen years working in the sex industry in Alexandria, the vice capital of the region. But unlike most women trapped in the sex industry, her biographies emphasize that she chose this life and had no regrets.

Finally, bored with the Alexandrian vice scene and expressly mocking Christians, whose faith she considered ridiculous, Mary decided to travel to Jerusalem. Scandalously, she paid for her journey by sleeping with pilgrims traveling along—a reminder of the prevalence of cultural views about sex among Christians, a topic we explored in chapter 3. When she tried to enter the Church of the Holy Sepulchre in Jerusalem, she encountered a miracle: an invisible force barred her entry. Confronted in this unexpected way by the weight of her sinful life, she repented. Immediately afterward, she was able to enter the church, where she received a divine message telling her to move beyond the Jordan. So for the remaining nearly fifty years of her life, Mary lived in the desert across the Jordan, just like John the Baptist, who had originally preached in that very area. In fact, it was in the monastery of St. John the Baptist that she received communion before retiring into the desert for good, bringing with her nothing but three loaves of bread. Just as the meager five loaves that Jesus once blessed were able to feed thousands for a day, so too did Mary's three loaves last a lifetime.

Reading about the lives of the desert saints, such as Antony or Mary, is fascinating because they seem so bizarre to us, just as they did to their original audiences, albeit for different reasons. After all, who wants to live on three figs a day and one cup of water per week in the middle of the desert? Mortifying the flesh in a variety of ways—sleep deprivation, deliberately uncomfortable clothing and environment, self-denial of food and drink—is a constant in the stories of the desert saints, even if the precise shape that these themes take in each saint's life is different. But there is a surprise yet in store.

Even as these aspiring saints fled churches and people, aiming to live counter-cultural lives utterly devoid of sin, we see sin follow them nevertheless, personified in the *Life of Antony* by his continued battles with demons. Furthermore, this solution of moving into the desert was clearly not sustainable for increasing the holiness of the church at large. Living in community allows us to provide for others in a way that a life of solitude does not. We are left asking: Were saints like Antony or Mary ultimately choosing to act in self-interest? As it happens, we live in a society with a growing number of aspiring desert saints today, even though they may never have heard of the original movement.

In March 2017, the Barna Group, a private organization that studies "cultural trends related to values, beliefs, attitudes, and behaviors," published a profile of the growing segment of American Christians who "love Jesus but not the church."[1] These individuals, the study noted, tend to retain fairly orthodox beliefs, and agree that religion is positive. The largest difference between their lives and those of practicing Christians had to do with church attendance and related activities versus solitary spiritual practices. While a markedly greater proportion of those who "love Jesus but not the church" spent time "in nature for reflection," in meditation, and "practicing silence and/or solitude," practicing Christians and evangelicals were significantly more likely to read Scripture regularly, and attend groups or retreats. Like Antony, they have entered their fort and have chosen to live alone, at least as far as their spiritual lives are concerned. Many may have been burned by the church, its hypocrisy and sinfulness. So they long to follow God on their own. They wonder: How could this be wrong?

As we conclude this book about sinners and cultural Christians in early churches, this chapter examines stories of ascetics and desert saints as an alternative to the other stories considered throughout this book. One way to view them is as the quintessential what-if scenario that existed already in antiquity. If

---

1. "Meet Those who 'Love Jesus but Not the Church,'" *Barna*, March 30, 2017, https://www.barna.com/research/meet-love-jesus-not-church/.

churches have always been filled with people who longed for holiness but were cultural Christians all too prone to sin, what if the most dedicated faithful were to separate themselves wholly from the world and, therefore, all forms of temptation and cultural sin? Would this not be the key to living a holy life in this world?

As it happens, we have enough evidence to be able to see how such decisions turn out. Antony was not alone in his decision to seek solitude in the desert. Rather, a large number of desert saints, both male and female, elected to live such holy lives in the fourth and fifth centuries CE, and their stories enticed the imagination of believers from that time on. These stories of extravagant faith that still stemmed from deeply cultural sins allow us to confront the essential conundrum that we face in our churches today: people are sinful, and whenever (and wherever) sinners gather together, there will be sin. Because people are rooted in the culture around them, much of that sin will be inspired by cultural beliefs, so deeply ingrained that we cannot easily separate them from the gospel. At the same time, a Christian cannot live alone without the church, so the stories of the desert saints, varied yet similar, provide us with a poignant response to the growing number of individuals today who self-identify as Christians yet reject the church. Renouncing the church to serve God alone was then, and still is today, yet another form of cultural Christianity.

A Christian Theme Park:
Late Antique Christian Tourism

In the 420s CE, a Syrian holy man feeling beleaguered by the crowds that he attracted everywhere he went—so strong was his aura of holiness—decided to take a radical step to get some solitude at last. He moved to live in nearby ruins, selecting the top of a tall pillar, ten feet up from the ground, as his new permanent abode. To his surprise, the crowds only intensified, forcing him to move to increasingly taller pillars to separate himself from the people below. He settled, at last, on a pillar fifty feet high, where he spent the remaining thirty or so years of his life. The crowds, undeterred, kept on coming. The holy man ultimately resigned himself to a life of teaching the crowds all day, every day, spending the rest of his time in prayer until a peaceful death claimed him mid-prayer in 459 CE.

Simeon Stylites, the Pillar Saint, exemplifies the new phenomenon of saints as spectacles and tourist destinations in Late Antiquity. The steady stream of pilgrims who came to visit him from as far away as Constantinople is typical of this new phenomenon of Late Antique Christian tourism. His many visitors even included two different Byzantine emperors—Theodosius II and Leo I.[2] Ironically, because of his decision to move away from people and live atop a pillar, he only became a greater attraction than he was before, when his fame as a wise holy man and teacher was regional rather than international.

The image of a man delivering homilies, lectures, and advice from the top of a fifty-foot pillar seems more like a performer rather than a saint. Indeed, people like Simeon became common tourist attractions, whom pilgrims of various levels of religious devotion visited, much as we might visit a zoo or a museum. Similarly to Simeon, the objects of attraction themselves were not always thrilled, but that only made them all the more fascinating for prospective visitors, who desired to get a glimpse or a blessing. One of our best sources for this complex relationship between the desert saints and their tourist visitors comes from *Inquiry about the Monks of Egypt* by Rufinus of Aquileia.

From September 394 to early January 395, seven monks from Rufinus's monastery on the Mount of Olives in Jerusalem traveled around Egypt. They visited many individual monks and monastic communities from the Thebaid in the south to the delta town of Diolcos in the north. It appears that at least one of them kept copious notes from the trip, for after returning to Jerusalem he composed in Greek a travelogue account of the trip in first-person narrative. As one modern scholar describes it, "This work is one of the most innovative Christian writings to have been composed during the fourth century CE, and to this day it remains an indispensable primary source for contemporary Egyptian monastic practice and lore." But the author, for reasons we do not know, released it anonymously. Rufinus, himself a long-time devotee of asceticism and an experienced tourist of the Egyptian desert to boot, translated this work into Latin a little less than a decade later, demonstrating and facilitating the appeal of the travelogue for both Greek- and Latin-speaking audiences across the Roman Empire. More than a mere translation, Rufinus saw it as "a self-standing piece of monastic propaganda."[3]

Strikingly, Rufinus had spent years earlier in his life traveling around Egypt and had presumably seen some of the same sights. For whatever reason, he did not write a travelogue of his own. His personal familiarity with the locations

---

2. For a study of the desert saints as spectacles, see Georgia Frank, *The Memory of the Eyes: Pilgrims to Living Saints in Christian Late Antiquity* (Berkeley: University of California Press, 2001).

3. Andrew Cain, *Rufinus of Aquileia, Inquiry about the Monks in Egypt* (Washington, DC: Catholic University of America Press, 2019), 11–13.

and saints included in the volume, however, perhaps spurred him to translate it, assuring a much wider dissemination for the work.

Whatever his reasons for this translation, Rufinus's text provides us with a crucial window into understanding two different groups that were exhibiting culturally influenced Christianity in different ways. First, the monks who traveled with the original narrator, whose work Rufinus translated, present to us the perspective of the Christian tourists of the age and allow us to come up with a profile: Who traveled? Why did they take this trip? And in what ways does their act of tourism represent cultural Christianity? Second, Rufinus's narrative, supplemented by the many famous sayings of the Desert Fathers and Mothers reduced to pithy soundbites, provides insight into these desert saints themselves and their own mode of cultural Christianity. Ultimately, we will see that each of the two groups, while earnestly seeking God, was also proceeding from a deeply ingrained cultural background that had provided a framework for their actions.

Christian Tourism as the New Grand Tour

In the mid-second century CE, a pagan Greek writer with little imagination but an interest in meticulously documenting the culture, mythology, and history of his ancestral homeland, now long under Roman dominion, wrote an extensive travelogue and geographical treatise, *Description of Greece*. Pausanias's work is packed with information but extremely dry. He seems to have specialized in deglamorizing some of the most famous places and stories associated with them. For instance, in identifying the Spring of Narcissus, associated with the myth of a man who wasted away after falling in love with his own reflection in the river, Pausanias matter-of-factly states: "They say that Narcissus looked into this water, and not understanding that he saw his own reflection, unconsciously fell in love with himself, and died of love at the spring. But it is utter stupidity to imagine that a man old enough to fall in love was incapable of distinguishing a man from a man's reflection."[4] Indeed.

Few have ever accused Pausanias of having a sense of humor. Yet his work's popularity already in antiquity is a testament to a new phenomenon that came into being in the Roman Empire: the tourism industry. One of the advantages of the Pax Romana, the peace over the Roman Empire from the late first century BCE on, was the rise of arguably the first booming tourist industry in the

---

4. Pausanias, 9.31.7.

world. True, travel in the Roman world required a commitment of months or years, as one could only travel about twenty-five miles in a day by cart and horse. But then Roman aristocrats could afford this investment, especially because visiting particular locations, such as Athens and Delphi, was a mark of prestige and refinement. Thus, the original grand tour of the Greco-Roman Mediterranean was born.

With a more-or-less set default route, the original tour included travel southward through Italy, down the Appian Way, and then visits to such famous locations in Asia Minor and mainland Greece as Troy, Athens, Delphi, and Olympia. Also included, much to the travelers' chagrin, were the features of travel that Pausanias downplays, although they have always been an authentic part of tourist experiences: cranky lodge-owners, restaurants specializing in food poisoning, and the occasional criminal element, such as pickpockets. And then there were the dangers of travel, which even the Pax Romana could only diminish and never eliminate: highway robbers on land, pirates on sea, and the challenges of weather and wild animals on any routes.[5]

The original version of the grand tour was also decidedly a pagan affair that featured a number of religious sites. For example, Delphi specialized in the sacred and had been a center of religious tourism since well before the Roman Empire. It was crammed to the brim with temples and altars to every major and minor divinity in the Greek pantheon. Located there was the *omphalos*, which Pausanias described with reverence and still attracts tourists today: a decorated stone that was considered to be the navel of the world—thence its name. As a graduate student at the American School of Classical Studies at Athens, I recall the irresistible nature of the *omphalos* for tourists, including nerdy graduate students, to pose next to it for a picture with their own belly buttons on display. Another major attraction of Delphi in the pre-Roman period was the oracle of the Pythia. The most famous oracle in antiquity, the Pythia had been getting high on laurel leaves and reciting mysteriously confusing prophecies of the future in perfect hexameters to bewildered visitors since as early as the eighth century BCE. To take the grand tour, ultimately, was to travel through a world filled with old gods.

The pinnacle of the grand tour was usually a visit to Egypt, complete with a luxury cruise down the Nile. Such cruises did not look quite like the hedonistic party barges in Hollywood's *Cleopatra*, but that flavor could be provided upon

---

5. For the history of the Roman grand tour through the eyes of a modern journalist who attempted to re-create it himself, see Tony Perrottet, *Pagan Holiday: On the Trail of Ancient Roman Tourists* (New York: Random House, 2003).

demand. For example, the Nile cruise toward the end of the Emperor Hadrian's trip to Egypt in 130 CE was a wild party, albeit one that went terribly wrong at the end. Hadrian's cruise, meant to be an extended romantic date with his lover Antinous, unfortunately ended with Antinous's accidental drowning—a further reminder of the dangers of travel, ancient or modern. Hadrian consoled himself, it appears, by declaring the deceased Antinous a god.

Of course, the pagan grand tour, with its emphases on the pagan sacred sites, was unsuited for Christians. Yet the narrative of the monks' tour through Egypt echoes the work of such travel writers as Pausanias in ways that make it clear that we have a Christian grand tour on our hands. Were these particular monks doing something new on their own voyage, or were they following the established route? We can answer this question from the *Inquiry about the Monks of Egypt*. First, the narrator notes at each stop of the monks that other tourists were present there and had similarly come there to see the particular saint on display at each exhibit. Also, the travelogue notes the challenges that the monks found in particular locations, whether because of weather or, in some cases, the threat of robbers. In the epilogue, the narrator explains why they did not take particular roads and did not visit certain regions. For example, the seven monks did not visit the monks in the Upper Thebaid for the following reason:

> We were unable to make our way to them on account of the peril of the journey, for even though all the areas of that region are infested with highway robbers, the ones beyond the city of Lyco are plagued by barbarians. We had no way of getting to them, and indeed it was not without peril that we saw the men I recalled earlier. During the journey we were in danger of losing our lives seven times, but "the eighth time trouble did not touch us," as God protected us through it all.[6]

Because of other travelers that the monks encountered at each stage and the dangers of the trip, which precluded travel to some areas altogether, it appears that the monks took the road most traveled—the Christian grand tour route for all who were fascinated with ascetics and wished to see them.

Overall, the evidence from Rufinus is that by the 390s, the Christian tourists had taken a pagan cultural concept and made it into something distinctly their own. The original grand tour of the Roman Empire had a religious dimension, as it allowed individuals to visit particularly famous shrines and other locations

---

6. Cain, *Rufinus of Aquileia*, 213.

imbued with significance for pagan worshipers. Similarly, this new Christian grand tour of the Egyptian desert built on the previous pagan idea of such travel as a spiritual experience. But instead of great buildings and cities, the attractions around which this new tour was built were the desert ascetics themselves. They were, in their own ways, quite spectacular, as the following few examples will demonstrate.

The object of the very first stop described is John of Lycopolis, who lived in a hermitage on a cliff. The narrator notes the steep mountain that visitors had to climb to reach him. Once they did, however, a guesthouse was available for those who needed it. John did not leave the hermitage and rarely allowed visitors inside. Women, in fact, were not even allowed to enter his field of vision—a detail that suggests that some women did go on the grand tour. Male visitors, nevertheless, were allowed to view him through the window of his hermitage, and he would "give them either a word from God to edify them or answers to encourage them."[7]

Another stop involved Or, an illiterate ascetic whose diet fascinated visitors: he mostly lived on roots and herbs from the desert. On rare occasions, only after long fasts, he ate vegetables from his garden. He is one of many of the ascetics, the narrator notes, to whom miracles and supernatural powers were attributed. First, in his old age, he miraculously received the gift of reading. And second, also in his old age, he received the power to drive out demons.

Other ascetics' miracles included driving wild animals (a hippo and a crocodile) out of the region in the name of Christ, and the miracle of healing. Theon, for example, who had been living in complete silence in his cell for thirty years, "would reach his hand toward them through the window, rest it on everyone's head, give his blessing, and send them away cured of all illness."[8] Didymus, the object of another stop on the tour, was renowned for his ability to walk barefoot over scorpions and poisonous snakes without suffering harm.

Not all stops involved an individual desert saint. Some destinations were monasteries or similar communities filled with monks, which effectively transformed the desert landscape. For example, one of the sights in the travelogue was a mountain filled with caves, in which many monks lived under the leadership of a holy man, Pityrion. In another location in the region of the Thebaid, the travelers visited a monastery led by one Isidore. This monastery was surrounded by a wall, like a city, and housed one thousand monks. They lived in utter silence

---

7. Cain, *Rufinus of Aquileia*, 64.
8. Cain, *Rufinus of Aquileia*, 101.

and never left the walls of the monastery, growing and making virtually all that they needed. Only two monks were designated for running errands in the outside world.

Especially striking is the delegation's description of the city of Oxyrhynchus in the Thebaid. It was "filled with monks on the inside and completely surrounded by monks on the outside. Whatever public buildings had been in it, along with the temples devoted to ancient pagan religion, now were the dwellings of monks, and throughout the entire city one could see many more monasteries than houses."[9] Boasting twelve churches, the city has been transformed "into something of a unified church of God. For no heretic or pagan is found there, but all the citizens are Christians, all are catholics, such as that it makes absolutely no difference whether the bishop conducts liturgical prayer in the street or in church."[10]

Overall, we find that every stop on the grand tour had something exciting to offer, as one could find ascetics living in a variety of improvised habitats, varying from caves to monasteries, and even an entire city, in the case of Oxyrhynchus. Travelers along that route appear to have been many. As a result, the seven-monk delegation whose voyage Rufinus translated kept running into other travelers on the same tour. Still, not all Christians were able to make this difficult voyage around the desert. And yet the same desire to experience the ascetics—the heroes of faith of the day—consumed those who could not travel to see them. Perhaps in response to the desire to know and experience the ascetics from a distance, various collections of the Desert Fathers' and Mothers' quotable aphorisms and stories—social media style—began circulating during this period as well. The existence of these sayings in Greek, Latin, and Coptic suggests their popularity across the Mediterranean world, including Egypt.[11]

Social Media (Desert) Saints

A pithy anecdote survives about the desert father John the Dwarf: "The same abba was very fervent. Now someone who came to see him praised his work, and he remained silent, for he was weaving a rope. Once again the visitor began to

---

9. Cain, *Rufinus of Aquileia*, 98.

10. Cain, *Rufinus of Aquileia*, 99.

11. See, for example, the new collection of sayings of Antony: Lisa Agaiby and Tim Vivian, *Door of the Wilderness: The Greek, Coptic, and Copto-Arabic Sayings of St. Antony of Egypt. An English Translation with Introduction and Notes* (Leiden: Brill, 2022).

speak and once again he kept silence. The third time he said to the visitor, 'Since you came here, you have driven away God from me.'"[12]

As this story exemplifies, the sayings of the desert saints and ascetics are short and to the point. Reading them, we cannot expect to know the real people—the sayings are much too formulaic. But their words reveal deep hunger for God and the conviction that the best place to find God was in the desert. Among the many sayings attributed to Abba Arsenius, who abandoned a life of political prominence and moved into the desert in the late fourth century CE, is this anecdote: "While still living in the palace, Abba Arsenius prayed to God in these words, 'Lord, lead me in the way of salvation.' And a voice came saying to him, 'Arsenius, flee from men and you will be saved.'"[13] And the Desert Father Or is reputed to have said: "If you are fleeing, flee from men; or the world and the men in it will make you do many foolish things."[14]

Perhaps the most popular topic in the sayings is the rigor of ascetic practices, such as minimizing food, sleep, and all bodily comfort, in conjunction with the need for solitude. "It was said of Abba Theodore of Pherme that the three things he held to be fundamental were: poverty, asceticism, flight from men."[15] Other sayings comment on particular types of ascetic practices alone. For example, "Abba Arsenius used to say that one hour's sleep is enough for a monk if he is a good fighter."[16] The travelogue *Inquiry about the Monks of Egypt* notes that some monks would sleep sitting instead of lying down. And a saying attributed to Abba Poemen ("Shepherd") states, "Because of our need to eat and sleep, we do not see the simple things."[17] On another occasion, Abba Poemen is reputed to have said in the same vein, "There are three things which I am not able to do without: food, clothing and sleep; but I can restrict them to some extent."[18] A desert mother, Amma Syncletica, likewise commented that "just as the most bitter medicine drives out poisonous creatures so prayer joined to fasting drives evil thoughts away."[19]

The continued repetition of the same motifs about different ascetics only serves to distance the real people from the ideal. In fact, nearly identical sayings

12. Benedicta Ward, *The Desert Christian: Sayings of the Desert Fathers* (New York: MacMillan, 1975), 92.

13. Ward, *The Desert Christian*, 9.

14. Ward, *The Desert Christian*, 248.

15. Ward, *The Desert Christian*, 74.

16. Ward, *The Desert Christian*, 11.

17. Ward, *The Desert Christian*, 186.

18. Ward, *The Desert Christian*, 193.

19. Laura Swan, *The Forgotten Desert Mothers: Sayings, Lives, and Stories of Early Christian Women* (Mahwah, NJ: Paulist, 2001), 44.

exist about multiple Desert Fathers and Mothers. For instance, one saying about Amma Sarah noted that "for sixty years she lived beside a river, and never lifted her eyes to look at it."[20] A similar saying exists about Abba Helladius: "It was said of Abba Helladius that he spent twenty years in the Cells, without ever raising his eyes to see the roof of the church."[21] Focusing their eyes and minds fully on God, they did not even see the world around them, desert and all.

This formulaic nature of staging the ascetics on the tour, or of staging their representation in collections of pithy sayings, shows that for the Late Antique audiences the desert saints' austerity and discipline was what made them so fascinating. Besides, there was surely something special about being able to boast about visiting them—just as there was the element of prestige and boasting for those who had taken the pagan grand tour. As Rufinus (and his anonymous Greek source) put it at the end of the prologue to his travelogue,

> Blessed be God, "who desires everyone to be saved and to come to the knowledge of the truth," and who guided our journey to Egypt and showed us great and extraordinary things, the memory of which it will be beneficial to preserve for posterity, so that these things not only may be a source of salvation for us, but also may form the basis of a salvific narrative that is eminently suitable for teaching holiness and that opens up, to those keen on making the journey towards virtue, a robust path paved by the deeds of those who came before us in faith.[22]

For Rufinus and his source, the verdict was clear: any self-respecting Christian should either go see the ascetics or read about them to achieve sanctification. Whether through seeing the ascetics or hearing about them, those who were not quite ready to move into the wilderness themselves could still reap the advertised spiritual benefits of the grand tour and boast about it to others.

"What Did You Go Out into the Wilderness to See?"

The phenomenon of ascetics and saints as tourist attractions and objects of quotable moments, however, was not entirely new to the world of Late Antiquity.

---

20. Swan, *The Forgotten Desert Mothers*, 38.
21. Ward, *The Desert Christian*, 62.
22. Cain, *Rufinus of Aquileia*, 59.

Rather, the phenomenon brings to mind the uncomfortable question that Jesus asked people who came to see him about their interest in the original desert saint, John the Baptist: "What did you go out into the wilderness to see?" (Matt 11:7).

Jesus provided the intended answer: the onlookers wanted to see a true prophet. One wonders, were some people motivated less by their respect for John's holiness and simply took a day-trip to look at a man who dressed himself in camel hair and ate locusts? Such curiosity likely describes many of those Late Antique tourists who traveled to see Antony, Simeon, and others who became stops on the grand tour of the Egyptian desert. Then we have the disturbing story of Mary of Egypt, who, before embracing a life as a desert saint in John's old territory, was able to find enough pilgrims to support her through prostitution as she traveled alongside them on pilgrimage from Egypt to Jerusalem. Clearly, what happened on the grand tour was meant to stay on the grand tour. And not everything that happened on the tour was spiritually edifying.

Ultimately, we find that the Christian tourists' desire to visit the desert saints and ascetics was a manifestation of cultural Christianity, rooted in the pagan tradition of the grand tour. Just because the new grand tour involved visiting Christian "sites," it did not become a spiritual practice for all. The experience of Mary of Egypt may be a stark reminder, but the hints are elsewhere. Cultural Christians were everywhere, even on pilgrimage trips. These travelers internalized pagan ideas about travel, prestige, and a desire for entertainment and found a way to make them respectable, at least on the surface. This cultural manifestation of the Christian tour was facilitated, first and foremost, by the staged nature of this phenomenon.

The desert saints in Rufinus's narrative and in the many biographies of them that survive come across as staged displays for viewers. They place themselves in fixed locations, such as pillars, tiny huts, caves, and hermitages. Set on this stage, the ascetics resign themselves to their fate as exhibits. We imagine Simeon on his pillar, for instance, who was surprised that moving off the ground only increased traffic to come see him.

But it was not only the act of staging that was pagan-inspired. The locations that many of the desert ascetics inadvertently selected were imbued with pagan meaning. In particular, the pillar to which Simeon moved most likely belonged to a pagan temple. Originally, such pillars supported the temple ceiling or, in the case of shorter pillars, a cult statue of a pagan god. In repurposing the pillar, therefore, Simeon appropriated a pagan structure, stationing himself on it as a figure of entertainment. One might extend the analogy to see Simeon raising himself up almost as a god, stationed on this old statue plinth.

Further similarities can be drawn between the ascetics' self-staging and museum exhibits or staged performances. Like performances, audiences on tour can look but (most often) cannot touch. Audiences can see and hear them teach or pray but (most often) cannot talk to the ascetics. The audiences knew, at least, what the "performance" was that they could expect at each stop of the tour: seeing the names of the particular saints at each stop of the seven monks' tour in Rufinus's book reminds us that such travelogues existed. But this was not all the entertainment that the visitors craved from the ascetics. The continued obsession of visitors with the ascetics' diet brings out an additional, less flattering parallel: the zoo.

Zoos or menageries seem to us a thoroughly modern concept, but they existed in the ancient world. Normally part of a wealthy individual's property, zoos were particularly popular in Egypt, a land that teemed with animals considered exotic for visitors, from crocodiles to camels to elephants and more. Furthermore, in antiquity, just as today, one of the greatest attractions for visitors of zoos was to see those animals eat. Here we see a direct parallel to the desert ascetics.

In the case of these ascetics, as we saw earlier, their dietary habits receive a remarkably high level of attention in their biographies, in the sayings of the Desert Fathers and Mothers, and in Rufinus's travelogue. Just as visitors today can offer zoo animals food (albeit with permission, and usually purchasing it at the zoo), ancient visitors brought the ascetics they visited food and commented on whether any of it was eaten. Of course, this obsession with the desert ascetics' dietary habits is visible already in the fascination of first-century Jews with John the Baptist. What did the onlookers go into the desert to see? For some, perhaps getting to see a man who lived on locusts and wild honey was worth the price of the (figurative) ticket.

Overall, the stories Rufinus and his original Greek source collected about the monks' grand tour provides us with an insight into Late Antique Christian tourists' motivations in visiting the human attractions in the desert. While it was easy for Christian travelers to attribute profound spiritual motivations to such trips, the reality was that the Christians, just as the pagans, craved entertainment and enjoyed the experience of travel to exotic locales. But the world of antiquity was a world filled with pagan gods. So the ascetics, without intending to provide such an alternative, allowed the trips to become respectable. At the same time, cultural Christians who were inspired to take such a trip were still profoundly superficial in their belief, as the story of Mary of Egypt and her "customers" on the pilgrimage to Jerusalem so poignantly reminds us.

But this story is not just about the tourists themselves and their culturally influenced Christianity. What about the saints who unwittingly became the objects of these voyages? How might we understand their thought process about their decision to embrace the desert life? Even more than John, the original desert tourist destination, these Late Antique holy figures' lifestyle choices raised obvious questions that enthralled their audiences: How does one live atop a pillar? Food—here is that obsession with feeding the ascetics again!—was no problem. Biographies of Simeon note that boys from the area brought him food, which he was able to lift up in a basket to his very cramped residence. But what about bodily functions? Presumably, the immediately surrounding area of Simeon's pillar was not the most salubrious after a while. Is this the real reason for the wall that was constructed around his column rather than the pretext that this was to keep the crowds from getting too close?

These practical questions emphasize the strangeness of the ascetics for us and for their original gawkers. They are the key for understanding these desert saints as cultural Christians. By asking the practical questions connected to their chosen lifestyle, we are able to connect our spectacle-prone saints to their two very different cultural predecessors: low-brow comedy and farce, as well as the earlier philosophical movements that advocated asceticism. And it is to this cultural baggage that casts the desert saints as, ironically, cultural Christians that we now turn.

Desert Saints as Cultural Christians: Jars, Barrels, and Stages

In the fourth century BCE, a philosopher temporarily living in Athens discovered asceticism. Fascinated by the idea of poverty and not relying on anyone or anything else, he gave away all his possessions, including much of his clothing, keeping barely enough to cover his body. At first, he kept a little wooden bowl as a drinking dish, but eventually he even got rid of that, after seeing someone else drink from cupped hands. Needing somewhere to live, he adopted as his abode a massive jar, *pithos*, which he requisitioned from a temple precinct.

Something got lost in translation, and many English-speakers today have heard of Diogenes and his barrel. There was no barrel, however—just a *pithos*. These massive storage jars were used for bulk storage and transport of both liquid goods (e.g., wine or olive oil) and foods (e.g., grain or olives). A *pithos* had added significance from earlier Greek mythology. In the myth of Pandora, the container that Pandora opened, which unleashed all evils upon the world, was actually a *pithos*. Yet another loss in translation, it is known as Pandora's box, but Diogenes and his contemporaries surely knew better, and the association was not lost on them.

For many fourth-century Athenians who had the misfortune to encounter him, Diogenes may indeed have seemed like one of Pandora's evils unleashed upon their society. Living as a spectacle, Diogenes roamed the city nearly naked, performing in public all acts that others performed in private—urinating and defecating on the streets, eating in the agora (highly scandalous), and sleeping outside in his jar year-round.

Diogenes's extreme asceticism was an obvious predecessor of the asceticism that the Christian desert saints embraced. An additional cultural norm that the desert saints inherited from Diogenes and other Greek philosophers was the concept of a life of relative solitude as the best way of acquiring a true life of the mind. To be fair, Diogenes, did not live entirely apart from people. Yet he lived apart from society and social expectations, even while living inside a city.

By the fourth century CE, stories about Diogenes had become ingrained as cultural heritage for many in the Greek-speaking world, and his legacy of asceticism, processed through many generations of other philosophers, was appealing to Christians as well. But this was not the only cultural influence on the desert ascetics. In addition to philosophy, we can discern in the ascetics' stories the influence of farce and low-brow comedy, defined with its irreverent and sometimes scatological humor, and the placing of people on display in exaggerated form.

Popular comedy was a feature of Greco-Roman entertainment culture since at least as early as fifth-century BCE Athens. Selecting topics of obvious political and cultural significance, the comedies placed people on the stage for the purpose of comic relief and entertainment. For example, the philosopher Socrates was the object of ridicule in Aristophanes's comedy *Clouds* (423 BCE). Related types of comedy proliferated in the subsequent periods, from the "New Comedy" of the fourth century BCE, to its translations and adaptation in the Roman Republic. Stories of mistaken identity and romance abound in these. Thankfully, the boy usually gets his girl at the end. In addition, while we know less about it, the genre of the farce was a feature of both comic performances in Athens and in the Roman world. By placing its subjects on stage, comedy and farce served to objectify them as entertainment, emphasizing bodily functions and food in ways that were humanizing and dehumanizing all at once.

By placing themselves on pillars and other "stages," the Late Antique ascetics connected themselves to these traditions, molding themselves into new objects of farce and combining humanizing (and maybe even superhuman) characteristics alongside dehumanizing ones. To take again the example of Simeon and his pillar, while rumors emphasized repeatedly his wisdom and holiness in living for thirty years atop a pillar, there was also a farcical dehumanizing element in witnessing (as visitors must have done) a saint urinate or defecate from a fifty-foot pillar. Even Diogenes, who performed such actions in public, did not do so from a stage. The same farcical staging can be seen in the story of Mark the Fool, who for eight years roamed around the streets of Alexandria wearing only a loincloth and pretending to be insane. Mark intended his actions to be penance for his previous fifteen years of sinful living, ironically as a monk in the desert. His story evokes Diogenes's model of asceticism in the city. Finally, the obsession with the ascetics' dietary practices likewise fits into this comic staging. The story of Abba Isaac comes to mind, for instance, who mixed the ashes from incense offering with his meager food. Such an act would, yet again, have been a spectacle naturally fit for a farce.

There is also a gendered dimension to the elements of staging comedy and farce in the public displays of ascetics. A number of stories survive about women cross-dressing as men to join monasteries. For example, Eugenia of Alexandria joined a monastery disguised as a man and eventually rose to become its abbot. Euphrosyne of Alexandria likewise disguised herself as a man and joined a monastery, claiming to be a eunuch. Remarkably, the beauty of this ostensible eunuch stirred up fights among the brothers—a reminder of the pervasiveness and inescapable nature of sin—leading her to move into a solitary cell in the desert. Even more striking is the story of Marina, who disguised herself as a man and did not reveal her true identity even when falsely accused to have fathered a child out of wedlock. These stories flip the dramatic stage standards in antiquity that required men to cross-dress and play women's roles on stage. In light of these stories, the saying of Amma Sarah acquires an added nuance: "According to nature I am a woman, but not according to my thoughts."[23]

Ultimately, whether or not the saints themselves recognized the cultural baggage associated with their ascetic life in the desert, they certainly did acknowledge, even while encouraging others to follow their example, that moving into the desert could not drive all trouble and sin away. The Desert Mothers seem to have been particularly outspoken on the futility of such escape. Amma Syncletica, the mysterious Desert Mother to whom an immense number of sayings is attributed, is supposed to have said, "There are many who live in the mountains and behave

---

23. Swan, *The Forgotten Desert Mothers*, 39.

as if they were in the town, and they are wasting their time. It is possible to be solitary in one's mind while living in a crowd, and it is possible for one who is solitary to live in the crowd of personal thoughts."[24] Similarly, Amma Theodora is supposed to have said, "There was an ascetic who, because of the great number of personal temptations said, 'I will go away from here.' While putting sandals on, saw another ascetic who was also putting on sandals. This other ascetic said, 'Is it on my account that you are going away? Because I go before you wherever you are going.'"[25]

But these concerns were not limited to the Desert Mothers. Ammonas, a Desert Father and disciple of Antony said, "I have spent fourteen years in Scetis (a solitary desert area) asking God night and day to grant me the victory over anger."[26] *The Inquiry about the Monks of Egypt* echoes similar sentiments on a number of occasions. One leader of a monastic community, Pityrion, is reported to have a theory that each individual, monk or no, has particular demons associated with particular sins, always following that individual. Another monastic leader, Dioscorus, who led a community of one hundred monks, was particularly worried about temptation of sexual sin among his flock.[27] There is, ultimately, nowhere we can run to flee our own culturally ingrained sinful dispositions and our sinful nature.

Cultural Sin in the Social Media Desert

The story of the saints and ascetics who populated the Late Antique desert landscapes brings out two new and surprising brands of cultural Christianity. First, the presence of these saints as new spectacles inspired a Christian yet culturally sinful version of the pagan grand tour of the empire. Indeed, the incredible fame that some of these desert saints acquired bears functional resemblance to the modern obsession with celebrities, whose homes and favorite haunts can also be tourist destinations. In other words, the church celebrity culture that Kaitlyn Beaty calls out in her recent book has this surprising ancient parallel.[28] The virtual desert that is social media has only amplified the farcical nature of the

---

24. Swan, *The Forgotten Desert Mothers*, 58.
25. Swan, *The Forgotten Desert Mothers*, 68.
26. Ward, *The Desert Christian*, 26.
27. Cain, *Rufinus of Aquileia*, 155 and 179.
28. Kaitlyn Beaty, *Celebrities for Jesus: How Personas, Platforms, and Profits Are Hurting the Church* (Grand Rapids: Brazos, 2022).

pillar saints of our days. But second, the desert ascetics themselves were, ultimately, fleeing the church yet unable to escape their own sinfulness. It may seem shocking to think of individuals such as Antony as cultural sinners, but if we examine their decision to pursue solitary lives apart from society and the church in light of the original biblical texts, this becomes clear.

The biblical descriptions of qualifications for elders provide a striking foil to the desert saints. The elders receive significant consideration in the New Testament because they are individuals who serve their local churches in a particularly intensive way. The qualifications for elders leave no room for the desert ascetics.[29] Only those married (husbands of one wife) and raising faithful children are deemed qualified for church leadership. In addition, there is discussion of the importance for older women to mentor younger ones.[30]

In essence, the New Testament repeatedly emphasizes that people should strive to live, lead, and serve in community rather than alone. We have noted on several occasions already that unlike the pagan world around, the New Testament and the early churches recognized that some men and women have a calling for singleness. They saw these singles, nevertheless, living out even this calling as part of the local church community, ministering to others in deed and prayer. The examples of Jesus and Paul, who both remained unmarried throughout the duration of their earthly ministry, only highlight this further. Both remained in close contact with people, ministering to individuals and communities. While Jesus, in particular, had spent time alone in prayer, he always returned to minister to people. His entire ministry, overall, was categorized by relationships. His repeated emphasis on valuing children, furthermore, highlighted the importance of the next generation.[31]

By leaving the church to move into the desert, the Desert Fathers and Mothers rejected that model. Even those who formed monastic communities with churches in the desert did not replicate the New Testament model, as they did not have families, but only single-gender communities (with the occasional secretly cross-dressing woman monk). This might not have seemed to be a problem if there was evidence that these exceptional communities were bastions of human perfectibility here on earth. But that is not the evidence that the stories in this chapter provide. Rather, not only were the desert ascetics themselves continuing to struggle in the desert with the same sins as before, but their action of moving into the desert provided others, the tourists, with new opportunities

---

29. 1 Tim. 3:1–7; Titus 1:5–9; and 1 Pet. 5:1–4.
30. Titus 2:3–5.
31. For example, see Luke 18:16.

for sinning. For some, the desert ascetics proved to be nothing but a stumbling block to spiritual growth.

More important, perhaps, by moving themselves away from churches, communities, and families, the desert ascetics took themselves out of the circulation of real human society. The requirements for elders and deacons, which cite marriage, highlight how by rejecting marriage, the ascetics rejected the enormous responsibility of discipling other image-bearers in their homes and communities. By rejecting cities and churches in those cities, they rejected the opportunity to help others. Ultimately, by choosing the desert, they chose themselves and their own desires, rather than striving to be a blessing to the world around them. And that is exactly the choice for anyone today, who thinks that they could leave the church and follow God alone. In a world of ever-greater opportunities to work from home, worship from home, and live a life of solitude, anyone's home could become a hermitage. But whenever you lock yourself inside that fortress in the video-call desert, you will, like Antony, still bring your demons along.

The siren call of the desert and its peace sings beautifully to me some days in my home, filled with the chaotic noises of three children. Someone is often upset with someone else. Very often, someone is yelling at someone else. There is much laughter, which is as wondrous as it is loud. As a result, sometimes, I have been known to say, "I cannot even hear myself think." And that is the point. People are difficult. The ascetics were right. People, with all their incessant noise and sinfulness, distract us from God. Yet it is by serving other people, these noisy and distracting image bearers, that we are daily forced to confront our own sinful nature and can daily pursue sanctification. This is what countercultural Christianity looks like.

Conclusion

THE LEGENDARY MID-TWENTIETH-CENTURY HISTORIAN OF the Greco-Roman world Moses I. Finley was reputed to sit in the back of a room during lectures by other scholars and then boom a question during the Q and A: "So what?" This is an intimidating question, but it is a pertinent one to consider in wrapping up any book. If you are not thinking about it, you should.

So what is the significance of the many stories and case studies of different cultural sins present in the early churches? Why is it important for us to recognize that there were cultural Christians in the church since its earliest days? What should you, long-suffering reader who made it this far, take from all of this, other than great historical anecdotes for future parties? Although, to be fair, one should never underestimate the value of such anecdotes. As I assure my students, dropping ancient history facts at parties is, in fact, the key to robust social life.

But the material presented in this book has much more serious implications than mere anecdote gathering. Ultimately, any issue that impacts our thinking on the self in light of eternity is serious. A nuanced and complex understanding of the history of the church and its people is important. Augustine certainly thought that having a proper understanding of history for Christians was inextricably connected to having a healthy understanding of theology as well.

I believe that the overall argument—that cultural Christians were present in all periods of the early church, from the first century to the fifth—has significant ramifications for Christians today. This is, indeed, the first obvious takeaway that I hope readers get from this book: we should be thinking more about cultural Christianity as an important dimension of the history of the church. The early church had plenty of cultural Christians, just as churches do today. And this takeaway leads us to two more that are related.

Toward the end of my time in graduate school, I read a book that pushed me to rethink some basic assumptions that I had held up until that point about the Classical Athenian democracy. In the process, that book had implications for my broader methodological thinking about the people of the past. That book was Matthew Christ's *The Bad Citizen in Classical Athens* (and no, he is not related to Jesus Christ, to the best of my knowledge).[1] Christ's book laid bare to me for the first time the ugly underbelly of Athenian democracy, which was much less smoothly run than we might imagine at first glance because its citizens were much less committed to the success of the democratic enterprise than I had ever imagined.

We often idealize Athens as the world's first democracy—a misleading statement omnipresent in introductory textbooks. Yes, this was a democracy in which citizens wrote and spoke repeatedly about their pride and trust in their government and legal system, which included an impressive structure of trials by a jury of one's peers. And yet plenty of Athenians held grudges for decades, were overly eager to sue each other, and were loath to serve on those juries of which they were seemingly so proud. These same citizens were eager to criticize politicians who led them, while turnout at democratic assemblies and for voting was, as the comic playwright Aristophanes quipped, much lower than at comedy performances.

The citizens wanted the safety that the Athenian army provided, but many were eager to shirk military duty. Some citizens who were drafted subsequently deserted on campaign or even during battle. Such behavior was sufficiently common that the term *shield thrower* became an insult—since the hoplite shield weighed close to twenty pounds, it is no wonder that someone eager to run away from battle would have jettisoned it. Having walked around some ancient battle-fields in the mid-summer Mediterranean sun, when these battles were originally fought, I am frankly amazed that anyone would have wanted to keep on fighting.

Matthew Christ's argument involved questioning something that I had taken for granted. Sure, I had known about the robust tradition of intellectual criticism of popular rule in Classical Athens—we need only think of such philosophical figures as Socrates, who effectively made a career of this. Plato's *Republic*, in fact, presented a picture of the ideal state that effectively criticized how Athens, his not-so-ideal state, handled every aspect of life and government. But I had never

---

1. Matthew Christ, *The Bad Citizen in Classical Athens* (New York: Cambridge University Press, 2006).

considered that while some citizens in the Athenian democracy criticized the government and its rulers, including even the very notion of popular rule, some of these same citizens along with many others were also terrible citizens.

It may seem shocking, but clearly it is possible for individuals and groups to possess the right view of the ideology of how the state and its citizens should act and yet act in a way that is completely contrary to that ideology. Sometimes, everyone, past and present, would love it if none of the rules applied to them, all while applying those same rules to others.

I think that the difficult question that Matthew Christ asked about the Athenian democracy—how good was its typical citizen?—parallels the main argument in this book. And this leads us to the second takeaway I hope this book imparts: we should never idealize the people of the past. Such heroization is dangerous, as we are dealing with real, flawed, and deeply sinful people.

On the one hand, we all have read both Jesus's and Paul's rebukes to many believers in the New Testament. Nonetheless, it is still tempting to idealize early Christians as better than us, maybe just because they were first. But as this book shows chapter by chapter, the "typical" Christian in the early church was not a superhero of faith and was actually much more negatively influenced by their culture than we might like to think. If we think about it theologically, we are much worse than we would like to think too. That is why we, the sick who pretend to be healthy, so desperately need the good news.

It is a natural instinct to search for role models, but it ultimately tends to lead us down the slippery slope of bad history. Matthew Christ's study of bad citizens provides helpful illustrations in this regard. As an ancient historian fascinated with the Athenians, I was inadvertently idealizing these people, whom I had spent years studying in detail. This idealization made me overlook some portions of the primary sources that were always right in front of me, like the anecdotes that Christ highlighted in his own argument about duty-shirking soldiers and the bitter jokes about the citizens who did not show up to vote.

Many modern churchgoers and students of the early church think in the same idealistic way about early Christians as I was once tempted to do with Athenian democratic citizens. On many occasions, I have heard my students and Christians at church note that the early Christians were much more devout than we are today. They were the real people of faith, as the argument goes, the ones who were willing to go to the lions rather than renounce Christ. To some extent, that's true.

We certainly can think of many examples that showcase the dedication of early believers. Over the course of this book we considered examples such as

Perpetua, Felicity, and Cyprian. It is easy to idealize the earliest followers of Jesus simply because they were the earliest—after all, they had a real connection to the Son of God. Some of them got to see and hear Jesus teach, witnessed miracles firsthand, and were willing to give up so much to follow the truth. Yet if we look closely, as we did in this book, we see that already from its earliest days the church has been filled with sinners. At the root of so many of the most common sins of these early believers was the surrounding culture that gave those sins a distinct Greco-Roman flavor. Eager to follow Christ, these men and women were cultural Christians nevertheless. And this makes them not so different from us.

The idealization of the early church and, in general, of the past seems to be a timeless human instinct. Nostalgia is a powerful force, and it leads us to idealize some of the past as a much better time than the present in which we live. The goal, then, could be to get back to that idealized past—when Christians were genuine, fully devoted, and not like ourselves. But this ideal past when the church was fully holy and blameless is, in fact, a myth. To be sure, Revelation assures us that this will happen in the future. We cannot get back to this ideal time in the past because it never existed.

So the third takeaway from this book is an exhortation to all Christians today to resist this nostalgic longing to restore the church to a time when (they imagine) it was perfect. The temptation to pinpoint such a time in the past is ever present, but it is always a culturally sinful impulse, especially as it leads us to restore an imagined past that is false and reflects our own cultural baggage.

American history has been filled with these restorations—times when people have genuinely worked hard to restore the first-century church. One example is the Stone-Campbell movement of the early nineteenth century. Plenty of those who conflate Christianity with American patriotism, in particular, have been tempted to call for such revivals and restorations, encouraging today's Christians to recover a Christian America that they ostensibly had lost. While such movements can have much love for the gospel and a genuine desire to get to something good, the desire to restore the church of the past is unnecessary. After all, as this book showed time and time again, the Christians of the early church, from the New Testament era to the age of Augustine, looked a lot like us in their attraction to the sins of the surrounding culture.

Strikingly, a desire to restore the church to its imagined previous glory is a phenomenon largely absent in the early church. The early Christians, from the Thessalonians of Paul's day to Cyprian slogging through crisis after crisis in the mid-third century, imagined they were living in the last days of the world. Everything was passing away and would surely come to an end soon, they thought, as they bemoaned the "old age" of the world around them.

The realizations from these takeaways should change how we think about the people of the early church. In turn, that may have an impact on how we think about our own practices and behavior. This leads us to our final and most uncomfortable takeaway. Where do we fall short and act as cultural Christians? The recent culture wars surrounding certain topics provide a mournfully fertile ground for discussion, as the select examples in the rest of the conclusion will demonstrate.

Pricing Human Life: Cultural and Countercultural Approaches

In September of 2021, right as yet another COVID-19 wave was beginning, the state of Texas, where death rates were some of the highest in the country at the time, proposed a 10,000 dollar reward offer to anyone who successfully prosecuted an abortion provider. The law was proposed as a thoroughly Christian and pro-life measure. I was troubled at the time over an ancillary question that the law raised, with its 10,000 dollar reward offer for those who successfully prosecute abortion providers: How does one put a price on a human life?[2]

As it happens, the church has been thinking about this question for a long time, providing both theological and practical responses. Theologically, evangelical Christians agree on the key doctrine of redemption—the "buying back" of sinful humanity through Jesus's sacrifice on the cross. But the Texas law showed that in practice, valuing human life is more difficult to quantify in concrete terms.

In chapter 6, we came briefly across a crisis that Cyprian, bishop of Carthage, was asked to resolve: buying back Christians who had been kidnapped by native tribes and were going to be sold into slavery, or even prostitution, if not ransomed. As Cyprian noted in his letter of response to the small-town bishops who contacted him for help, enclosed with it he sent 100,000 sesterces for the buying back of the captives, estimated to be as much as a million dollars in modern currency.

---

2. Nadya Williams, "Pricing Human Life," *Current*, September 30, 2021, https://currentpub.com /2021/09/30/pricing-human-life/.

That Cyprian was able to raise these funds in short order for this emergency in a time when he and his church were dealing with many other emergencies, including an Ebola pandemic, shows just how critical the Carthaginian Christians considered their responsibility to buy back fellow Christians, even at a time of deep suffering when no one could be certain when their own life might be taken from them by either the plague or through martyrdom. Yes, sometimes human life has a literal price, but then, as Christians, perhaps we should be more aware of this than the world around us.

I think that there is a useful analogy for us today, as the pandemic's effects continue to reverberate in our society. What is a human life worth? And how do we show that we value it? Cyprian's call to a countercultural pro-life ethic involved supporting those who needed support with money and resources, providing for the widows and the destitute. How crudely, by comparison, the Texas law, with its monetary reward for informing on abortion providers comes across, even as the state's COVID-19 death rates have been among the highest in the US.

As the Supreme Court has recently overturned *Roe v. Wade*, the call to Christians to support life in practical ways with finances and resources is no less urgent than ever. Redeeming the lives of others should take such practical forms as providing for single mothers, widows, orphans, and others who suffer in our midst, precisely because of the theological assumptions that Christians share. "He who redeemed us on the cross through His blood is now to be redeemed by us through the payment of money," reminds Cyprian matter-of-factly.[3]

Leggings and Blaming Bathsheba

A culturally inspired view of humanity is pervasive in how many Christians in our society view women. Particularly alarming in these days of #metoo and #churchtoo and following the release of the Southern Baptism Convention's report on sexual abuse in the congregation is the tendency to blame women for sins committed against them by men. This attitude, however, is not biblical. Rather, it stems from the modern cultural assumption that since relationships involve two people, any problems are the fault of both. In the process, this assumption has led to mistrust of victims of rape and other violence, tragically and unjustly holding them culpable for sins done against them. Coming full

---

3. Cyprian, *Epistle* 62.2.

circle, such a culturally inspired view of abuses today has also influenced some evangelicals' reading of the Bible. Here is an example.

Recently, there was yet another social-media kerfuffle about interpretations of the story of David and Bathsheba in 2 Samuel 11. Twitter veterans noted that like so many trends, this topic cycles through with remarkable regularity. The chief question at hand: Was Bathsheba raped or was this a consensual affair and, therefore, blatant adultery? The answers among the general evangelical public were divided. Maybe, some argued, we shouldn't blame David alone for what happened. As the adage stemming from modern egalitarianism goes, it takes two to tango. Besides, Bathsheba seems to have been bathing naked in public, so wasn't she kind of asking for it, given her lack of modesty?

Several thoughtful theologians, including Carmen Joy Imes, provided insightful responses to these arguments, highlighting the ways the rebuke from God that the prophet Nathan delivered to David made it abundantly clear that the guilt was one-sided.[4] Nathan began, after all, by telling David what seemed to be a story about someone else: a rich man who slaughtered his poor neighbor's only lamb to serve as dinner for a guest. Only when David exclaimed in outrage that this man must die did Nathan tell him that he is the man. In this analogy, the reader realizes that David is the wealthy man. Bathsheba's husband, Uriah, is the poor neighbor. As for Bathsheba, she is the lamb that was led to its slaughter. She is the victim in this scenario.

In her analysis of portrayals of Bathsheba in children's Bibles from the late twentieth century, art historian Elissa Yukiko Weichbrodt noted the parallels between the suggestive ways Bathsheba's body is emphasized in these illustrations and such other culturally accepted portrayals of, say, bare women's limbs in women's razor commercials.[5] In other words, our culture has so influenced our perceptions of women, that these views have seeped even into children's Bible illustrations. By emphasizing women as objects of gaze, our culture suggests that they are culpable, at least in part, for the sins of the beholder. This attitude is also visible in the obsession with women's modesty, popularized especially by the evangelical purity culture of the 1980s and 1990s. Toxic vestiges still reverberate, as the following example shows.

In late spring 2022, Owen Strachan, who is no stranger to such controversy,

---

4. Carmen Joy Imes, "Blame David, Not Bathsheba. The Prophet Nathan Did," *Christianity Today*, July 18, 2022, https://www.christianitytoday.com/ct/2022/july-web-only/rape-david-bathsheba -adultery-sexual-sin-prophet-nathan.html.

5. Elissa Yukiko Weichbrodt, "Seeing Bathsheba," *Current*, July 25, 2022, https://currentpub.com /2022/07/25/seeing-bathsheba/.

criticized women's leggings as immodest in a podcast episode.[6] His assumption was that when women dress immodestly, they lead men into sin. Should any assault result to such women, it is entirely their fault. By reverse logic, one might also logically ask any victims of assault, as has sometimes happened as well: What did you do to cause this to happen to you?

The attitude of evangelicals like Strachan is remarkably similar to the perspective of such pagan Romans as Ovid, who too saw women as nothing more than objects of prey to pursue and seduce. Such an attitude is one that Jesus and leaders of the early church, such as Tertullian and Cyprian, fought against, as they highlighted women's clothing, instead, as most significant for women converts themselves. God is the one looking at you, not men, Cyprian especially emphasized in his treatise *On the Dress of Virgins*, which we mentioned in chapter 5.

A countercultural and biblical view of women today, just as in any previous period of the history of the church, involves seeing them not as sexual objects—a standard of society—but as God sees them. Seeing women through God's eyes rather than the sinful lens of the world is as difficult to apply today as in the first century CE. And this challenge extends also to how we see immigrants, foreigners, and those who do not look like us in our society.

Immigration, CRT, and War

In spring 2020, as everyone worldwide was struggling to understand the deadly pandemic raging all around, I had to take my then one-year-old daughter to the pediatrician for a regularly scheduled checkup. The nurse was asking me various basic newly standard questions during the initial screening: Has the family been exposed to COVID-19 recently? Has anyone in the family traveled internationally of late? And then came the grand finale: Has the child recently been "around anyone sick or dirty," such as (the nurse added in clarification) an immigrant? The question, and the atrocious way it was phrased, stopped me in my tracks.

As I mentioned in the introduction, I immigrated to the United States in high school. When I speak English, my strange hybrid accent—not quite Russian, not quite Hebrew—is mostly gone. Or, at least, most people who meet me for the first time assume that I simply hail from a different part of the United States. In other words, I do not sound like a foreigner to most people. As a white woman of

---

6. Owen Strachan, "Should Women Wear Tight Leggings?," *Antithesis*, April 22, 2022, https://podcasts.apple.com/us/podcast/should-women-wear-tight-leggings-a-biblical/id1152518569?i=10 00558336598.

Jewish descent, I do not look "different" either. But the nurse's inadvertent revelation of her assumptions—that it is the outsiders from whom diseases and threats arrive—showed the powerfully ingrained prejudices in the culture around us.

For a nation composed of immigrants, the United States has certainly had an unusually conflicted relationship with immigration and immigration policy. From the various quotas that limited certain types of immigrants in the late nineteenth and the first half of the twentieth century, to the prejudices that various immigrant groups have faced at different time periods, the story of American immigration is more mournful than celebratory.[7]

Particularly mournful within this larger story is the refusal of some Americans, including devout Christians, to see the face of Jesus in the immigrants who do not look like them. In the recent book *Heathen: Religion and Race in American History*, Kathryn Gin Lum shows how white American Christians from the eighteenth century to the present have defaulted to seeing anyone nonwhite as, effectively, an inferior and uncivilized "other." This means, in religious terms, also seeing these individuals *en masse* as heathens in need of salvation—material and religious—rather than fellow heirs in God's kingdom.[8] This default view, which conflates Christianity with American identity, also overlooks the reality that the center of gravity for Christianity has been shifting to the global south for a while now.[9]

This view, the result of Christian nationalism and the belief in the superiority of white Americans to all others, has a destructive impact on our ability to pursue accurate biblical anthropology. In other words, this distorts our ability to love others the way Jesus did and the way he called us to do as believers. This has a destructive impact both at home, such as in the obsessive opposition to the concept known as Critical Race Theory (CRT) by certain groups of American politicians who claim to be Christians, and abroad, such as in many American Christians' refusal to welcome refugees and victims of wars.

CRT remains a concept that most people cannot define (or definitions vary absurdly), but this has not stopped the strife around it. It has become a

---

7. I wrote about the anti-Jewish immigration policies in WWII-era United States in this *Anxious Bench* post: Nadya Williams, "Israel and Immigration: A Christian Reflection on the Consequences of Past Sins," *Anxious Bench*, May 19, 2021, https://www.patheos.com/blogs/anxiousbench/2021/05/israel-and-immigration-a-christian-reflection-on-the-consequences-of-past-sins/.

8. Kathryn Gin Lum, *Heathen: Religion and Race in American History* (Cambridge, MA: Harvard University Press, 2022).

9. Few have done as much to explain this phenomenon as historian Philip Jenkins. See *The Next Christendom: The Coming of Global Christianity* (New York: Oxford University Press, 2002); and *The New Faces of Christianity: Believing the Bible in the Global South* (New York: Oxford University Press, 2008).

divisive curse, whose briefest mention is enough to foment angry debates among Christians within the same church—I know this because I have seen it firsthand. Which is the (worse) heresy, one is left to wonder? CRT itself or opposition to it? To Christians who are bewildered over this question, I particularly recommend John Fea's piece, "An Open Letter to American History Teachers: Stop Teaching Critical Race Theory."[10] Faithfully teaching American history from its genocidal and enslaving beginnings requires discussing horrific sins, and no additional theory or divisive terminology is needed to convey the point about the depth of the nation's cultural sins, which have distorted its view of entire groups of people during different periods. Of course, healthy patriotism should have a place in our hearts as well, as another historian, John Wilsey, exhorts Christians to remember, but it should never become idolatry.[11]

If we have a gospel-centered view of humanity and its preciousness to a loving God, then this should make it abundantly clear to us that structural racism continues to be a national cultural sin. But the other side of this same distortion of our perception of humanity impacts our treatment of others abroad. Recent American history abounds with examples of turning away refugees—from ships of Jews fleeing the Nazis during the Holocaust, to Syrians fleeing ISIS. Meanwhile, during the brutal ongoing (as of this writing) Russian invasion of Ukraine, certain prominent political voices, such as a self-proclaimed Christian nationalist congresswoman from my current home state of Georgia, Marjorie Taylor Greene, have thrown their full support behind Russia, the invader. Augustine would not be impressed.

Looking Forward to the City of God

Ultimately, as people of God, we live in this world, even as we look forward to the city of God. In the meanwhile, try it as we might to fight against it, the culture around us has always managed to permeate the church in various insidious ways. While I can identify some cultural sins in people around me, I undoubtedly am guilty of others of which I am not aware or whose magnitude I do not accurately

---

10. John Fea, "An Open Letter to American History Teachers: Stop Teaching Critical Race Theory," *Current*, May 28, 2021, https://currentpub.com/2021/05/28/an-open-letter-to-american-history-teachers-stop-teaching-critical-race-theory/.

11. John D. Wilsey, "Whatever Happened to Patriotism? A Healthy Love of Country is Nothing to Disdain," *World*, August 9, 2022, https://wng.org/opinions/whatever-happened-to-patriotism-1660044135.

perceive. But what I keep coming back to again and again is the beauty of this imperfect and corrupted body of Christ, where each Sunday I get to worship the risen Lord with fellow sinners, with whom I may have deep, fundamental disagreements about issues related to war, gun control, structural racism, the best ways to respect and promote a culture of life, and so much more. At least, we all have the same stance on leggings: they're fine. Some in the congregation even wear them to church.

Jokes aside, in this divided country and world of ours, where else might one be able to spend time regularly with people with whom one has such deep disagreements and yet still love one another deeply? This glimpse of God's city here on earth is ours to enjoy every Sunday, and for that I am profoundly grateful. The fact that we are able to gather together each week because we all believe in the Lord Jesus Christ, who died for our sins—including our cultural sins—and rose again and is eager to have an eternal relationship with us, is the most countercultural idea of all.

Acknowledgments

BOOKS DO NOT EXIST IN A VACUUM BECAUSE THEIR WRITERS do not. In the process of writing this book, I have benefited from an extraordinarily generous community of scholars and friends, who gave kindly and lavishly of their own time and wisdom to read parts of the book and provide thoughtful comments that greatly improved it: Meghan DiLuzio, Jeff Dryden, Jen Ebbeler, Jay Green, Andrew Hendley, Bruce Lowe, Steve Walton, and John Wilsey. Katya Covrett was a dream editor to work with. A gifted scholar in her own right, she provided thorough comments and reading recommendations that improved the manuscript.

I am very grateful for their gift of time and expertise. I also emphatically claim ownership of any mistakes and errors that remain. After all, writing books may feel sanctifying at times, but the process assuredly does not result in perfection for either the book or its author.

But my debts go far beyond those incurred to the colleagues who read and commented on portions of the book. The *Anxious Bench* blog on Patheos and, especially, *Current* magazine provided me with a nurturing Christian intellectual community that equipped me to find a stronger voice as a writer and offered opportunities for test-driving ideas in progress. Thinking alongside seasoned public writers whose work I admire has been a blessing and the best learning experience I could have asked for. Special thanks are due to Eric Miller, who has been a kind mentor and friend.

The University of West Georgia granted me research leave in Spring 2021, which allowed me time to draft the first six chapters. King's Chapel Presbyterian Church (PCA) in Carrollton, Georgia, has been a loving and nurturing church home for my family for the past seven years and counting. It has been a wonderful blessing to think through the challenging questions in this book alongside wiser Christians who clearly seek to live counterculturally in this world.

Most of all, I am grateful for my husband, who lovingly created time for me to write by doing so much to take care of our kids during a busy season for him as well. His gift of time for me to write is one that I cherish, along with the cute pictures he has snapped along the way of the kids digging for dinosaur fossils in our backyard, jumping in the leaf pile, or riding bikes. But his help and support has extended far beyond loving our kids and me in practical ways. As a seasoned historian of both antiquity and modern American evangelicalism, he repeatedly pointed me in helpful directions, suggested books, and asked questions that ultimately transformed this project for the better. Thank you, Dan.

Subject Index

Index Locorum